WOMEN
GUARDING
MEN

WOMEN GUARDING MEN

LYNN E. ZIMMER

Foreword by James B. Jacobs

The University of Chicago Press
Chicago and London

Lynn E. Zimmer is assistant professor of sociology
at the State University of New York at Geneseo.

The University of Chicago Press, Chicago 60637
The University of Chicago Press, Ltd., London
© 1986 by The University of Chicago
All rights reserved. Published 1986
Printed in the United States of America

95 94 93 92 91 90 89 88 87 86   5 4 3 2 1

Library of Congress Cataloging-in-Publication Data

Zimmer, Lynn Etta.
  Women guarding men.

  (Studies in crime and justice)
  Bibliography: p.
  Includes index.
  1. Prisons—United States—Officials and employees.
2. Women correctional personnel—United States.
I. Title. II. Series.
HV9470.Z56 1986   365'.6   85-28857
ISBN 0-226-98339-0

For Joseph and Mark

Contents

Foreword

At the broadest level, Lynn Zimmer's account of women breaking into the all-male world of maximum-security prison guards is a contribution to our understanding of social change. Back in 1964, very few Congressmen would have imagined that the monumental Civil Rights Act, which was meant as a charter for minority rights, would eventually force the officials of prisons like San Quentin, Attica, and Stateville to hire women for almost all posts and job categories. This is a "reform" that had no constituency, one which hardly anyone wanted. Nevertheless, the mixture of rights consciousness, legal logic, and individual courage fundamentally transformed the landscape of America's male maximum-security prisons.

In the 1970s I often encountered top corrections officials who dismissed out of hand the possibility that they would ever be required to assign women to the tiers of their toughest prisons. Despite pressures from their affirmative action officers and sometimes from their unions, they frequently remained steadfast, allowing the issue to go to litigation. In 1977, the matter reached the United States Supreme Court in the *Dothard* v. *Rawlinson* case. The Alabama Department of Corrections sought to vindicate its policy of excluding women from positions involving contact with inmates in men's maximum-security prisons; its attorneys argued that being male should be recognized as a bona fide occupational qualification for such positions. The Supreme Court agreed, concluding that maximum-security prisons were too dangerous for women.

However, the trend toward sexual integration of the prisons did not falter. Lawyers for women's rights refused to take no for an answer. They continued to charge that correctional hiring and assignment policies illegally discriminated against women and, remarkably, they chalked up one victory after another in the lower courts. Time and again, the Supreme Court's decision was interpreted narrowly and limited to its facts, as if it were a precedent from an obsure county court. The post-*Dothard* lower court decisions demonstrate how powerful is the social and legal momentum toward racial and sexual equality even in the face of such obstacles as an unfriendly national government and a skeptical Supreme Court.

Professor Zimmer's study illuminates how the trend toward equal employment opportunity is being played out in the trenches. The story that she tells so well is not a romance about superwomen beating down closed doors, vanquishing their opponents, and triumphing in their new correctional jobs. It is the story of ordinary people thrust into the role of occupational pioneers by economic and social circumstance. The women's voices that speak to us from these pages about their aspirations, trials, and travails are extraordinarily modest. For many of the women guards, this job is simply better than other options such as waiting on tables. Many of the women are not out to strike a blow for sexual equality; in fact, they are content to accept the male guards' judgment that they are less capable than men.

Whatever their own ambitions, values, and attitudes, the women guards are playing an important part in the dramatic transformation of women's roles in American society. If women can successfully carry out the necessarily authoritarian duties of a prison guard in penal institutions which house the most frightening and dangerous people in our society, where can they not perform? These women guards will serve as a symbol of equality for new generations of young women who will grow up telling themselves that "if women can guard dangerous men in maximum security prisons, then I can . . ." Nor should we forget that Lynn Zimmer's work itself provides an encouraging model for women social scientists who want to undertake research in traditionally all-male settings.

This study is also, and perhaps most fundamentally, a contribution to our understanding of the prison in modern American society. The prison has probably been buffeted by more change in the last two decades than in its entire previous combined history. The prisoners' rights movement has led to a penetrating examination of the prison's every nook and cranny, and of its every rule and regulation. Prison officials' complete autonomy in running their institutions has been lost, perhaps forever. The incredible closedness of the prison has been steadily breaking down. Now the tightly knit homogeneous guard corps and its subculture are being transformed by the introduction of minorities and women.

The result is a prison far more integrated into mainstream American society than it ever was before the mid-1960s, and a prison far more accountable to outside rules and institutions. All this change makes prison administration much more complicated and demanding, especially in light of the prison crowding crisis of the past decade. Prison officials have made great strides in obtaining more funds, rationalizing procedures, and conforming practices and conditions to humane standards. New organizational equilibria are beginning to emerge, especially in some of the federal prisons.Nevertheless, for the foreseeable future, our prisons will face extraordinary challenges; most important of all is the recruitment, training, and development of career staff at all levels. It is fortunate that women have broken down the walls of discrimination. Their energies and talents will be a key factor over the rest of this century and beyond in meeting the extraordinary demands that are constantly being made of our institutions of confinement and punishment.

JAMES B. JACOBS

Acknowledgments

I owe special thanks to all of the participants in this study who gave unselfishly of their time and shared with me their knowledge, insights, and experiences. To those women who have worked so hard to become the first female guards in men's prisons, I want to express my deepest respect and admiration.

There are two sociologists who were particularly important in bringing this study to completion. First is Rose Goldsen, who gave me encouragement and helpful suggestions during some critical stages of data collection. She kept reminding me that I had to work hard to see the world from the perspective of those I was studying; I thank her for keeping me "on track." To James B. Jacobs I want to express my utmost appreciation and warmest affection. His work has influenced my own in immeasurable ways and has always stood as a model for what I hope to achieve. As a teacher and friend he has provided a perfect blend of criticism and support. I thank him for years of encouragement for this project as well as others.

I am also indebted to my friends, teachers, and colleagues who read and commented on drafts of various chapters and provided limitless encouragement: Ellen Auster, Spencer Cahill, Gil Gillespie, Craig Little, Doni Loseke, Peter Meiksins, Robert Stern, and Robin Williams, Jr. Special thanks to Ron Pointer for his patience and support, to Arno Zimmer for his valuable editorial assistance, and to Sally Harrington for typing (more than once) the entire manuscript.

The research for this book would not have been possible without the financial support of the Edna McConnell Clark Foundation and the Educational Foundation of the American Association of University Women. I also want to express my gratitude to John Moran,

Director of the Rhode Island Department of Corrections, and Thomas Coughlin, Commissioner of the New York State Department of Correctional Services, for their support in carrying out this research.

Introduction

Before 1972, the practice of hiring only men to guard male inmates in the nation's prisons was unquestioned and unchallenged. In fact, women were excluded from virtually all criminal justice jobs that required the exercise of authority over men. Police departments used women only to supervise female arrestees, investigate cases of juvenile delinquency, and perform clerical duties (Fleming 1975; Tenny 1953). Female probation and parole officers generally were restricted to supervising female and juvenile offenders (Stout 1973). In prisons, women were employed as guards only within women's facilities, where inmates' isolation from men was viewed as necessary for rehabilitation (Freedman 1974), or within juvenile institutions, where women's capacity for "mothering" was considered a tool for inducing good behavior from boys (Polsky 1962).

Today, women work in all criminal justice occupations and perform many of the same tasks as their male counterparts. Every large urban police department now hires women as full patrol officers (Price and Gavin 1982; *Handbook on Women Workers*, 1975). Probation and parole departments assign mixed-sex caseloads to female employees (Schoonmaker 1975), and nearly all state prison systems and the Federal Bureau of Prisons employ women to guard male inmates.

The number of female guards who work in men's prisons varies from state to state; nationwide, they constitute approximately 6 percent of the guard force in men's prisons. As of December 1978, the last time systematic data were gathered, at least three states (Louisiana, Wyoming, and Kentucky) filled over 15 percent of guard positions with women (Morton 1979). In less than a decade, then, the situation changed from one of the virtual absence of female guards in men's prisons to one in which their presence is the norm. However, the change has not been an easy one either for the women or for the correctional systems they have entered.

This study offers the first in-depth, empirical examination of the integration of America's prison guard forces. It presents a "natural history" of the movement of women into men's prisons, focusing on three critical areas: the social and legal forces that prompted the change; the manner in which integration policies have been implemented in two states (New York and Rhode Island); and the subjective experiences of key participants. Although particular attention is paid to female guards themselves and the problems they face in adjusting to this highly nontraditional job, the concerns of prison administrators, male guards, and inmates are examined as well. It is hoped that this study will prove useful in meeting the practical needs of prison administrators, many of whom are still struggling to implement the integration process. It is further hoped that, by adding to the current body of literature on women in nontraditional occupations, this study provides new insight into the evolution of sex roles in the 1980s, particularly the ways in which women incorporate changing notions of womanhood into their work behavior.

Women in Nontraditional Occupations

In recent years, researchers have documented the experiences of women who have entered a variety of traditionally male occupations and have discovered, almost unanimously, that these women faced discriminatory hiring, promotion, and assigment policies, opposition and sexual harassment from male co-workers, and inadequate on-the-job training and socialization (Kanter 1977; Martin 1980; Rustad 1982; Westley 1982; Deaux and Ullman 1983; Drolet 1976; Horne 1980; Walshok 1981). While female guards who work in men's prisons have faced many of the same occuptional barriers as women in other nontraditional occupations, their experiences have, at the same time, been unique. For one thing, the prison is a work environment qualitatively different from other work settings. The job of guarding itself is highly sex-typed male, both by tradition and by definition. Also, the sexual integration of the prisons has taken place within a rather peculiar legal framework that has allowed, and to some extent required, continuing inequality between male and female guards.

The occupation of prison guard is not merely one more tradition-ally male occupation in the process of becoming sexually integrated. It is an occupation that is highly sex-typed male and has long been thought to require the traditional male qualities of dominance, au-thoritativeness, and aggressiveness. It is a job in which the tradi-tional female qualities of nurturance, sensitivity, and understanding are thought to be not merely unnecessary but actually detrimental. The occupational subculture itself stresses the importance of "ma-chismo" for successful job performance, and even some researchers into the guard role have supported the view that the prison guard "who cannot muster some version of this masculine image before both inmates and peers is in for trouble" (Crouch 1980:217). The job of prison guard is rivaled perhaps only by the job of combat soldier as being the epitome of a "man's occupation," by definition as well as by tradition. In fact, the continuing debate over the desirability of using women in combat (Goldman 1982; Nabors 1982; Quester 1982; Segal 1982; Tuten 1982) encompasses the same issues raised with regard to women's employment in men's prisons: Can women meet the psychological and physical requirements of the job, and will their presence decrease the overall effectiveness of the work force? Cer-tainly among male guards, and perhaps even within the population as a whole, there is a belief that regardless of women's suitability for the large majority of traditionally male jobs, women simply cannot perform effectively in a job that requires daily, face-to-face contact with male inmates, many of whom have committed crimes of vio-lence.

The experiences of female guards differ markedly from those of other nontraditional working women because the prison itself is a work environment characterized not only by periodic episodes of extreme violence but also by almost constant disruption, turmoil, and confusion. In fact, when the integration process began in the 1970s, American prisons were going through a particularly tumultuous period in which inmates were challenging guards' authority, admin-istrators were challenging guards' autonomy, reformers were chal-lenging the prison's traditional goals, and the courts were challeng-ing traditional methods of control. Although administrators, inmates, and guards alike were affected adversely by the changes that were taking place in the prison system, guards were most vehement in their opposition to their changing occupational world, often respond-ing with insubordination, militant demands for unionization, and a tightening of the guard subculture. For most guards the "battle cry" of the 1970s proclaimed a return to the "good old days" when they ran the prisons unencumbered by rules, regulations, and procedures; guards opposed virtually every change imposed by legislators, judges, or prison administrators, regardless of its purpose or value. When women first began working as guards in men's prisons, then, they entered an already problem-ridden work environment, the remnants of which can still be seen today.

The sexual integration of many traditionally male occupations occurred primarily as a result of legal prohibitions of sex discrimination, and the sexual integration of the prisons was no exception. The prison administrators surveyed by Joann Morton (1979) overwhelmingly cited legal requirements as the main reason for their abandonment of male-only hiring practices. However, a number of courts, in recognition of the special problems of implementing sexual integration in the prisons, have ruled that absolute equality among male and female guards is not required and, in fact, may be prohibited under some circumstances. Thus, female guards, unlike women in other nontraditional jobs, have entered men's prisons to work under a legally sanctioned system of "near-equality."

The Legal Context

Women's legal right to seek guard jobs in men's prisons is guaranteed by the 1964 Civil Rights Act, as amended in 1972.[1] Title VII of the Act proscribes employment discrimination on the basis of race, religion, sex,[2] and national origin. By extending the obligation of nondiscrimination to public sector employees, the 1972 amendments mandated an end to the exclusion of women from the heretofore male-dominated occupations in criminal justice agencies. These amendments also increased the enforcement powers available to the Equal Employment Opportunity Commission (EEOC), the federal agency established in 1964 to oversee implementation of Title VII's mandates. The EEOC was given the power to prosecute Title VII violators in the federal courts, a power it quickly utilized. Within eight months, the EEOC had filed twelve cases claiming employer discrimination on the basis of sex compared with only four sex discrimination cases filed in the eight previous years when the Justice Department was responsible for initiating Title VII lawsuits.[3] Thus, the 1972 amendments were crucial to women's advancement in corrections work in two separate ways: first by covering public sector employment, and second by increasing the enforcement power of the EEOC.[4]

Even after passage of the amendments to Title VII, some prison administrators refused to hire women as guards because they hoped that the job of guard in men's prisons would be declared an allowable exception to Title VII's mandate of nondiscrimination. An important provision of Title VII states that some discriminatory practices might be allowed if there is "a bona fide occupational qualification [BFOQ] reasonably necessary to the normal operation of that particular business or enterprise."[5] The EEOC had already ruled that this exception would be narrowly defined, stating that the BFOQ exception could only be claimed "where it is necessary for the purpose of authenticity or genuineness, e.g., an actor or actress, " and could not be claimed because of assumptions about the characteristics of women in general or the preferences of co-workers, the employer, clients, or customers.[6] The federal courts had upheld this narrow interpretation of Title VII's BFOQ with regard to private employment,[7] but prison administators presumably hoped that the job of prison guard was distinguishable. When women began to file Title VII lawsuits against corrections agencies that refused to hire them, prison officials regularly used Title VII's BFOQ as an affirmative defense. When these cases were heard in the lower federal courts, the women generally won,[8] and it seemed as if their movement into guard jobs in men's prisons could not be halted.

In 1977 this apparent momentum toward equality slowed when the Supreme Court ruled, in *Dothard* v. *Rawlinson*,[9] that at least under some circumstances guard jobs in men's prisons qualified for a BFOQ exemption. In this case, the State of Alabama had refused to hire Dianne Rawlinson for the job of prison guard because she failed to meet the minimum weight requirements. Rawlinson filed a class action suit, claiming that such regulations violated Title VII. While the case was pending, Alabama instituted a new regulation that barred women from all contact jobs in men's prisons.[10] Rawlinson challenged this regulation as well.

A federal district court held that Alabama's height and weight requirements constituted a violation of Title VII. The court also struck down the no-contact rule on the grounds that the state presented no evidence that women could not perform effectively as prison guards.

The State of Alabama appealed this district court decision, and in 1977 the Supreme Court, in an opinion written by Justice Stewart, reversed the part of the decision that invalidated the no-contact rule. The Court held that the job of prison guard in Alabama's male maximum-security prison qualified for a BFOQ exemption as provided by Title VII. As James Jacobs (1979b) points out in his analysis of *Rawlinson*, the Supreme Court had no evidence that women actually were unable to perform the job. Instead, the court relied on the assumption that the mere presence of women decreases prison security:

> Although Justice Stewart acknowledged that Congress intended the BFOQ exemption to be very narrow, he found that the deplorable conditions of the Alabama prisons, fueled by the presence of "predatory male sex offenders, " justified the exclusion of women. He reasoned that a woman could not successfully serve as a prison guard in the Alabama prisons because womanhood itself made female officers uniquely vulnerable to sexual assault, thereby increasing the instability of the total prison environment. [P. 402]

Rawlinson presented the first serious blow to women's movement toward equal employment opportunity in corrections, and because it was the only female guard case to reach the Supreme Court, one might have expected it to have far-reaching consequences. Shortly after the *Rawlinson* decision was handed down, Jacobs pointed out that it could be used as a precedent to limit the advancement of women in all men's prisons:

> The deference paid to claims of prison officials by the *Rawlinson* majority strongly suggests that women will be held legally excludable from all maximum security prisons, and perhaps from medium and minimum security institutions as well. Prisons, by definition, are populated by individuals who pose serious threats to the community, and all maximum security prisons hold at least some "predatory sex offenders." Unless prospective women guards are able to prove the negative—that they will not be more vulnerable to attack and will not destabilize the prison regime—the momentum of the *Rawlinson* decision will probably lead other courts to conclude that the role of women in men's penal facilities should be limited. [P. 394]

Ironically, no other state correctional department has been successful in relying on *Rawlinson* to deny jobs to women.[11] For example, in *Gunther* v. *Iowa*[12] the district court declared that, although a BFOQ existed in the "peculiarly unhospitable" environment of Alabama's maximum-security prisons, the same was not true in the medium-security Iowa reformatory where correctional administrators were seeking to deny guard jobs to women. In *Harden* v. *Dayton Human Rehabilitation Center*,[13] another lower court declared that the state had not supplied the preponderance of evidence necessary for the BFOQ claim. The only corrections case to reach the Supreme

Court, then, did not provide definitive guidance for administrators who were trying to determine their Title VII obligations; consequently, many of them remained unsure of the exact conditions under which they might legally deny guard jobs to women.

The confusion over Title VII's applicability to corrections was heightened by numerous court decisions upholding inmates' claims that the use of opposite-sex guards violates their constitutional right to personal privacy. Not all such cases have been decided in favor of inmates.[14] But in *Bowling* v. *Enomoto*,[15] the court declared that "prisoners in all-male inmate institutions had limited right to privacy which included right to be free from unrestricted observations of their genitals and bodily functions by prison officials of opposite sex under normal prison conditions." Similarly, the court ruled in *Hudson* v. *Goodlander*[16] that an "inmate's privacy rights were violated by assignment of female guards to posts where they could view him while he was completely unclothed." Although *Hudson* neglected the issue of how women's employment rights might be balanced against inmates' right to privacy, *Bowling* declared that California officials themselves were responsible for devising a plan that would protect inmate privacy while maximizing equal opportunities for women.

More than a decade after the 1972 amendments to Title VII, no single court decision has provided guidelines for a clear, legally acceptable balance between the sex discrimination and the inmate privacy issues. In *Gunther*, the court claimed that correctional departments *could* develop assignment procedures to protect inmate privacy while meeting the requirements of Title VII but did not suggest that prison administrators *must* protect inmate privacy. In *Forts* v. *Ward*,[17] a case filed by female inmates in New York State, the court ruled that when inmate privacy is protected through other means, inmates have no constitutional right to same-sex guards. In this case, however, the employer voluntarily agreed to make changes in prison rules that would allow more inmate privacy. It is not known how the privacy and employment issues might have been balanced if correctional administrators could not or would not alter prison routines and procedures.

It is still not certain, then, exactly how equal employment opportunity is to be achieved in the prisons. Other than *Rawlinson*, the case law demands equality in matters of hiring. But in matters of deployment, the case law is clearly contradictory. Many prison officials—especially those who have not been directly involved in litigation—remain uncertain about their legal obligations to all parties.

Because legal justification can be found for almost any deployment policy, a wide variety of policies prevail, with some states deploying male and female guards in a nearly identical manner and other states using women only for a limited number of non-inmate-contact positions.

Although Title VII provided the impetus for the sexual integration of America's guard forces, then, it has not mandated full equality among male and female workers in the prison. Instead, a system of legally sanctioned "near equality" has emerged which not only has been detrimental to many female guards themselves but also has affected negatively the male guards with whom they work and the administrators who must design and implement integration policies. What has emerged is a situation somewhat analogous to that in the armed forces, where women are permitted to serve but are denied access to all combat-related roles (Binkin and Bach 1977). In most other newly integrated occupations, the goal of male-female equality is at least conceivable, even if not yet attained. In the prisons, male-female inequality is allowable and, under some circumstances, required. As the case law continues to evolve, this disparate situation may change.[18] In the meantime, some degree of overt inequality continues to set the context in which women work as guards in men's prisons.

Coping with Sexual Integration

For the first women struggling for equal employment opportunity in corrections, the legal battles were only the first obstacles. By winning the right to work as guards in men's prisons, women were, in effect, winning the right to enter a hostile work environment in which many questioned their right to be there and nearly everyone doubted their ability to perform the job.

Male guards were most vehement in their opposition to women, and many of them, in fact, hold two sets of beliefs that virtually preclude their acceptance of women as equal co-workers. First, many of the men believe in natural, immutable differences between males and females. Second, many believe that the job of guarding requires those traits associated with masculinity. They therefore conclude that women should not be hired to work as guards in men's prisons. As the number of women guards has grown, these men increasingly worry about the security of the prisons, about the women's personal safety, and about their own safety should they ever have to rely on a female partner for support. In other work settings where mutual dependency among workers is important to job performance and safety, male opposition to sexual intergration has also remained strong. For example, in the military (Larwood et al. 1980; Durning 1978; Priest et al. 1978; DeFleur et al. 1978; Adams 1980) and in police work (Martin 1980; Horne 1980; Price and Gavin 1982), male opposition to women has not decreased to the extent it has in many other newly-integrated occupations (McIlwee 1982; Epstein 1980; Schrieber 1979). From the perspective of most male guards, women simply cannot be counted on to fulfill many of the job's requirements.

Males guards have also shown anger and resentment toward newly-hired women guards for what they perceive to be women's preferential treatment in matters of assignment. In some states, assignment guidelines aimed at protecting inmate privacy effectively exclude women from many of the high-contact posts that all guards wish to avoid because they are the most unpleasant and dangerous in the prison. Male guards generally have to accumulate considerable seniority before obtaining preferred posts; many women have been able to obtain them by virtue of their female status alone. Thus, many male guards conclude that, because equal assignment of men and women is inappropriate and because differential assignment is unjust, women should be prohibited altogether from working as guards in men's prisons. Many male guards, in fact, remain convinced that the "powers that be" will eventually reverse the integration policy and remove all currently employed female guards. While they wait for this reversal, many of these men openly harass the women, refuse to work with them, and undermine their efforts to perform the job as required.

The requirement to hire women as guards in men's prisons was thrust upon prison administrators with little warning, and they were, for the most part, both ill-prepared and ill-equipped to meet the challenge. Forcing sexual integration upon a reluctant male work force is a difficult task in itself. For prison administrators the practical problems of sexual integration were exacerbated by the ambiguous (and ever-changing) legal situation and the failure of existing case law to clearly define women's proper employment role. The task of dividing prison posts into privacy-invading and non-privacy-invading categories is not easy,[19] and administrators have found that almost every division generates complaints from someone—male guards, female guards, or inmates. Sexual integration has also caused administrative problems by decreasing management flexibility in deploying the guard force efficiently because although they have been forced to hire women, administrators have not been allowed, in most cases, to use them interchageably with men. Every woman hired, then, puts an additional constraint on managers' ability to assign personnel to posts in the prisons.[20]

Although court-mandated inequality has created some genuine problems for prison administrators, it is also the case that most administrators have not worked diligently to implement the maximum amount of male-female equality that is allowed under the law. Like most male guards, male administrators remain unsure whether women are capable of supervising, disciplining, and physically controlling male inmates; they are concerned about the effect of women's presence on overall prison security. Consequently, they have often interpreted prisoners' privacy rights more broadly than the case law requires, thereby restricting unnecessarily the posts on which women can be placed. They have ignored a great deal of informal discrimination against women at the local prisons—even when it violates administrative policy. They have also been apathetic to the problem of sexual harassment and how it adversely affects women's performance. Put simply, administrators have not developed affirmative plans for successful sexual integration of the guard force.

Male inmates have been divided in their opinion of the hiring of women to guard them, but most strongly favor and only a few strongly oppose women's presence. On the positive side, inmates claim that women treat them better and that women's presence substantially improves the prison environment. These prisoners have been extremely cooperative with women guards, providing job-related information and assisting them in the performance of their control functions.

The most common complaints about female guards focus on the privacy issue and the need (or perceived need) of inmates to change their behavior to accommodate women's presence. Some inmates have openly harassed female guards and engaged in various forms of sexual misconduct in an effort to discourage women's employment. Although such behavior causes problems for women, they are somewhat better equipped to cope with inmate oppositional behavior than with that of male co-workers because they can, at least, take disciplinary action against prisoners. In general, neither those prisoners in favor of women's presence nor those opposed disregard female guards' sexual status, and, as will be seen in later chapters, the ways in which women adapt to the job reflect the sex-bound nature of their interactions with inmates.

Because of the unique legal guidelines framing women's employment in the prisons, and because of treatment by male guards and inmates alike, women have not been able to routinely "fill" the existing guard role in the male prison. At the same time, women entering these jobs have had no established "female guard role" to follow. As a consequence, women have had to create a role for themselves—and have had to do so with very little support or assistance and often in the face of overt discrimination, opposition, and sexual harassment. Some women failed to adapt and left prison employment; but many have remained, gradually developing styles of performing the job that fit their own personalities and abilities while still meeting the basic requirements set by their employers. Their modes of adaptation indicate that the categories of liberated and nonliberated, feminist and nonfeminist are not distinct; nor are they especially meaningful to women faced with the need to make practical decisons regarding their work behavior. Although these women are working in a nontraditional job, many of them hold traditional sex-role attitudes; in fact, such attitudes often prove functional for female guards in their adjustment to the job. In the prisons, women with the most liberated sex-role attitudes have more work-related problems and more difficulty in establishing good relationships with co-workers and inmates than do more traditionally oriented women. Even in a typically male occupation such as that of prison guard, then, there are rewards for typically feminine behavior. This indicates not only that nontraditional jobs fail necessarily to attract women with nontraditional attitudes, but also that work in a nontraditional job may, under some circumstances, actually encourage and reinforce women's traditional sex-role behaviors.

For women working in the prisons, then, sex remains an important factor in their treatment by others and in their adjustment to the job. More than a decade after integration, many problems remain. The case law continues to allow and require some degree of male-female inequality, and many administrators have designed policies that severely restrict women's role in men's prisons. Male guards remain opposed to women's presence and are often openly hostile to them. Only inmates—the most powerless group in the prison—have supported women's presence, but even then that support seems to be predicated on women's willingness and ability to perform the job differently from men.

Understanding Women's Occupational Behavior

Female guards differ widely in their job behavior and strategies for dealing with inmates, but virtually no woman performs the job "like a man," a finding that is consistent with nearly every other study of women who work in a traditionally male occupation. At the present time, there is no well-accepted theoretical framework for explaining women's differential occupational experiences or their behavioral responses to those experiences. However, two opposing theoretical trends can be found in the literature on women and work, one focusing on male-female differences and the other on structural conditions inherent in the work settings women have entered. Relying on the terminology of Roslyn Feldberg and Evelyn Glenn (1979), some research uses the "gender model" and other uses the "job model" for explaining women's occupational behavior.

The gender approach focuses on how typically female attitudes, behaviors, and prior experiences negatively affect women's ability to achieve equality on the job. For example, it has been reported that many women give priority to interpersonal and family relationships rather than to their careers, thus hampering their career advancement (Nieva and Gutek 1981; Sobel 1963; Haller and Rosenmayer 1971; Epstein 1975). Other women presumably fail to achieve equality on the job because they suffer from an "anti-success syndrome" (Smith and Smith 1970; Horner 1970; Hoffman 1974). Barbara Forisha and Barbara Goldman (1981) attribute women's occupational behavior to the fact that they are guided by the interpersonal sphere of love rather than the productive sphere of work organizations. Carol Ireson (1978) presents the basic thesis that "socialization, particularly socialization into a female sex role, negatively affects girls' achievement patterns" (p. 177). Margaret Hennig and Anne Jardim (1977) likewise blame socialization, particularly girls' lack of team sport experiences, for women's failure to obtain the skills necessary for advancement into high-level management ranks. Studies such as these suggest that if women can only learn to "act like men," then barriers to their occupational equality will be removed.

Other researchers have rejected the individualistic gender model in favor of a more structural explanation of women's inability to achieve equality on the job. Joan Acker and Donald VanHouten (1974), for example, argue that what appear to be sex differences in worker behavior can be accounted for by the different control mechanisms to which men and women are subjected. Rosabeth Kanter (1977) identified the factors inherent in the low-level organizational positions women normally fill as the major force behind women's corporate behavior. The same basic analysis is applied by Michael Rustad (1982) to women's experiences in the military and by Susan Martin (1980) to women's experiences in police work.

Changes in women's occupational behavior and the achievement of sexual equality in the workplace are assumed to rest on the removal of all remaining structural constraints and barriers.

Feldberg and Glenn (1979) criticize both the gender and job models, suggesting that the occupational behavior of both women and men might be better understood by integrating the two approaches. Few researchers seem to have taken their suggestion to heart, although in their study of female truck drivers, Muriel Lembright and Jeffrey Riemer (1982) found that the job model assumptions with which they began the research were inadequate for interpreting their data; they eventually incorporated assumptions from the gender model into their data analysis. The data on female guards are likewise incomprehensible without an understanding of the structural factors inherent in the job model, the individualistic factors inherent in the gender model, and the interrelationships between them.

When women work as guards in men's prisons, the primary structural barrier they face is a legally sanctioned system of inequality that allows different assignment policies for men and women. This system has important consequences for women's occupational behavior and for male guard attitudes toward the integration process itself. But it is also clear that both men and women bring to the job individual, gender-related characteristics and attitudes that affect their occupational behavior and their relationships with each other. Male guards overwhelmingly believe that women are innately unsuited to the job of guarding, and those beliefs guide male guard behavior in ways the critically affect women's ability to perform the job effectively. In addition, women bring to the job certain attitudes and beliefs that affect their reaction to both the structural barriers that confront them and male guard behavior toward them. Neither male nor female guards are mere cogs in the organizational machine, responding to structural preconditions in a uniform way. Instead, they are workers coming into the prison from a society in which sex roles and sex-role attitudes are currently in flux. Among both male and female guards, some find that there are personal advantages to retaining stereotypical sex-role patterns on the job; and although those patterns are related to and reinforced by continuing structural factors, they are not totally dependent on them. This study will show that it is the interrelationships among men, women, and the critical structural preconditions that account for women's occupational experiences and their behavioral responses to those experiences. It therefore suggest that the developing theory of women's occupational behavior must incorporate both job-related and gender-related factors if it is to be useful for understanding and explaining the occupational behavior of female prison guards.[21]

Note to the Reader

The primary data-gathering technique used for this study was the unstructured interview, and throughout the following chapters, the presentation of data reflects the method of collection. (For a more detailed description of the research methods used, see Appendix.) A large portion of the data is descriptive. Whenever possible, the actual words of the participants, taken from the interviews, are used. A tape recorder was used in only a few interviews, so most of the quotations included are constructions from field notes. The quotes represent the ideas and, in most cases, the actual phrases used by interviewees. I have added bridging material primarily to achieve grammatical correctness.

In both presentation of my own ideas and quotes from the interviews, I have standarized much of the prison jargon in order to spare the reader the task of juggling two or more sets of terminology. There is sometimes a great deal of variation in the terminology used between state prison systems (and sometimes between individual prisons within a single system). In New York, for example, the top administrator at each local prison is called a "superintendent." In Rhode Island, the title used for the same position is "associate director." I have chosen to use the term "warden" to refer to all prison heads. I also use the term "guard" throughout the book, although in New York and Rhode Island (and in most other states) "correction officer" is the official title. The change from "guard" to "correction officer" if fairly recent, and many persons in the prison, including many guards, continue to use the older term. My decision to use "guard" is also based on the belief that it, more than "correction officer," describes the occupational role; that is, occupants of the role do more guarding than correcting.

Standarization of terminology serves the additional purpose of helping to protect the anonymity of individual participants. In some cases, it is important to differentiate between the New York and Rhode Island systems, but whenever it is not necessary, the state in which an incident occurred is not identified. I have also used fictionalized names throughout the book and, in a very few cases, have changed insignificant details so that individuals may remain anonymous.

Setting: The American Prison

Women who work as guards in men's prisons have many of the same occupational experiences as women who have broken into other traditionally male occupations, but the experiences of female guards are also molded by the unique environment in which they work. Prisons offer a work environment that under the best of circumstances is unpleasant and under the worst of circumstances is highly dangerous. In addition, at the time women began entering men's prisons, in the mid-1970s, the job of guarding was itself in a state of turmoil, resulting from nearly two decades of institutional change, much of it affecting the guards' job and the techniques they could use to maintain control over inmates. Guards' hostility toward these changes was reflected in increased alienation and conservatism, a strengthened occupational subculture, and a movement toward unionization. Women were entering not only a male-dominated occupation but one that was troubled by internal tensions and dilemmas.

The Structure, Organization, and Goals of the Prison

No two prisons are alike. Each of the fifty states operates a distinct correctional system under its own set of penal laws, regulations, and procedures. Within states, individual prisons differ substantially for reasons of size, security classification (i.e., maximum, medium, minimum), and location; to some extent, each prison also reflects the characteristics of its staff, the management style of its warden, and its own unique history. Nevertheless, some generalizations can be made about American prisons that apply to the penal institutions in the New York and Rhode Island systems where most of the women in

15

this study work.[1] These generalizations are based on the literature on prison organization, especially the works of James Jacobs (1977), John Irwin (1980), Gresham Sykes (1958), Leo Carroll (1974), and Gordon Hawkins (1976). This chapter also draws on my own experience doing research in the prisons over the last few years.

Prisons are highly bureaucratic organizations that operate under a wide range of legal and administrative constraints. Each state correctional system is governed by the laws and budget guidelines established by its state legislature.[2] Rules and procedures for daily operation are promulgated by a central administrative agency but are subject to legislative override or reversal by state and federal courts. A substantial increase in federal judicial control over state prisons began in the late 1960s, as the courts gradually expanded their recognition of prisoners' civil rights; prison administrators, for the first time, were forced to develop correctional practices that would not violate the constitutional rights of inmates (Jacobs 1980).[3]

Unlike their autocratic predecessors,[4] the wardens at each prison largely execute rather than design correctional policy. They receive their instructions from the central administrative offices, and their communications to high-level administrators are mainly in the form of information, progress reports, and recommednations. The ability of today's warden to set poloicy and create rules is rather limited.

The internal organization of each individual prison is hierarchical and bureaucratic. Depending on the size of the institution, there may be several assistant or deputy wardens directly responsible to the warden; the typical prison has at least a deputy warden in charge of custody and another in charge of programs and "treatment." The security branch of prison personnel resembles a military structure, with the deputy warden supervising captains, lieutenants, sergeants, and rank-and-file guards.[5] Because guards are on the lowest rung of a paramilitary ladder, they are subject to the rules and directives established at each higher level. They are the staff members furthest removed from the decision-making process and the ones least likely to affect it; as such, they have very little input into the rules and procedures that govern the prison.

Coexisting with this formal organizational structure of prison personnel is the informal organization of the prisoners. The nature of prisoner subcultures has changed over time as prison conditions and population characteristics have changed.[6] In today's large maximum-security prison, many prisoners are organized into racial and ethnic gangs that perpetuate a great deal of inmate-to-inmate violence (Jacobs 1977, 1979a; Carroll 1974; Irwin 1980). In California, for example, where gang warfare is especially intense, the rate of violent incidents involving inmates rose from 1.36 per one hundred inmates in 1970 to 4.30 per hundred in 1974 (Park 1976). Gang members fight for sex, status, control over public areas of the prison,[7] and control over the distribution of prison contraband (Irwin 1980).[8]

According to John Irwin (1980), the new "convict identity" is based on toughness and unlimited exploitation of fellow inmates: "Toughness in the new hero in the violent men's prison means, first, being able to take care of oneself in the prison world. Second, it means having the guts to take from the weak" (p. 193). Leo Carroll (1974) also describes the view of manhood that is shared by many of today's young inmates:

> Prison, in their eyes, is the ultimate test of manhood. A man in prison is able to secure what he wants and protect what he has: "In here, a man gets what he can," and "nobody can force a man to do something he don't want to," are key elements of their belief system. Any prisoner who does not meet these standards is not a man, "has no respect for himself," and is therefore not entitled to respect from others. [P. 69]

In this world of mutual exploitation and struggles for power, only a few prisoners are able to remain independent—unaligned with any organized gang—and they must be both physically able to protect themselves against attack and willing to avoid open confrontations with gang members (Irwin 1980). Many physically weak and un- aligned inmates seek refuge by withdrawing from the general population and entering the prisons' protective custody units (Irwin 1980; Conrad and Dinitz 1977).

Prison officials have been ineffective in significantly reducing violence among inmates. Segregating gang leaders or the most vio- lent offenders is of limited utility because violence and gang fighting are pervasive and widespread. In some prisons, innovative programs that encourage a few inmates to act as arbitrators between gangs have been tried but have had only limited success (Sumner 1976; Bennett 1976). Violence between inmates thus remains a fact of life for the administrators and line personnel who must manage and operate the prisons.[9]

Over the years, the prisons have taken on more responsibility for rehabilitating, educating, and training inmates,[10] but today, as in the past, "custody and control are the nucleus, the paramount considera- tion of the entire institutional apparatus" (President's Commission on Law Enforcement and Administration of Justice 1972:45–46).

Maintaining custody—keeping prisoners in—is the easiest goal to fulfill because the walls, fences, and guard towers that surround most prisons present a formidable obstacle to any inmate contemplating escape (Nagel 1973). Maintaining control (or internal order) is much more difficult, given the violent nature of the inmate organization and the limited number of control options available to prison officials. In some states, the change to indeterminate sentencing and the elimination of parole has meant that prison officials can no longer manipulate release dates as forms of reward and punishment.[11] Court decisions in recent years have further limited the range of punishments by, for example, outlawing the use of corporal punishment[12] and restricting the use of disciplinary segregation.[13] In addition, inmates are now entitled to a disciplinary hearing, with some due process rights before serious punishments can be implemented at all.[14] Inmates seldom prevail at these hearings (Jacobs 1977; Irwin 1980), but because they make it necessary for prison officials to charge inmates with specific rule violations, "potentially troublesome" prisoners cannot be as easily controlled as in the past. Rather than segregating or punishing selected inmates to prevent misconduct, prison officials must now wait for actual infractions to occur and follow standardized disciplinary procedures before ordering punishments. Both prison officials and guards complain that those restrictions hamper their ability to prevent misconduct, reduce inmate-to-inmate violence, and maintain order within the prisons (Irwin 1980; Jacobs 1977; Carroll 1974).

The Guard's Job

Prison guards are the staff members directly responsible for preventing escapes and obtaining inmate compliance to prison rules and regulations. The guard is, according to Gordon Hawkins (1976), "the key figure in the penal equation, the man on whom the whole edifice of the penitentiary system depends" (p. 105). In spite of their critical role, there has been very little indepth examination of guards and the way they carry out their duties.

Much of the early sociological research on prison guards reinforces the stereotype of guards as aggressive, stupid, and sadistic men who have serious personality and psychological problems (Barnes and Teeters 1943; Clemmer 1940; Rouceck 1935). Prison scholars and reformers have often blamed guards for being rigid opponents of reform (Cressey 1973; McCleery 1960; Cantor 1939) and have suggested that because guards are at the root of much that goes wrong in the prisons, prison conditions can be improved only by recruiting different types of guards, upgrading their training, and instilling in them a sense of professionalism (Regoli et al. 1981; Attica 1972; Joint Commission on Correctional Manpower and Training 1969; Frank 1966). Most of these critics, however, have failed to examine the role requirements of guards or the specific conditions under which they must perform their job. Gresham Sykes (1958) was the first to examine the occupation of guarding rather than the occupants themselves, and only recently has additional research begun to focus specifically on the guards' role, including its historical development, position within the organizational structure, and response to changing legal mandates (Crouch 1980; Jacobs 1977, 1978; Jacobs and Retsky 1975; Carroll 1974; Fox 1982; Lombardo 1981; Hawkins 1976). The following portrayal of guards and their role within the typical American prison is shaped predominantly by this recent literature.

Because guards are both unarmed[15] and outnumbered,[16] they are not able to maintain order and security in the prisons by physical force alone. Some guards use force illegitimately, to punish particularly unruly or disrespectful inmates (Bowker 1980; Toch 1977; Marquart and Roebeck 1984), and sometimes legitimate force is necessary to break up fights between inmates, but guards are motivated to use physical force sparingly because it carries with it the risk of being injured or killed themselves. Furthermore, force is simply less effective than other techniques. According to Sykes (1958), force "will be of little aid in moving more than 1200 inmates through the mess hall in routine and orderly fashion. . . . The ability of the officials to physically coerce their captives into the paths of compliance is something of an illusion as far as the day-to-day activities of the prison are concerned and may be of doubtful value in moments of crisis" (p. 49). Instead of force, guards rely primarily on a system of preventive control aimed at averting inmate rule violation and a system of institutionalized punishments aimed at deterring inmate misconduct.

An important aspect of preventive control is the constant regulation of all inmate movement, a task that is facilitated by the architecture of prisons and the placement of doors, gates, and checkpoints at all strategic locations. These physical barriers are staffed by guards who allow inmates to pass only if they are going to scheduled programs, work details, meals, or some other specifically authorized designation.

At certain times during the day all inmates are required to return

to their cell (or dormitory) for the "count," a highly ritualized procedure designed to guarantee that no inmate has slipped through the
"preventive net" of control. If the count does not clear (i.e., if the
number of inmates in their cells does not equal the official population
figure), all activity within the prison ceases until a numerical mistake
is discovered, a missing inmate is found, or an escape is detected.
Guards take the count very seriously because they know that all
escapes will be thoroughly investigated and that ultimately they will
be blamed.

The movement of outsiders is monitored nearly as closely as that
of inmates, primarily to prevent the entrance of contraband (especially weapons and drugs). Every visitor is viewed as a potential
carrier of contraband and may be subjected to a thorough body
search before being allowed into the prison. Inmates' personal visitors are particularly suspect and will be allowed only in the official
visiting room, where guards can constantly watch to see that no
contraband is passed. As inmates leave the visiting room and return
to their cells, strip searches may be conducted as an additional
precaution. Noncustodial personnel (nurses, teachers, counselors)
and general visitors (politicians, lawyers, researchers) are also suspected carriers of contraband and may be searched by guards as they
enter the prison.

In addition to regulating and controlling the movement of all
people in the prison, guards are responsible for monitoring the movement of all physical objects. Packages arriving for inmates are thoroughly searched for contraband before they are delivered. Alcohol,
drugs, weapons, and money are deemed the most dangerous items,
but food, cigarettes, toiletries, and clothing are defined as contraband
if in excess of the allowable amount. Money and cigarettes are
considered dangerous because they can be used for barter or gamb-
ling, activities strictly forbidden in prison.

Guards are also responsible for making sure that inmates do not
confiscate prison equipment and supplies. This task is especially
difficult because it entails the constant searching of inmates as they
move through the prison. Items that are particularly appealing to
inmates are watched closely and guards may have to account for all
cooking and eating utensils, food, tools, and sporting equipment
before prisoners are allowed to leave certain areas. Of greatest concern is that inmates will try to conceal items that can be later
fashioned into weapons; their creativity and ingenuity in so doing is a
constant topic for prison folklore. During my research, one guard
working at a checkpoint claimed that he caught three inmates in one

day with identical metal rods, prompting him to search for their source. He discovered a newly acquired prison wheelchair sitting in a corridor with no spokes remaining on either wheel. That most of the spokes were never discovered suggests that the constant searching of inmates is inadequate. This is because checkpoint guards sometimes tire of searching the same inmates who pass them several times a day and may be overwhelmed when large numbers of inmates pass at one time, such as going to or from the mess hall.

Just as the daily count is a check on the guards' success in controlling inmate movement, the occasional "shakedown" is a check on how well they have prevented the entrance of contraband or the confiscation of prison equipment. At irregularly scheduled times (or when there is an indication of impending trouble), prison authorities may order a thorough search of cells and/or prisoners to uncover contraband. Such shakedowns are never unsuccessful, and most prisons have a display of confiscated weapons with which to impress new guards of the importance of preventive control.

In addition to these primarily preventive control and monitoring functions, guards are responsible for detecting and adjudicating inmate violations of prison rules. Forbidden behaviors range from illegal acts (such as murder, rape, assault, and theft)[17] to those peculiar to prison life (grooming and clothing standards, smoking regulations, use of profanity, failure to obey a guard's direct order, and the like). Many of these rules are obviously necessary to ensure security and internal order, but the purpose of some of the more petty regulations is far from clear and they remain both a source of anger and frustration to inmates and a point of constant friction between staff and inmates.

Guards would find it virtually impossible to enforce the large number of prison rules were it not for the cooperation of the majority of inmates. That cooperation is achieved not only by the threat of punishment but also through tacit agreements between guards and inmates as to which rules will be strictly enforced. Different guards have different rule enforcement standards, but most guards are willing to ignore some minor rule infractions by those inmates who voluntarily comply with the more critical rules and regulations. These arrangements are beneficial to guards as well as inmates, but they are also potentially dangerous because as guards depend increasingly on the voluntary cooperation of inmates to keep basic order, inmates are in a position to "up the ante," forcing even greater concessions. At such a point, guards may have their authority "corrupted" (Sykes 1956, 1958; McCorkle 1970) and may find it more and more difficult to enforce even the most important rules.[18] But in spite of the problems associated with these arrangements, they are probably necessary if a small guard force is to maintain relative order and stability in the potentially explosive prison environment.

The real danger for the guard lies in the possibility that prisoners will for some reason withdraw their voluntary compliance. Anger at a particular guard or general frustration may lead to an unexpected attack. Since the 1960s, inmate attacks against guards have increased in number and seriousness (Bowker 1980; Park 1976). Such duties as breaking up fights among inmates, taking custody of rule violators, and conducting shakedowns carry especially high risks (Bowker 1980).

In the prisons, there is also the ever-present possibility of collective violence. Inmates may simply refuse to obey orders, go to work details, or return to their cells. Since they are outnumbered and unarmed, guards have few options when prisoners rebel en masse. They can give up control of the prison to inmates or they can move the troublemakers into detention and try to reassert their authority over the remaining inmates. If this fails, guards may be taken hostage, assaulted, raped, or even killed. These very real possibilities provide an additional motivation for guards to forfeit total authority, avoid direct confrontations, and ignore some inmate rule violations.[19]

The dilemma for guards trying to perform this job is that both "corruption of their authority" and "toughness" have negative consequences and neither provides protection against physical harm. Most guards settle for an unstable accommodation with inmates and live with the fear that pervades the job of guarding. In a recent study of Illinois guards, James Jacobs (1978) found that more than 50 percent felt danger to be the most serious disadvantage of the job.[20]

Coinciding with the periodic episodes of violence is the boring routine that marks much of the guards' day. The tower guards and those assigned to patrol the external perimeter of the prison, for example, may spend an entire eight-hour shift alone except when relieved for meals or breaks. Guards who work at manual or electronic control room posts may be busy during the day if they are located in a central area, but they will have little sustained interaction with inmates or other prison workers. Guards who work the gates in peripheral areas see few people throughout their entire shift. These assignments offer protection from the danger and harassment associated with working directly with inmates but offer little stimulation, challenge, or excitement. These also are "dead-end" jobs that do not usually lead to movement up through the ranks.

A few jobs in the prison do offer variety, challenge, and the opportunity for positive interaction with others. Although dangerous, assignments in the cell house—the busiest part of the institution—entail constant activity. Assignment to a work detail, where the entire shift is spent supervising the same inmates, may be desirable because it is less monotonous than many other guard jobs and offers the opportunity to develop personal relationships with prisoners. The front desk is another active post; the guard at the main entrance screens visitors and often meets state and local politicians and prison officials.

Even though there is a wide variety of posts, and some assignments may be enjoyable, the prison remains a generally unpleasant working environment for most employees, but especially guards. Many prisons are old, dark, and dirty. Guards must work nights, weekends, and holidays, disrupting normal family life. The job of guarding carries very little prestige, and in some communities a stigma. Although there is some opportunity for advancement, competition for promotions is intense. And for those who do get promoted, the working conditions may be even worse since, as middle-level managers, sergeants and lieutenants are caught between rank-and-file guards (with whom they share basic conditions of employment) and prison administrators (who control their advancement opportunities). In addition, although these are technically supervisory positions, sergeants and lieutenants have little more opportunity to affect prison policy than rank-and-file guards.

Probably the worst aspect of the guards' job is that they must work directly with inmates who suffer from and resent the deprivations and restrictions inherent in imprisonment (Sykes 1958). Prisoners see guards as the ever-present symbol of the state's coercive power, and guards, more than any other members of the criminal justice system, bear the brunt of the felon's frustration and anger. Even the "best" guards, those who try to be fair and just, cannot escape the hatred of prisoners. Some inmates express this hatred through constant verbal abuse and harassment (Bowker 1980); others may throw food, urine, or feces on guards (Toch 1977; Jacobs 1977). And always, no matter how good a guard's rapport with inmates, there is the chance of serious injury or death.

The Prison Guard Subculture

In contrast to the wide attention prison scholars have given to inmate subcultures (Irwin and Cressey 1962; Cloward et al. 1960;

Sykes 1958; Sykes and Messinger 1960; Clemmer 1940; Bowker 1977), they have devoted very little to the occupational subculture of the prison guard. Yet, without an appreciation of this subculture, one cannot fully understand the nature of the occupation of guarding in today's prison or the guards' attitudes toward the many changes that have occurred in prisons over the last few decades, including the hiring of women.

The concept of subculture has been widely used by sociologists but remains only vaguely defined. In a collection of essays specifically on subcultures, the authors refer to them as "cultural innovations" (Cohen 1970), "total cultures in miniature" (Arnold 1970), "variant life styles" (Irwin 1970a), and "subdivisions of the national culture" (Gordon 1970). J. Milton Yinger (1960) points out that the "subculture" is a difficult concept to define because it carries with it all the ambiguities associated with its parent concept of "culture." In spite of this confusion over conceptualization, there is general agreement that a subculture does not refer to the people who may be members but to the set of cultural definitions shared by members—including norms, values, attitudes, symbols, myths, and beliefs—that differ in some way from those in the dominant culture. These subcultural definitions must exist over an extended period of time, even as individual "believers" come and go. Although somewhat ambiguous, the concept of subculture can be used as a way of sensitizing us to the special combinations of norms and values shared by certain subgroups in society and the special ways in which members understand the world and seek solutions to common problems. It is with this meaning in mind that the term "subculture" will be used as an aid to understanding the occupation of guarding and the cultural definitions many guards share.

Industrial sociologists have been interested in the development of occupational subcultures because workers' informal social networks have been found to affect overall productivity, both positively and negatively (Homans 1969). The development of an occupational subculture seems to be largely spontaneous and unaffected by management efforts to promote or impede them, but some occupational environments appear to be more conducive to their emergence than others. Many of the criteria identified in the literature as facilitating the appearance of a strong occupational subculture exist in the occupation of prison guard.

Occupations that expose workers to fear or danger in the workplace are especially likely to foster worker subcultures (Fitzpatrick

1980; Haas 1977; Skolnick 1969; Lucas 1969). Because overt displays of fear by some members can be detrimental to the entire work group, subcultural norms and values stress the importance of overcoming fear through displays of masculinity and machismo. Jack Haas (1977) found that high steel construction workers continually demonstrate their fearlessness by flaunting danger and taking unnecessary risks. For coal miners, fearlessness is equated with masculinity and a masking of one's inner feelings:

> Through the years the men's definition of their role had extended from the notion that the miner must be a (real) man to the prevalent ideal that (real) men were miners. The intensified and highly restrictive role taken over by men who worked in the mine was identified as a man's role. This male role, which had to be maintained at all times, envisaged a toughness and fortitude that ruled out public admission of fear or discussion of danger, and (as in combat) every effort was consciously extended to control anxiety and inhibit the symptoms of anxiety—tremors and sweating—and to remain, outwardly, as cool and calm as possible so that the job could be carried on. [Lucas 1969:22]

Arthur Niederhoffer (1967) found that the occupational subculture of the police often takes on a "locker room" aura that reflects not only the nature of the occupation but also the general nature of the male subculture, in which displays of aggressiveness and sexuality are expected.

The prison is, of course, also a dangerous work environment, and guards continually stress the importance of masculinity for performing the job. Questioning a worker's masculinity is tantamount to challenging his ability to perform the job. The terms "faggot" and "pussy" are used for guards who show fear on the job, for those who frequently make errors in judgment, and for those who do not participate in the nearly constant banter among guards (much of it involving a questioning of each other's masculinity). When male guards discovered I was in the prison to interview female guards, they would invariably tell me about some "female" on their shift who should be included. This comment was sometimes meant as a joke (referring to a buddy) but was also used to identify guards whom they did not consider "man enough" to do the job.

In addition to stressing masculinity as a way of overcoming fear, the subcultural norms include advice for decreasing the threat of danger on the job. "Never turn your back on an inmate," "never trust an inmate," and "never let your guard down" are popular occupational norms in the prison. In short, the subcultural definitions teach guards that inmates can never be trusted (Irwin 1980) and that they must never be complacent about security.

A second variable that favors the development of an occupational subculture is intense interaction among workers, off and on the job. This usually occurs in "one-industry towns," such as coal-mining communities, where nearly all residents are connected with the same employer (Lucas 1969; Kerr and Siegal 1954). In this kind of environment, work and social contacts coincide and many families become related through marriage.

Prisons surely fulfill this requirement. They are commonly located in small rural communities, where the prison is the primary employer. This accounts, in part, for the intense social interaction found among prison workers (Esselstyn 1966). Even in urban settings, however, the prison guard subculture develops because guards spend a great deal of time socializing with each other, most often in bars and taverns, without other family members (Fogel 1975). Ralph Gardner (1981), who studied occupational stress among prison guards, speculates that this camaraderie develops because of guards' feeling that only other guards can understand their problems and concerns.

A third factor that encourages the growth of occupational subcultures is employee opposition to organizational goals and management strategies (Crozier 1964). The police subculture, for example, promotes opposition to the administration and socializes new recruits into the belief that efficient police work would be impossible were officers to follow administrative rules and procedures to the letter (McNamara 1967). Prison guards are also highly critical of their administrators (especially central office personnel), who "don't know what it's like in here," and of the myriad rules and regulations that "tie their hands" and prevent them from doing their job. New recruits are often told by old-timers to forget everything they learned in the training academy and to rely instead on their own common sense and the wisdom of experienced co-workers.

Low status attached to a job is a final factor that promotes the development of an occupational subculture (Fitzpatrick 1980; Seidman et al. 1958; Gouldner 1954). Workers who feel unappreciated by the public often draw together, defensively, to provide mutual support and to reinforce for each other the importance of their occupational role. The police subculture, for example, stresses the idea of police as the "thin blue line" between chaos and order. The guarding of inmates is an even more stigmatized occupation, and prison guards report feeling unrecognized and unappreciated by the general public as well as by their own superiors (Jacobs and Retsky 1975). Only among other guards do they receive support for the notion that the job is a difficult one, requiring a "special breed" of individual. Thus, prison guards frequently describe their job as "impossible," but with a certain pride that is reinforced by the subculture.

Occupational subcultures can be functional for employees by increasing solidarity, providing enjoyable social interactions on the job, improving morale, and helping workers find solutions to common problems (Ritzer 1977; Cohen 1970). But while they may benefit some workers, subcultures may be dysfunctional for the organization itself (Blau et al. 1955; Gouldner 1954). Several researchers have suggested, for example, that the police subculture encourages cynicism and a lack of commitment to organizational goals (Van Maanen 1975; Reiss 1971; Niederhoffer 1967). Hans Toch (1977), in his study of violence among both police officers and prison guards, maintains that subcultural norms often condone physical violence and encourage protection of individual aggressors: "Subcultures of this kind reflect alienation or an absence of community. They reflect an ethnocentric or egocentric orientation of men who sense no rewards, and suspect anger, in departing from parochial goals. The loyalty of such men is to their own kind, no matter how individually reprehensible they are, because the larger setting is seen as impersonal and threatening" (p. 123). So, although the occupational subculture may be a response to deeply felt employment dilemmas, it is not always a positive or helpful influence on workers. If it encourages an exaggerated notion of masculinity, it can increase aggression and violence on the job. If it is primarily oppositional in nature, it promotes a cynicism among workers that lowers morale. Such a subculture may also inhibit communication and cooperation between administrators and low-level employees, decreasing the opportunity for mutual problem solving.

To some extent, the prison guard subculture demonstrates each of these negative consequences. According to David Duffee (1980), the guard subculture was born of commonly felt conflict and confusion over the changing occupational role as prison rehabilitative programs were increased throughout the 1950s and 1960s. At the time, prison critics suggested that guards should be educated about "treatment philosophy" so that they could incorporate rehabilitation directly into their job. In this new, alternative role,

> correction officers would see themselves as agents of change dedicated to moving inmates toward acceptance of themselves as

law-abiding citizens. The officers would prefer persuasive techniques of influence and would selectively utilize coercion only as a last resort for a short-term effect. They would convey messages of tolerance, initiative, and acceptance, instead of messages of the custodial prison: repressive control, punishment of socially stigmatized criminals, and isolation from the free community. Impersonal carrying out of control duties *only* would be replaced by establishment of psychological *contact* with inmates. The officers would be full-fledged partners in the overall effort to restore inmates to the free community, prepared and ready for socially constructive lives. [Johnson 1981:83]

Thomas Murton (1979) suggested that prison systems should take more care in recruiting guards with the appropriate concern for inmate rehabilitation:

A primary consideration in the reform of the prison should be personnel selection. . . . The major personnel criteria should be that the correctional workers have personal integrity, concern for others, and sincere commitment. . . . A deep, personal commitment to the reform movement allows no compromise of integrity. In addition, it requires a willingness on the part of the officer to subordinate personal goals of tenure, promotion, retirement, recognition, and other indications of professional success for the welfare of the inmates if necessary. [P. 34]

Although a few guards have incorporated rehabilitative goals into their job (Johnson 1977) and a few prison systems now include inmate counseling as a formal guard responsibility (Ward and Vandergoot 1981), there has been no major transformation of the guards' role. Guards themselves were unmotivated to make such role changes, in part because they realized that, despite the rhetoric of prison critics, they would continue to be judged on their success in maintaining order and security, not on their ability to relate to inmates. In short, even as broad prison goals have changed, the job of prison guard has remained primarily one of custody and control.

Efforts to change the guards' role did not succeed, but the move toward increased rehabilitation itself had a great impact on the job of guarding. During the 1970s, as prison officials responded to the suggestions of reformers, administrative directives increasingly proscribed specific forms of guard behavior (e.g., verbal and physical abuse of inmates), while the rules for inmate behavior became more vague and ambiguous: "Under the role prescriptions dictated by the rehabilitative ideal, the guard is to relax and act spontaneously. Inmates are to be understood, not blamed, and formal disciplinary mechanisms should be triggered as infrequently as possible" (Jacobs and Retsky 1975:7). Guards became unsure what constituted acceptable inmate behavior under the new rules and how they were to obtain compliance. They complained that inmates constantly questioned orders because the rules were always changing:

> The idea of what a prison should be like has swung from one end of the pendulum to the other. No one really knows what the answer is. A lot of people think they do. One day this is o.k. and the next day it's not o.k. And the next day . . . well, maybe it's o.k. There are no rules, no regulations for the correctional officer himself . . . there is no directive and he more or less fends for himself. [May 1976:12]

Leo Carroll's (1974) study of a Rhode Island prison during this period of change found that anomie and normlessness pervaded the guard force. Upset by the conflicting demands placed upon them and by the institutional changes that limited the means for obtaining inmate compliance, guards rebelled against their superiors and refused to enforce any of the rules; conditions deteriorated until control of the prison was virtually transferred to the inmates.

The guards' loss of control during the 1970s was exacerbated by the entrance of a "new breed" of inmate who refused to negotiate an acceptable bargain with guards:

> Contemporary prisoners—especially black prisoners, who comprise a majority of the prison population in a number of states and about 50 percent nationwide—are no longer "buying all the bullshit"; they are unwilling to accept the kinds of mutual accommodations and understandings between inmates and staff that, in the past, had kept the pressures toward anarchy and violence under some sort of control. In effect, inmates have withdrawn the consent on which prison government has always rested; they have shifted the measure of an individual's worth from adjustment back to rebellion. [Silberman 1978:246]

Moreover, the inmate population during this period was increasingly made up of blacks and other minorities (Mattick 1976) who were more likely than their predecessors to have been convicted of violent crimes (Toch 1977). They tended to be more politicized, questioning both the conditions in the prison and the fundamental right of the state to imprison them (Crouch 1980; Jacobs 1977). Rather than seeking mutual accommodation with guards, this new breed of inmate used intimidation to control both guards and weaker inmates. In many large prisons, organized gangs of inmates, some formed inside prison and others imported from the streets, virtually ran the institutions. Because of the formidable physical structure of most American prisons, guards were able to prevent mass escapes but could maintain only minimal internal order. Thus, guards were being encouraged by prison reformers to help, counsel, and understand inmates, while they were finding it more and more difficult to carry out their primary control functions (Jacobs 1977; Irwin 1980; Carroll 1974).

Guards also felt betrayed by the public, who showed a new concern for the plight of inmates (Murton 1979; Irwin 1980), and by their own superiors, whom they accused of "siding with the inmates" (Jacobs 1977; Duffee 1974; Carroll 1974). Prison administrators did not shift their loyalty from guards to inmates, but many did endorse prison reform (Berk and Rossi 1977) and most at least tried to comply with the new law concerning inmates' constitutional rights, if only to avoid lawsuits (Jacobs 1977).

Guards were also angered by the increase in privileges and material goods that became available to inmates during this period. As early as the 1950s, many amenities, such as movies, radios, sports and recreational activities, and increased smoking privileges, were introduced into the prisons (Reckless 1955). Today, even more humanitarian reforms are evident: some prisoners are allowed to wear street clothes instead of uniforms; more personal items, including decorations, radios, televisions, food, and toiletries, are allowed in the cells; visiting hours have been extended; and the physical barriers that had separated inmates and visitors have been removed in most prisons. Some states have authorized conjugal visits, allowing an inmate's wife and children to join him for a weekend in a trailer on the prison grounds. In general, the entire prison routine has become less regimented. Inmates have more time out of their cells and more freedom to congregate in the yard, recreation rooms, and cell blocks.

Some of these newly instituted humanitarian reforms clearly made the guards' job more difficult than it was in the past (Mattick 1976; Thomas 1972; McCleery 1960). A large group of conversing inmates is harder to control than a company of inmates silently walking in single file. The right to more personal possessions makes shakedowns more time-consuming and the control of contraband more difficult. But the implications of these reforms for guards have, in a sense, been more emotional than practical. It seems that many guards have interpreted public and administrative concern for inmates as a lack of concern for them and their occupational problems

(Weber 1961). Any inmate gain is interpreted by guards as a personal loss.

Donald Cressey (1973) has suggested that guards' opposition to changes in the prison routine can also be attributed to the "law and order" attitudes consistent with most guards' class background:

> A working class prison guard who has learned what is "right" and "proper" in the world is likely to implement in his work a strong moral code that stresses righteous indignation about crime, hatred of robbers and rapists, intolerance of slovenliness and laziness, disdain for acquisition except by the slow process of honest labor, and "self-discipline" rather than self-expression. . . . Any prison reformer who tries to implement a program at variance with such attitudes must expect resistance. [P. 142]

Lucien Lombardo (1981) found that guards are still opposed to many prison reforms; furthermore, they blame the changes on administrators who prefer to "coddle" rather than punish criminals.

At the same time that prisoners' daily existence was becoming less regimented, the guards' was becoming more so as prison bureaucratization and centralization increased (Jacobs 1977) and guards were ordered to document and justify formerly routine decisions.[21] New York State, for example, requires guards to report all uses of force on a special form, filled out in triplicate and signed by any witnesses.[22] Not only must guards become proficient at writing these reports,[23] but they are keenly aware that such reports allow administrative review and criticism of decisions that once went unnoticed and unquestioned. Guards tend to interpret this increased supervision not as a result of bureaucratization but as an expression of administrators' lack of confidence in their competency and integrity (Silberman 1978; Irwin 1980).

In response to these institutional changes affecting the guards' role and responsibilities, the guard subculture became increasingly defensive, conservative, and opposed to reform[24] (Duffee 1974; Poole and Regoli 1980; Irwin 1980). Guards remained cynical about the concept of rehabilitation as well as their role in it (Regoli et al. 1979), and many new guards quickly joined older ones in longing for the "good old days" when they ran the institutions and inmates knew their place.[25]

Not all guards become equally enmeshed in this occupational subculture,[26] but its definitions and values remain powerful because they provide the only clear, consistent occupational philosophy for guards. There is substantial pressure on new recruits to adopt the subcultural values, beliefs, and moral outlook, and if they do so they are rewarded with the collective support of many of their peers. Guards who reject the subculture tend to do it more as isolated individuals and without a shared definition of the occupation to contradict that supported by the subculture. Consequently, the guard subculture, with its negative evaluation of the job, the inmates, and the administration remains a powerful force in the prison regardless of the actual number of guards who actively support it.

Unionization of Prison Guards

The same anger and disillusionment with changing prison conditions that led to a tightening of the prison guard subculture also led guards to form unions (Jacobs and Crotty 1978). By the mid-1970s, guards in nearly half the states, including New York and Rhode Island, were unionized (Wynne, 1978a), and many of the unions succeeded in negotiating contracts that substantially increased wages. In New York State, for example, the annual salary for new guards rose from $7,571 in 1970 to $11,981 in 1977 (Jacobs and Crotty 1978). By 1981, newly hired guards in New York and Rhode Island earned about $14,000 a year, which they could easily supplement by working overtime.

Neither guards nor their unions were satisfied with merely increasing the compensation for working under what they considered deteriorating conditions, and guards pressured prison administrators to institute changes that would improve their working conditions. Through both contract negotiations and collective protest (including strikes, walkouts, and "sick-outs" in several states),[27] guards demanded stricter rules and harsher punishments for inmates, an increase in the staff-inmate ratio, and a reversal of many of the prison reforms that had been implemented by correctional departments (Jacobs 1977; Wynne 1978a; Carroll 1974; Christianson 1979; Staudoher 1976; Potter 1979; Irwin 1980). Most of these demands could not be met by prison officials because the conditions that most frustrated guards had been the result of legislative action or judicial decree; prison officials lacked the power to reverse them, even if they desired to do so.

Guards also used the formal collective bargaining process to challenge administrative assignment policies and, in ten states, have been successful in negotiating provisions that require seniority to be used as the basis for all job assignments (Zimmer 1985). Under these seniority systems, guards are able to bid for all internal vacancies and receive the assignment of their choice as long as they are the most senior bidder.[28] For any unbid posts, supervisors can assign the least senior guard or a new guard who is still on probation (and therefore not yet covered by the seniority provision).[29]

Guards favor strict seniority systems that give prison administrators little direction over job assignment for a variety of reasons, including the fact that such systems prevent nepotism, favoritism, and bribery. Guards also prefer to control their assignments because family or other obligations may make some shifts and pass days preferable. And because the actual tasks that guards perform are so varied—ranging from the gun tower to kitchen supervision to cell block duty to clerical and administrative tasks—many guards prefer to choose an assignment that best fits with their own interests, skills, and expertise. These factors alone make a seniority system especially desirable to prison workers, but the real pressure for seniority occurred because of the deteriorating working conditions of the late 1960s and early 1970s as changes in the prison regime were being implemented more quickly than could be accommodated. During this period, guards lost many of their traditional means of control, and the job became more difficult and dangerous (Jacobs 1977; Toch 1977; Bowker 1980; Carroll 1974; Irwin 1980). Under these working conditions, many guards preferred to remove themselves from direct inmate contact as much as possible; assignments in the administration building, in enclosed control booths or gun towers, or on the night shift when inmates were locked in their cells therefore became the most desirable. Only a seniority system could guarantee that those guards who had "put in their time" in direct-contact jobs could move into jobs that offered relative safety and an escape from the changes that many guards resented.

Measuring the overall impact of guard unionization on working conditions is extremely difficult. Unionization has given guards a voice in the administration of the prisons and both prison officials and state political leaders must now listen to the concerns of guards as well as to those of inmates.[30] This may be of some psychological importance to guards because it helps to counterbalance what they have always perceived as excessive public and administrative concern for inmates. On the other hand, James Fox (1982) argues that unionization has increased guards' frustration because it raised expectations without being able to fulfill them.[31] It is clear that unionization has led to some decrease in administrative authority, especially in matters of personnel assignment (Jacobs and Crotty 1978;

Wynne 1978a; Christianson 1979), but the guards' increase in power
has not been translated into substantially better working conditions.
The guard's job is constrained by the goals and organization of the
prison and these cannot be changed through collective bargaining.
Nor can collective bargaining reverse any of the changes in the
prison that have so frustrated guards over the past few decades,
especially those that have resulted from judicial or legislative decree;
nor can it improve the disposition and behavior of inmates. And even
seniority fails to improve working conditions for all guards; it merely
provides relief to guards who have served some period of time.[32]

The job of guarding in today's prisons, then, remains difficult and
unpleasant. Job morale continues to be low and job stress high
(Brodsky 1977). Perhaps more important, guards remain angry. In
1979, New York State guards "struck out" at the entire system by
walking off the job for seventeen days (Zimmer and Jacobs 1981). In
Michigan, guards rebelled against their superiors, locked up prisoners without orders to do so, and triggered a prison riot that resulted in
160 injuries (Hart 1981). Guards still complain that they are given
insufficient tools with which to carry out the organizational goals of
order and security. Thus the role strain that emerged during the
turmoil of the last few decades has not been ameliorated by unionization. The guard's job remains filled with tension, confusion, and
danger.

Conclusion

When women entered male prisons they were entering a dangerous work environment in which the possibility of injury or death is
always present. Greatly outnumbered and given few reliable tools for
guaranteeing inmate compliance to prison rules, guards are engaged
in a continual struggle with inmates for control of the prisons.

The decade of the 1970s was a particularly volatile period for
prisons because important changes were occurring in the formal
organizational structure, the legal rights of inmates, and the role
requirements of guards. Many guards responded to these changes
with an anger and hostility that led to unionization, collective protest,
and a strengthening of the guard subculture already based on conservatism, cynicism, and machismo.

Male guards generally viewed the introduction of women into
their all-male world as one more liberal change imposed from without. The idea of women as co-workers threatened a basic assumption

they held about the job: that "masculinity" is a primary job requirement. The tightly knit subculture to which many guards owed alle-
giance closed its ranks. Women breaking into this traditionally male
occupation were not to receive the assistance or support of the male
co-workers with whom they shared basic working conditions.

Becoming a Guard

Title VII's proscription of sex discrimination in employment gave women the legal right to seek employment in traditionally male occupations. Although the large majority of women continue to work in predominantly female occupations (Smith 1979; *Handbook on Women Workers*, 1975), some women have begun to obtain positions previously reserved for men. When women choose to become guards in men's prisons, they are moving not only into an occupation from which they have long been excluded, but also into one whose duties contradict those traditionally seen as appropriate for women. Theirs is the epitome of a nontraditional occupational choice. One might wonder whether women who choose to guard male prisoners are different from women who make more traditional occupational choices. What qualities or characteristics lead them to choose this job? Are they different from the "average" woman in some noticeable way? And what implication does self-selection have for the capacity of this subgroup of women to perform a job for which most women might be ill-suited?

Women and Occupational Choice

Industrial psychologists have attempted to identify why particular individuals choose the jobs and careers they do.[1] Some researchers have suggested that individuals choose occupations rationally, weighing the advantages and disadvantages and giving primary consideration to wages and other extrinsic rewards (Clark 1931; Tiedeman 1965; Davis and Moore 1945), but the largest body of research has focused on the unconscious, psychological needs that people attempt to fulfill through their choice of an occupation.

John Holland (1959, 1973) expanded upon the early, psychologically oriented theories (Brill 1949; Forer 1953, Roe 1956) by defining the specific characteristics that are important in an individual's choice of an occupation. He identified six types of "occupational environments" and six "modal personality orientations" that typify people's "habitual or preferred methods for dealing with environmental tasks" (Holland 1959:35). According to him, people make "adequate" occupational choices to the degree they choose a job with an environment that corresponds most closely to their own values, interests, skills, role preferences, and life-style. Holland suggests further that individuals with accurate self-knowledge are most likely to make adequate occupational choices.

Holland's theory has been widely tested, and those tests confirm that his vocational preference inventory (VPI) successfully differentiates persons already working within his six different occupational groups (Lacey 1971; Hughes 1972; Gaffey and Walsh 1974; Fishbourne and Walsh 1976). What these studies cannot confirm, however, is whether workers possessed these personality orientations before beginning employment or adopted them as a result of the work experience. Still, the VPI continues to be widely used by schools and vocational counselors to guide individuals into specific occupational categories (Prediger and Hanson 1976), and the assumption that people self-select for occupations according to both personality characteristics and special areas of expertise remains largely unquestioned.

As early as the 1940s researchers interested in occupational choice began to search for the differences between men and women that might account for their different career choices. Studies indicated that women workers seek intrinsic rewards, such as a pleasant work environment, the opportunity to engage in social interactions with co-workers, and the opportunity to be of service to others, rather than the extrinsic rewards of pay and prestige that guide male choices (Jurgensen 1947; Singer and Stefflre 1954; Bendig and Stillman 1958; Centers and Bugental 1966; Wagman 1965). Ralph Turner (1964) and George Psathas (1968) have further suggested that girls' occupational aspirations are largely dependent on future marriage plans. More recently, researchers have claimed that women make different choices than men because early socialization has provided them with different traits, skills, and abilities (Mischel 1976; Hetherington and Parke 1979) and encouraged them to have lower occupational expectations and aspirations than men (Walum 1977; Bem and Bem 1970; Ireson 1978). Over the years, then, explanations for why women's career choices differ from men's have shifted from "natural" predispositions, to different needs, to differential socialization and training.

During the 1960s and 1970s, some researchers turned their focus away from differences between men and women and directed it toward differences among women. First, attempts were made to differentiate between women who choose a career and those who prefer not to join the labor force. Researchers generally found that career-oriented women possessed more stereotypically masculine qualities—they tended to be more competitive, more aggressive, and more achievement oriented than women who remained homemakers (Gysbers et al. 1968; Rand 1968; Wagman 1966). Women who join the labor force have also been found to have more liberal sex-role attitudes than those who choose homemaking careers (Dowdall 1974; Waite and Stolzenberg 1976).[2]

Alice Rossi (1965) was the first to suggest the importance of studying differences among career-oriented women. She hypothesized that there would be significant differences between women who choose male-dominated occupations ("pioneers") and those who work in traditionally female occupations ("traditionals"). Using Rossi's conceptualization, Donna Nagely (1971) found that pioneers are more committed to their careers, are more likely to endorse the basic principles of the women's movement, and are less likely to have traditional attitudes about male and female roles. Kenneth Wolkin (1972) found that pioneers had a greater desire to work and valued work situations that offered the opportunity for mastery and independence.

In his research, Jim Crawford (1978) set out not only to identify but also to account for the factors that differentiate pioneer and traditional women. He hypothesized that pioneers would have less stereotypic perceptions of the female sex role and less traditional attitudes toward marriage and women's place in society. He also hypothesized that differences in women's family background would account for differences in their sex-role attitudes and, ultimately, in their occupational choices. He found no support for the family background hypothesis,[3] but he did reaffirm that pioneer women had less traditional attitudes toward "proper" female sexual behavior, women's work roles, and women's family roles. Pioneer women also engaged in less sex-role stereotyping about appropriate and inappropriate behavior for males and females. Crawford concludes that "there is indeed a connection between feminine role perception and vocational choice in females" (p. 136).

The Bem Sex-Role Inventory (BSRI), which measures accept-ance of typically masculine and typically feminine characteristics, has also been used to differentiate traditional from pioneer women. Because the masculinity and femininity scales are separate (rather than opposite ends of a single continuum), individuals can score high on one, neither, or both. If high on both scales, respondents are said to be androgynous (Bem 1974). Jan Vandever (1978) gave the BSRI to nursing students and found that 51 percent could be char-acterized as "highly feminine." When the BSRI was given to workers in a masculine occupation (attorney), a neutral occupation (journal-ist), and a feminine occupation (librarian), it was found that the more masculine the occupation, the higher female occupants scored on the masculinity and the androgyny measures (Fitzgerald 1976). In a study comparing female engineering and home economics students, Barbara Yanico and her colleagues (1978) obtained similar results. Women studying to be engineers were similar to home economics majors on the femininity scale but, unlike home economists, scored high on the masculinity scale as well, making them more androgy-nous. The BSRI tests, then, support the hypothesis that traditionals and pioneers have different sex-role orientations.

Recent studies of women who work in traditionally male blue-collar occupations also suggest that pioneer women have back-grounds and personalities that predispose them toward a nontradi-tional occupational choice. In her study of female police officers, Susan Martin (1980) claims that "what may distinguish many policewomen from other women in the population is the large propor-tion who describe themselves as having been independent, athletic, or 'tomboys' when they were girls" (p. 61). Several women in her study had considered military careers and a substantial number had long aspired to police work. Mary Walshok (1981) studied women in several different traditionally male blue-collar occupations and found that family backgrounds forced or encouraged these women to be-come independent and self-reliant at an early age. From childhood they enjoyed "male pursuits," described themselves as "tomboys," and claimed that their favorite hobbies required mechanical exper-tise. Walshok describes these women as especially articulate, reflec-tive, and risk taking and suggests that these characteristics account, at least in part, for their nontraditional occupational choices.

Using different measures and techniques and examining diverse samples of female workers, these studies agree that women who make nontraditional occupational choices are in some identifiable ways different from the general population of women. A major problem with these studies is that they apply their measures to women already working in traditional or nontraditional occupations and cannot control for any effect of the occupational experience itself. In spite of this shortcoming, these studies have been well accepted, probably because they support the more general theoretical litera- ture on occupational choice by finding some congruence between individuals' occupational preferences and their family background, personality, attitudes, and psychological needs. Relying on this sub- stantial body of literature, one might expect that those women who have chosen the job of prison guard—a highly nontraditional occupa- tional choice—to be different from women in typically female occupations and, to perhaps an even greater extent, different from the general population of women.

Women Choosing to Become Prison Guards

Some of the women currently working in men's prisons began their correctional careers in a women's prison and only later sought transfer to a male facility; other women joined the guard force after the integration order and have worked only in men's prisons. But whether women joined the force before or after integration, they have made a highly nontraditional occupational choice. Work in a women's prison is traditional only in the sense that such jobs have long been available to women; when one considers that the job requirements include the exercise of authority over (and the physical control of) others in an often dangerous and volatile environment, the job is, in a real sense, nontraditional. There may be some differ- ences between women who joined the guard force before and after the decision to integrate, but these two groups had virtually identical responses when asked why they had become guards.

Of the seventy women interviewed in New York and Rhode Is- land, not one had aspired to the job of prison guard. When asked about their career plans as teenagers, only two women said they had considered jobs in law enforcement, and both had anticipated work- ing for small police departments.[4] Most of the others mentioned typically female occupations (nurse, teacher, secretary) or claimed that as teenagers they had not planned to enter the work force at all. Several women had wanted to be social workers and feel that their job in corrections comes close to meeting that aspiration. Nearly all female guards claim, however, that their decision to take this job could not have been predicted even a short time before the actual decision was made.

Although many women guards were able to name aspects of the job that they found particularly rewarding, all women interviewed said their primary incentive was financial. Almost 40 percent of the women were single mothers with long-term financial responsibilities; many others felt that their salary was critical to their family's well-being. Female guards' emphasis on pay is similar to that of women in other nontraditional blue-collar occupations (O'Farrell 1980); women in the skilled trades (Baker 1975), police work (Ermer 1978), construction (Westley 1982), and mining (Drolet 1976) have also named monetary rewards as the most critical factor in choosing their jobs.[5]

Closely related to the promise of high wages is the lack of other opportunities, especially ones with the minimal education and experience requirements of guard work. In some of the small communities where many of New York's male prisons are located, the prison is the main employer. The opening up of guard jobs to women provided women in these communities with a new opportunity that could not be matched elsewhere.[6] Several women had formerly worked in the prison, performing clerical or administrative duties for much lower wages; these women were able to nearly double their salaries by becoming guards.

Many women who are now guards worked at several lower-paying jobs before seeking prison employment:

> When I got out of high school, I worked in a bank for a while. I hated that and the money was terrible. Next I worked for an employment agency, but that folded within a year. After that, I got a job in a day care center. I liked working with kids, and I got to take my daughter to work with me, but, again, the pay was really low. When this came along, I decided it was my best chance for a decent salary. Now I pay for a full-time babysitter and still come out ahead.

Women also find the benefits and security of state employment appealing, especially after long experience working in less stable and secure jobs:

> I've been a waitress for twenty years. The money was okay, but there's no security. If you get sick, you don't get paid. I'm getting too old for that. I work less now than I ever did the rest of my life—I even take a real vacation.

Although women recognized the advantages of guard work, the decision to actually take the job, once it was offered, was not an easy one for most. Until actually faced with the decision, many had not seriously weighed the advantages and disadvantages of becoming a guard:

> It came as a shock, really. I guess I never thought it would happen so I hadn't given it much thought. Once I started thinking about it, I started to worry. Me a prison guard? But I figured I might as well give it a try. I knew if it didn't work out I could always quit.

Most women decided to enter the academy only after serious contemplation and advice from friends and relatives. Some met strong opposition:

> When I told my husband that I might get assigned to a men's prison if I took a job, he blew his top. We had a raging battle for days. In fact, he didn't speak to me for weeks. But I couldn't be deterred—I knew this was the best job I would ever be able to get.

One woman who had relatives working as guards received the opposite advice:

> I took the test pretty much as a joke. I never really intended to take the job. But after it came through, everyone tried to convince me to take it. They said they'd watch out for me and make sure nothing happened. They said if other women can do it, so can I. And here I am.

Very few women seem to have begun their careers as guards with a personal commitment to the job or confidence in their ability to succeed at it. The most typical attitude was, given the lack of good alternatives, "I'll give it a try."

Theories of occupational choice often stress that self-selection for a career is a developmental process, extending over many years as individuals make decisions about their own abilities and potentials and make educational choices that ultimately narrow the range of future occuptional choices (Ginzberg et al. 1951; Super 1953; Psathas 1968). The employment histories of female guards may be closer to theories of "occupational drift" than occupational choice. In some cases, workers drift into jobs by accident or because of the lack of other options (Katz and Martin 1962; Caplow 1954). Ronald Pavalko (1971) suggests "that 'rational planning' as an explanation of the occupational decision-making process applies primarily to middle class youth who more often aspire to highly prestigious or professional occupations" (p. 50).[7] Research on male prison guards has stressed that few male prison guards have actively chosen this occupation; instead, they have drifted into it because of family tradition or prolonged unemployment (Jacobs and Retsky 1975; Crouch and Marquart 1980; Lombardo 1981). Perhaps female prison guards took the same route—they, too, "drifted" into it.

Even if no long-term planning was involved in their occupational choice, female guards may still represent a select group of women. The reasons people give for ultimately deciding to try a particular job may not reveal everything that made the decision possible. Despite a lack of other occupational options, many women would refuse even to consider the job of prison guard—in a female or a male prison. The women I interviewed were at least predisposed to "try" this highly nontraditional occupation.

The general theoretical literature on occupational choice (Roe 1956; Holland 1959, 1973) and the research on women in other nontraditional occupations (Tangri 1972; Martin 1980; Walshok 1981) would lead one to hypothesize that female guards, in comparison to women who make more traditional occupational choices, would have personality characteristics and skills that make this choice possible. This literature suggests further that the greatest divergence between female guards and other women would be their sex-role attitudes. Women in other nontraditional occupations have consistently displayed more liberal attitudes about proper male and female roles than women who choose traditionally female occupations (Nagely 1971; Crawford 1978; Fitzgerald 1976). Because the job of prison guard is an extreme example of a nontraditional job choice for women, we would expect female guards to have nontraditional attitudes about the role of women in the work force and in society as a whole.

In-depth interviews with women guards focused, in part, on their attitudes toward recent changes in the role of women in society and their attitudes toward potential changes. They were asked for their opinions on the Equal Rights Amendment (ERA), the proper role of women in the work force, the effect of working mothers on child development, and the degree to which marital equality was possible and desirable. Although the questions and techniques used in this study differ from those of previous research on women in nontraditional occupations, I sought to tap some of the same sex-role attitudes.

In contrast to other "pioneer" women, female guards have rather conservative sex-role attitudes. Out of seventy women interviewed, only twelve (17 percent) strongly favored passage of the ERA. Of the remainder, a few were adamantly opposed; the others felt it mattered little one way or the other. Only 38 percent of female prison guards felt that husbands and wives should have equal power within the family. Some women had extremely traditional views on this issue. One female guard, for example, explained:

> When a woman goes home she's got to act like a woman if she wants to keep a man. If I were married I would give my husband my paycheck and then have him give me money back for groceries.

Another woman, who claimed that she has had no trouble handling male inmates because she grew up in the city where "girls learn to be tough in order to survive," maintains that "equality" should not extend to personal relationships with men:

> I know how to handle myself on the streets. I'm not afraid to walk in the city alone at night. But if I'm with a man, I'm going to let him protect me.

A majority of female guards (56 percent) also held the traditional belief that mothers should not work during their children's formative years. Many of these women had worked at various jobs while their children were young, but only out of financial necessity.

The only statement that received nearly unanimous support from women (96 percent) was, "Men and women should get equal pay for equal work." But not all of these women favored equal opportunity for women in all employment areas. Some felt men should be given preference for jobs to which they are particularly well suited, such as those that require superior physical strength. Indeed, several women working in men's prisons claimed that men are much better suited for such employment and that women should fill only a very few of the available guard jobs.[8] One woman explained why she took the job in spite of her belief that women could not perform on an equal basis with men:

> Women don't really belong here, but if the department is stupid enough to hire women then I might as well take advantage of it. There's no other job in town where I could earn as much money.

Women with this attitude generally favor strict limits on the number of female guards in each prison and favor the assignment of women only to those posts that involve little or no direct contact with male inmates. They feel that women are useful for a few specialized tasks, such as searching female visitors, but should not be used interchangeably with male guards. Other women favor more egalitarian treatment of male and female guards, but only eleven (16 percent) felt that women could perform all jobs in the prison as well as men.

Only four female guards claimed that a prison could be run with a guard force that was 50 percent female.

Only a minority of those interviewed possess nontraditional sex-role attitudes. The majority have conservative attitudes concerning "proper" male and female roles and the remainder fall somewhere between the two extremes, perhaps having somewhat liberal attitudes about work-related issues and more conservative attitudes concerning women's family roles. There is no support for the hypothesis that women in this highly nontraditional occupation would have nontraditional attitudes toward women's roles in society.[9]

There is also nothing extraordinary about the backgrounds of these women, especially when compared to their male counterparts. Forty percent of both males and females who entered the New York State training academy in 1977 and 1979 came from the metropolitan New York City area. Fifty-one percent of the women, as compared to 41 percent of the men, are minority group members. Fifty-four percent of the male recruits have some college education, as compared to 55 percent of females. Of those with college credit, both males and females have completed a mean of 2.4 years.[10] Female recruits are slightly older than males. The mean age for women is 28.2 years; the mean for men, 26.1.

Female guards also have fairly traditional employment backgrounds. Before becoming guards, most worked at a variety of low-paying jobs, most commonly clerical work, other kinds of office work, and waitressing.[11] Many were unemployed before entering the training academy. No women had had prior work experience in which they were required to discipline and control others.

One interesting background factor is that thirteen female guards (18 percent) had male relatives—husbands, uncles, brothers, and fathers—who were guards. This is probably because many prisons are located in communities that offer few other employment opportunities, and there is no indication that having a relative in corrections predisposes women toward acceptance of this highly nontraditional occupation for themselves. In fact, the women who had relatives in corrections tended to have traditional attitudes about women's roles and to most strongly favor limits on the use of women in male prisons. Thus, it does not seem to be the case that male guards pass on to their female relatives a belief that women are suited to this occupation. It may be, however, that for some of these women, the mystique of prison employment was removed by having relatives employed at the prison, and this may have contributed to their predisposition to choose the occupation for themselves.

Women Choosing to Work with Male Inmates

There are two paths by which female guards continue to arrive at men's prisons. Some women previously worked in a prison for women and voluntarily sought transfer to a male facility; they make a *choice* to work with men. Others, who joined the guard force after the integration process had begun, are assigned to a male prison upon completing their academy training; these women chose to become prison guards with the understanding that they might *have* to work in a male prison, at least temporarily.

In both New York and Rhode Island, the first women to work as guards in men's prisons were those who used the union contract's seniority provision to voluntarily transfer from a female to a male institution. In both states, there continues to be a steady stream of women making such voluntary transfers. The reasons they give for doing so are quite varied, although most frequently they want to obtain better posts and shifts or better promotion opportunities than those available in the much smaller women's prisons. Many women prefer the day shift because of family obligations, but in the typical female prison as many as five or even ten years of seniority are required before it can be obtained. In a large male prison, guards with only a few years' seniority can obtain the shift of their choice (although not necessarily their most desired post).

In New York, with prisons located throughout the state, some women transfer to a male prison because it offers them a more desirable location. Several women claimed that they had cut their commuting time by more than half by bidding for a male prison closer to their homes.

Male prisons also offer more opportunity for advancement because there are more supervisory positions within the uniformed ranks. One woman currently working in a men's prison had passed the lieutenant's examination while assigned to the woman's unit but found that that facility had no lieutenant openings. To avoid delay in obtaining her promotion (she estimated she would wait one to three years if she remained in the women's unit) she took the first available lieutenant's opening in a male facility. Supervisory experience in a male prison has the added advantage of offering the opportunity to supervise a larger staff than is possible in the smaller women's prisons.

Women also claim that experience in a major male institution is necessary for advancement into prison administration:

I don't want to be a guard my whole life. Right now, I'm going for my degree in Criminal Science. Pretty soon, they'll be looking for more women in administration. The more experience I have in different types of prisons, the better I'll look. If I pass the sergeant's exam, I'll put in a bid for "minimum." . . . When the time is right, I'll be ready to move up.

A few women who had voluntarily moved from a female to a male prison claimed that the women's facility was too small and confining. One woman, for example, reported:

I just got tired of seeing the same faces every morning. Over at "woman's" everybody knows your business and there's always someone who is mad at someone else. It was constant gossip and bickering. . . . I guess it's the same here, but the place is so big that you can get lost if you want to. . . . I just needed some new scenery.

Another woman reported that at the women's unit it was difficult to be a "real guard" because of the "mothering mentality" that existed there. Many of the older female guards, she claimed, resented new women who possessed a professional attitude toward the job and expected female inmates to obey the same rules as males.

Only two women reported that they transferred because they preferred to work with male inmates. One woman claimed that men were more interesting and exciting. The other felt that male inmates were easier to control than females:

The women are much more violent than the men. And the worst part is, you never know when it's coming—all of a sudden they just fly off the handle and attack you. With men, you can at least tell when they're starting to get angry and do something before it gets out of hand.

This woman was also impressed by the tendency of many male inmates to treat female guards with respect and to refrain from using vulgar language in their presence. She claimed that female inmates openly displayed their contempt and hostility toward guards whereas male inmates were more respectful and kind.

Most women made the decision to transfer to a male prison only after a great deal of contemplation. Of greatest concern was the possibility of sexual assault:

I wouldn't say it is any *more* dangerous in a men's prison—I've been attacked several times by female inmates—but it's a different kind of danger. You always worry about getting raped if you ever get into a hostage situation. But, it seemed as if the benefits of moving over here outweighed the risks.

Other women were afraid that they would be more likely to sustain physical injuries in the male prisons. They believed that they were less able than most of their male counterparts to defend themselves against an inmate attack.

In many cases, friends and relatives tried to dissuade women who were contemplating the move, arguing that work in a male prison was too dangerous. One woman reported:

> My father was the most upset. He is a policeman and knows the kind of men who end up behind bars. I knew he would never approve but I did it anyway—I figured he would calm down after I had proved I could handle it. He still doesn't like the idea, but has stopped talking to me about it.

Another woman said:

> My husband was set against it—he was never too crazy about my working with female inmates. But I kept talking about how nice it would be to work on the day shift, and finally he gave in. At first, he would worry if I were five minutes late getting home. Now he's used to me being here and doesn't think about it anymore.

Only one woman claimed that her family was truly supportive of her choice:

> My family knows I'm going to do whatever I set my mind to do anyway, so they might as well approve. Besides, they know I'm not stupid—that I wouldn't have made the decision if I weren't sure I could handle it.

Some women worried less about the potential danger than about their own ability to control male inmates:

> I wasn't sure how they might react to a woman giving them orders. I thought that if they just flatly refused to do what I told them, I wouldn't have too many options. If you've got to call for help every time you issue an order, you can't be effective as a guard.

Only a few women claim they made the move to a male facility without hesitation. Some had accumulated a great deal of seniority at the women's prison and knew they would immediately be able to obtain posts with no direct contact with inmates. A woman who works in an outside control booth, screening visitors at a New York prison, claims:

It was no big deal to move over here. I've got 17 years seniority with the state. I got this job right away and have had no trouble. It gets pretty cold at times, but other than that, I can't complain.

A woman who had worked in a female prison for about a year before transferring found the decision easy because she was confident of her ability:

> I went through the exact same training as male guards, so I don't see any reason why I should have been apprehensive. I am in better physical condition than most men. I know how to do my job, and I enjoy doing it. It makes no difference whether the inmates are men or women—to me, they're still inmates.

Her attitude was rare, however; most women made the decision recognizing the risks and their own potential shortcomings in performing the job adequately. Most women made the change only after careful consideration and only because work in a male prison offered some tangible benefits, especially in the realm of increased opportunity.

The situation is, of course, different for those women who began prison employment after the integration process had begun because they have not chosen to work in a male facility in the same sense. In both New York and Rhode Island, women who choose to become guards are, in effect, choosing to work in a male prison because there are very few openings in the women's prisons, especially compared to the number of women entering the training academies. In New York, all new guards are assigned to the prison in their recruitment area that is most in need of new staff, and this is much more likely to be a male than a female prison. From January 1977 to June 1979, of the 293 female guards graduating from the New York training academy, 106 went to a women's prison for their first assignment while 187 were sent to a male facility. Of this latter group, more than half went to a maximum-security unit.[12] After a year on the job, all guards are free to bid for openings in the prison of their choice. Female guards can then ask for assignment to the state's only women's prison, but they might have to wait several years to obtain such an assignment because they can be outbid by both male and female guards with more seniority. Equal employment opportunity for male guards has resulted in fewer jobs for women in women's prisons. In Rhode Island, at least one shift in the women's prison is now filled predominantly with men.[13]

All new trainees in Rhode Island are immediately sent to the male maximum-security prison for initial on-the-job training. During their six-month probationary period, they serve in all prisons in the system.[14] A position in the one female facility can be obtained only after accumulating a good deal of seniority.

Few female guards, regardless of their avenue of entrance into a men's prison, express an explicit preference for working with men. New female guards accept the necessity of working in a male facility because they want the job of prison guard. Some of them hope to transfer to a women's prison as soon as possible; others do not, either because they have adjusted well to working with men or because, like those women guards who have transferred from a women's prison, they appreciate the additional job opportunities available in the male facility. Only a few women claimed to choose a male prison because they liked working with men or found male inmates easier to handle. For the others who planned to stay in a male facility, increased opportunity for advancement or increased opportunity to obtain preferred shifts and posts provided the major motivations.

Conclusion

The new occupational opportunities that Title VII opened up for women in corrections would have been meaningless if women themselves had not been willing to seek jobs as guards in men's prisons. Since 1972, the number of such women has grown steadily.

The job of prison guard is an extremely nontraditional occupation for women. Because the literature on occupational choice suggests, first, that people choose careers that match their personality and areas of expertise and, second, that women who choose nontraditional occupations tend to have nontraditional sex-role attitudes, one might expect female prison guards to espouse rather "liberated" attitudes concerning male and female roles in society. This is not the case. Female guards are a diverse group, especially with regard to sex-role attitudes.[15] Only a small minority defined themselves as "liberated" or claimed to favor major changes in sex-role patterns. Many have extremely conservative views about sex roles; a few even suggested that guard jobs in men's prisons should not be open to women. If there is one generalization to be made about these women, it is that they become guards primarily because of extrinsic rewards—money, security, and fringe benefits. In this respect, the women are probably quite similar to their male counterparts.

It is important to keep in mind, as we examine the experiences of female guards and the ways in which they have adjusted to the job, that although these women have made rather extraordinary job choices, they are, in many ways, not substantially different from the general population of women.[16] In addition, the differences among them clearly overshadow the similarities. Once they become guards, however, they all share one common experience: working on a job in which they are unwanted and unappreciated by nearly everyone in their work environment. The following chapter will examine in detail the attitudes of prison administrators, male guards, union leaders, and inmates with regard to women's presence in men's prisons.

Individual and Institutional Reaction to Women in the Guard Force

Women's use of Title VII to acquire guard jobs in men's prisons probably came as a surprise to nearly all observers. Such a dramatic challenge to occuptional segregation was not foreseen even by drafters of the original Civil Rights Act; the 1964 antidiscrimination bill included sex only as a result of accidental and perverse circumstances, and there was virtually no debate about the changes it might induce in women's employment patterns.[1] Debate over the 1972 amendments also failed to include discussion of the male-dominated law enforcement jobs this legislation would make available to women.[2] Perhaps no one seriously considered that women would want such jobs; even a *New York Times* editorial praised the law in the following simplified way: "The [EEOC] will thus be empowered to move against police forces and fire departments that don't hire enough black people and school boards that fail to promote women as readily as men into supervisory positions" (Rosenbaum 1972:3).

Had there been widespread recognition of the full consequences of Title VII and the 1972 amendments, both bills might have received considerable opposition. There had been some changes in public attitude toward women's causes during this period (Erskine 1971; Ferree 1974; Mason 1976), but as late as 1972, 49 percent of American women were unsympathetic to the demands of organized feminist groups and only 48 percent favored any efforts to strengthen or change the status of women (Harris and Associates 1972; Boles 1979). Debate over the Equal Rights Amendment during the early 1970s focused extensively on the suitability of women for military and combat duty (Schmitz 1972), and powerful antifeminist movements emerged to challenge the view that male-female equality was a desired goal.[3] So even in the population as a whole, there was probably not strong support for women's movement into guard jobs in men's prisons. In the prisons themselves, there was almost total opposition to changing the long-standing policy of hiring only men.[4]

The 1970s was not a particularly good time for forced integration of the nation's guard forces, but even under the best of circumstances, prisons may be highly resistant to change. Although Herold Hage and Michael Aiken's (1970) study of organizational change applied primarily to private sector organizations, many of the characteristics they identify as impeding adaptation to change appear to be applicable to prisons: (1) a work force plagued by low job morale and low job satisfaction; (2) an abundance of formalized rules to govern worker behavior; (3) a high degree of centralization, with decision making taking place almost exclusively at the top; and (4) a high degree of stratification within the organization, with wide differences between the highest and lowest ranking members. Furthermore, David Duffee (1974, 1980) suggests that the general problem of implementing change in bureaucracies is intensified in organizations such as prisons, which usually suffer from an overload of cases, conflicting goals, and inadequate resources: "In most cases, the prison as it stands is changed bit by bit, begrudgingly and slowly" (1975:39). Richard McCleery's (1961) study of change in the Hawaii prison system, George Weber's (1961) in a juvenile institution, and James Jacobs's (1977) in the Stateville penitentiary in Illinois all support Duffee's contention that prisons are especially resistant to change.

The mandate to hire women as guards was perhaps the most unwelcome of all the changes forced upon prisons in the last few decades. To understand the resistance met by women guards, it is necessary to examine the reactions of each of the key groups in the prisons: male guards, union leaders, inmates, and administrators.[5] Each group views this innovation from a different perspective; each has its own special fears and concerns.

Opposition of Male Guards to the Entrance of Women as Co-workers

Male prison guards have consistently displayed resistance to and resentment toward the many changes that have occurred in the prisons over the last decade or so (Zimmer and Jacobs 1981). Male guards are also overwhelmingly opposed to the hiring and equal deployment of women to all posts in men's prisons. Out of nearly a hundred men interviewed, only a handful were at all supportive of this change; the opposition of the remainder ranged from mild to intense. The most frequently voiced reasons for opposing the presence of women were that they impair the security of the institution as a whole and jeopardize male guards' own safety.

Many of these male guards hold deeply felt convictions that innate sex differences make women unsuitable for the job of guarding men. The most often mentioned difference was size and strength:

> How can you expect a woman to hold her own in this place? There's no way in the world a 100-pound woman can handle a 250-pound inmate. I don't care how much karate she knows.

Women are also viewed as emotionally and psychologically weaker than men:

> A woman can't take the abuse the way a man can. Many a time the inmates here have female guards reduced to tears—running off to the ladies' room.

And even if women's "differences" are not critical on a day-to-day basis, their weaknesses and special vulnerabilities are expected to arise during prison emergencies:

> As long as everything is going along smoothly, the girls are okay. But wait 'til this place blows—and it will! You'll have all the girls begging to get out of here. Christ, there are even some men who can't handle it.

In every prison, male guards have stories about female guards who have failed to respond properly during momentary crises. For example:

> We had a fight on the yard last summer and the female guard out there froze. The guard on the wall had to call inside for some men to be sent out. Even after they arrived, she just stood there—didn't even try to help. Now how much good do you think she's going to be if we have real trouble around here?

Stories such as this one circulate widely, even from prison to prison. This same story was told to me by male guards in three prisons located near each other. Only a few additional incidents involving women's actual faulty performance were recounted, but most guards felt them to be inevitable, especially as the number of women increased and they began to move into more direct-contact jobs.

Many men are especially fearful of what the presence of women will mean for the functioning of the institution during serious crises.

They are concerned over their own safety because they doubt that a female partner can be counted on to provide necessary support:

A lot of things can happen to you in here—guards get killed every day. When I go into a dangerous situation, I want to know that my partner is going to be there to help me. You just can't count on a woman. And even if you can, what is she going to do? Is she going to be able to pull an inmate off my throat before he has the chance to kill me? No way in hell!

Even women who seem to have sufficient physical strength are assumed to lack the aggressiveness that allows men to "jump into" trouble quickly:

When men spot trouble, right away the adrenaline starts flowing and they're ready for a fight. Women don't have "heart"—they have to stop and think and figure out what they should do. By that time, everything might be over. Men react and think about it later.

Male guards also feel that the presence of women diminishes their own safety because in time of danger, they will need to be concerned not only with self-protection but also protecting the women:[6]

If I go into a situation and there's a woman there, the first thing I've got to do is make sure nothing happens to her. If it's another man, I figure he can handle himself. But while I'm looking out for her, anything could happen to me.

This paternalism is motivated by a strong cultural tradition of man as the "protector of women." One male guard explained:

You can tell me I should treat women just the same as men, but it doesn't work that way in practice. If I let a women get killed in there, how am I going to feel about myself? What am I going to tell my wife and children?

Another man explained that paternalism is a natural, unalterable condition of manhood:

Men *have* to protect women—just like other species. If the female wolf is in trouble, the male wolves will protect her even if they get themselves killed in the process. It works the same way with humans.

Men who hold these views are unable to accept women guards uncritically or to treat them as equals. Their views about the nature of womanhood are deeply ingrained and perhaps go unchallenged (or even rewarded) in their nonwork lives. In that respect, male guards have attitudes that are not unlike those of a large portion of the American male population and are, in fact, quite similar to those found among men who work in the other blue-collar, male-dominated occupations into which women have recently intruded (Meyer and Lee 1978; Westley 1982; Drolet 1976; Vaught and Smith 1980; Walshok 1981; Schaeffer and Lynton 1979; Deaux and Ull-man 1982; McIlwee, 1982; O'Farrell and Harlan 1982; Durning 1978). Working-class males tend to have traditional sex-role atti-tudes (Hall and Keith 1964; Albrecht et al. 1977) and, because they often socialize in same-sex peer groups (Gans 1962), may have had little or no prior experience interacting with women as equals. For male guards who firmly believe that women are innately different from men in ways that critically affect their job performance, the presence of women is very unsettling and the request that they treat women as equals is virtually impossible to fulfill.

Not all of the male guards who are opposed to women as co-workers hold extremely traditional sex-role attitudes; many are, in fact, anxious to explain that they generally favor women's rights and equal job opportunity. They view this particular job, however, as a necessary exception:

> Now don't get me wrong, I like women all right—they just don't belong in a prison. There are lots of jobs women can do better than men—I even think women are smarter than most men. They can be presidents, but they sure don't belong in here.

Some men feel that although women are not capable of performing all jobs in the male prison, they can handle a few—particularly control room jobs and administrative positions—and can be useful for conducting searches of female visitors.

> We always needed a few women around here, especially to check the female visitors who come through. With female guards to do the searching, a lot less contraband gets into the prison.

Although many men agree that women are capable of working on the posts that do not involve direct contact with inmates, most feel that assignment of women to these "choice" positions is unfair be-cause male guards have traditionally "earned" these posts by accu-mulating years of seniority working directly with inmates. Indeed, many men in New York and Rhode Island complain that current administrative policies often allow differential assignment of male and female guards, with women invariably getting the easier assign-ments:

It used to be once you got to a control room post, you never had to go back into population. Now I get called to do strip searches all the time. If a woman can't do the whole job, she doesn't belong here.

Given these two sets of beliefs—first, that women cannot do the whole job, and second, that it is unfair for women to be placed automatically in the few jobs for which they are suited—the only logical solution is the removal of women from the prisons.

Some male guards seem to be as disturbed by women's successful performance as they are by their inferior performance, perhaps because successful job performance by female guards challenges male guards' belief that masculinity is a necessary requirement of the job. Peter Horne (1980) found this to be the case among male police officers, who were reluctant to relinquish the "macho" image of the job when women joined the force and performed the job adequately, presumably without "machismo." Mady Segal (1982) suggests that concern over masculinity is responsible for much male opposition to women in the military:

The military in general, and combat in particular, is a masculine proving ground. If women are fully integrated into the military, then this arena loses this function. A young man cannot prove he is a man by doing something that young women can do. The negative attitudes of men toward women in the military . . . can be attributed in large part to this desire to maintain the military as a mechanism for establishing adult male gender identity. [P. 283]

One male prison supervisor who was supportive of women's presence similarly suggested that the male ego was at the heart of male guards' opposition to women:

It really hurts these guys to think that a woman can do their job. They've been walking around town like big shots—like they're doing a job only "real men" can do. Well, if the woman next door can do your job, then maybe you're not so tough after all. You know, these men have been going home to their wives for years saying "you don't know what it's like in there." Now some of their wives are joining up. The jig is up, so to speak.

Male guards, however, remain reluctant to change their belief that masculinity is a necessary requirement of the job, probably because doing so would require them to develop a new definition of the nature of their occupational role. Consequently, rather than questioning the necessity of masculinity, most male guards question the ability of women to perform the job without it. And if a woman can perform the job, they question her "womanliness" and normality. The few female guards whose performance is praised by males are often described as "masculine."

> Sure, Clara can do the job as well as most men, but have you seen her? She may be a woman technically, but she sure doesn't look or act like one—doesn't talk like one either. She can curse with the best of 'em.

Another male guard added:

> Now, Clara, I'd take her any day as a partner. If an inmate starts to act up, she can sit on him. Believe me, he won't be going anywhere soon.

Although women like Clara are accepted in one sense, they are constantly discussed and joked about. It is suggested that they are lesbian or have "hormone problems." Indeed, it is these perceived abnormalities that make these few women acceptable as work partners but clearly not acceptable as women. And because they are defined as exceptions, their successful performance does nothing to assuage men's attitudes toward female guards in general.

Many men can see some logic in women such as Clara choosing the occupation of prison guard, but they are confounded by the motives of other female guards. During the interviews, male guards often asked me, "But why would a woman *want* to take this job?" They often claimed that a "real woman" or a "lady" would not expose herself to the seedy world of the prison:

> Believe me, you see and hear everything in here. These inmates will "jack off" in front of you without giving it a thought. It's just no place for a lady. Why, the language itself would turn any decent woman away.

Some men suggested that a woman must be "immoral" to want a job in which men must be occassionally unclothed in their presence:

> Do they get a thrill out of seeing naked men? I think it's disgusting. It's one thing to be a nurse, where patients have to get undressed to be treated. But why would any woman want to look at a man while he's taking a shower or using the toilet? They must be perverted or something. The inmates don't like it either; it's demeaning.

Female guards, then, are often viewed as deviant, abnormal, and unfeminine as well as incapable.

For some men, the belief that women are unsuitable for guard jobs is so strong that they are absolutely convinced the policy will be reversed as soon as its irrationality is detected by those in power:

> You've got all kinds of people making decisions about the prisons who have never set foot in one. It's easy for them to say, "go ahead, hire women"—what do they care if this place falls apart. Just wait 'til a woman gets raped or killed—they'll change their tune then, and the women will be out of here in no time flat.

Most guards have no clear sense of how or why this change occurred. They blame high-level administrators and judges for making uninformed decisions. One guard in New York claimed that this was just one more "crazy" decision by "those administrators up in Albany":

> What will they think of next? They've lowered the standards so *anybody* can get in. First they brought in these minorities; some of them can hardly sign their name. Now we've got these women who can't even protect themselves. How do they expect us to run a prison? Next thing you know, they'll be bringing kids in here to control inmates. We might as well give the inmates the keys to the place and go home.

These quotes reveal that guards' opposition to the hiring of women is often closely tied to their more general opposition to the professional administrators who manage the prisons, judges who "meddle" in prison affairs, black guards who were brought into the prisons under affirmative action plans, and the myriad of changes that have directly affected guards in recent years. Sexual integration of the guard force is resented in much the same way racial integration was (Jacobs and Grear 1977), perhaps because, like minorities, women threaten to reduce further the homogeneity of the guard force that was once all-male and nearly all white, rural, and recruited from the communities in which the prisons are located (Schwartz 1972; Attica 1972; Irwin 1980).

In short, most male guards oppose the hiring of women as guards in men's prisons. A few men feel there are some advantages to women's presence—that women have a calming effect on inmates or that they are more perceptive in anticipating problems between inmates—but these sentiments are not widespread. A few female guards are viewed by a large proportion of their male counterparts as capable but only because they are not "real women." Their success is not taken as indicative of the capabilities of women in general. The mistakes and failures of any woman, on the other hand, are attributed to the group as a whole. Thus, the slightest mistake by a female guard serves to prove what most men believed all along: that women are not capable of performing successfully as guards in men's prisons.

Mixed Reaction of Inmates to Female Guards

When inmates first heard that women would be hired to guard them, the most common reaction was amusement. Like men in general, many male inmates have stereotypic images of women, their capabilities, and their "proper" role in society. The idea of women working as guards in men's prisons is contrary to their commonsense notions of how the world is supposed to be organized.

Prisoners report that as women actually began to enter the prisons, their reaction changed from amusement to apprehension. They wondered, "What will it be like?" "How will they act?" "What will change around here?" "How will this change affect me?" Each new female guard became the focus of a great deal of inmate conversation. The most important information they sought concerned the woman's appearance; when a woman was judged by one inmate as "good looking" or "built," others were anxious to see her and add their own personal assessment to the gossip about her.

When asked about the behavior of their fellow inmates during this period, many men claimed that there was considerable rudeness and hostility toward the women:

> There are always a few guys who look for any chance to make trouble. When women first came on the block, they started flashing or masturbating—one guy peed through the bars whenever a female guard walked by. Others used a lot of vulgar language just to see if they could get a rise out of her. You know, it was something new—something to do.

An inmate on one housing unit where a woman had been assigned claimed that the inmates "drove her out" and then regretted it:

> Eggleston tried hard to make it but a bunch of the guys gave her a hard time. Instead of writing them up, she tried to talk to them about it—explain how they had to clean up their act. So they gave her an even harder time. They called her "mom," which she didn't like, especially if there was some brass [supervisory personnel] around because it made it sound like she was being too friendly with us. Then they did things like ask her to unbutton one button on her blouse so they could "get a peek." Finally, she left for another post. After she was gone, everyone was sorry; they said

"She treated us better than the men; we should have been nice to her." One guy even wrote her a letter, saying he would keep everyone in line if she came back. But it was too late.

In most prisons the novelty of women's presence wore off fairly quickly—within a matter of months, inmates claim. At that point, the harsh treatment of females decreased dramatically and remained confined to only a few "troublemakers."

Once women's presence becomes established in the prison, inmates develop one of three basic attitudes about them. One group is fairly neutral, one is adamantly opposed, and the third is rather strongly in favor of their use as guards. The attitude typical of neutral inmates is: "What difference does it make? The rules are the same no matter who's enforcing them. A screw is a screw is a screw."

Inmates who favor female guards give a variety of explanations. Some men claim that their presence represents a nice change—that it is pleasant to look down the hall and see a woman coming; it gives them a reprieve from the all-male world. When asked whether they view the presence of women as a "tease"—a sexual stimulation that cannot be acted upon—one inmate answered:

> Sure, that's a bit of a problem—especially with the good looking ones. But I would be a fool to try anything; my ass would be in big trouble. So I look, but I don't touch. Touching would be nice, but looking is better than nothing at all.

Some inmates claim to prefer female guards because they treat them better than do male guards—they are more helpful, more compassionate, and more understanding. Comparing male and female guards, one inmate remarked:

> The men are like police. They like to degrade you—to use their power to antagonize you and then hope you'll do something stupid and get in trouble. The women are more professional; they don't have anything to prove. If you do something wrong, a female guard will write you up, but she's not nasty about it; she's not glad you got into trouble.

Inmates also claim that female guards are easier to talk to and more willing to listen to problems:

> I did something real stupid one day—I just went crazy and started throwing everything out of my cell. Officer Helms just stood there a few minutes and said, "I hope you're about finished because the

more you throw out, the more you'll have to clean up." After things calmed down, she asked me if I'd like to talk out what was bothering me. The thing is, I think she really cared.

Other inmates say they can share family problems with female guards. They talk with them about their wives, girl friends, and children. For example:

> I don't get to see my daughter much and last time she came I was shocked because she looked more like a woman than a little girl. She had on tight pants and makeup and I got angry at her because I'm afraid she's trying to attract the wrong kind of boys. We didn't have much to say to each other; I asked her a few questions, but she just shrugged her shoulders and didn't want to tell me how she was doing in school. After she left, I was depressed and angry because I'm not there to tell her things that fathers should tell their daughters; and she can't count on her mother. But when I finally talked to Officer Marks about it, I began to feel better. She said a lot of it was just a stage all girls go through. She told me she used to wear gobs of makeup and her mother thought she was going to be a whore. And she gave me some ideas of questions to ask her in a letter. I didn't know what fourteen-year-olds are into these days.

Inmates who generally favor the presence of female guards feel that privacy is not a major issue:

> It took some getting used to. We had to stop sleeping in the nude and start covering up when we came out of the shower. Now I don't give it a second thought.

Another inmate claimed that the necessary adjustments were positive ones:

> Pretty soon I'll be out of here and I'll be around women all the time. If you live in a house with women, you can't walk around in the nude, using foul language. I figure this will be good practice for being around my wife and daughters again.

But even inmates who favor the use of women as guards recognize some disadvantages to their presence. Some fear is expressed that female guards will not be able to protect them if they are attacked by another prisoner. But, as one inmate said, "More than likely the male guards would just stand around and watch anyway." There is also some fear for the women's own safety:

> Most of the inmates here wouldn't hurt a woman, but there are always a few "crazies" you have to worry about. I'd feel terrible if anything happened to one of the women.

These inmates claim that they try to control potential troublemakers as much as possible. In a few cases, inmates have protected women from attack by other inmates, and they have offered to help female guards with their disciplinary duties:

> I told Officer Andrews that I didn't like the way one of the guys talked to her. I offered to teach him a lesson, but she said no, it would be better if she handled it. Otherwise, it would look like she couldn't take care of things herself. But, still, she knows she can count on me if there's ever any real trouble.

In contrast to these prisoners, who generally favor the use of female guards, others strongly dislike being guarded by women. One inmate claimed that it is humiliating to take orders from a woman:

> It's bad enough being locked up in here, but then, having a woman boss you around—it's degrading!

Being guarded by a woman not only threatens some inmates' "manhood" but violates their sense of the rightful place of men and women in society. Several inmates said, "it's just not right," or claimed that women belong either in the home or in female occupations. These inmates do not so much resent the presence of women as oppose, on the basis of their ideology, the hiring of women for all "male" occupations.

Some prisoners claimed that female guards are "tougher" than male guards and more readily write tickets for inmate misconduct:

> These women are treacherous. You never know what they're going to do. One day they're acting all sweet and the next day they write you up for nothing.

Female guards are accused of being petty:

> Female guards write bullshit tickets. They'll write you up for having your shirt untucked or your top button undone. None of the male guards will even notice those things. The women want you to follow every rule to a "T."

A number of inmates complained that the use of women as guards invades their privacy. In both New York and Rhode Island, some women work on posts in which they occassionally see inmates undressed—using the toilet or taking a shower. Some inmates find the women's presence especially disturbing:

> There's no way we should have to put up with having a woman guard here, gawking at you while you're on the john. It's just not right. I won't take a shower when Andrews is on duty. I don't see

why I should have to change my life around just so she can work in here. Let her go work over in the woman's prison if she wants a job so bad.

For other inmates, the issue is not so much protection of bodily privacy as protection of the all-male world. In a study by Cheryl Peterson (1982), 52 percent of the inmates responding to a questionnaire agreed they were not free to speak and act as they pleased when women were on duty. One inmate in the current study explained:

I can't be myself with women around. I've got to watch what I do and watch what I say. When there's just guys around you can relax. You don't have to worry about offending anybody.

Some inmates also feel that being close to women without the possibility of starting a sexual relationship is "torture":

When I see Percy go by, all I see are tits and ass. If they [prison officials] are going to make us get along without sex, then why do they want to go and dangle women right in front of our faces? Some of these guys don't have as much self-control as I do. Sooner or later one of these bitches is going to get it.

Forty percent of inmates in the Peterson (1982) study felt that women's presence makes the lack of sex more frustrating. The Federal Bureau of Prisons Task Force (1980) also found sexual provocation to be a problem for some male inmates, although the problem seemed to be generated more by the presence of nonsecurity workers (such as nurses and counselors) than by female guards. In a similar vein, a federal inmate wrote to *Corrections Magazine* complaining about a female teacher:

When men are compelled to remain celibate and are not permitted conjugal visiting rights, it can only create serious problems when female staffers choose to go half clad and arouse sexual feelings among their subordinates.[7]

Female guards, of course, are never "half clad" because they all wear standardized uniforms which are extremely nonrevealing (and are often identical to those worn by the men). But prisoners still see female guards as sexual objects, and some women may actually encourage this feeling through their general manner, style of walking, use of makeup and jewelry, and personal interaction with inmates. But even then, some male inmates seem to find this a pleasant consequence of the use of women while others interpret it as an unpleasant form of "teasing."

It is difficult to get a reliable reading of inmate attitudes toward the use of female guards, because in most prisons the number of women is so small that inmates' generalizations often reflect their experiences with one or a very small number of women. At this point, it is clear that a wide diversity of opinion among inmates exists, but only a small minority seem to be adamantly opposed to women's presence. Similar results were found by Holland et al. (1979) in their survey of male and female inmates' opinions regarding the use of opposite sex guards; they found only 11 percent opposed to the integration policy. Similarly, Peterson (1982) found that 63 percent of male inmates favored an increase in the use of female guards. Attitudes may change (in either direction) if the number of women increases and inmates have experience interacting with a larger sample of women. Also, any change in the role of female guards, and the types of positions they normally fill in the prison, can be expected to affect inmate attitudes. For now, inmate opinion toward the women is generally favorable, with a small minority voicing strong opposition.

Union Support for Female Guards

American unions have often been accused of contributing to women's limited employment opportunities. Many unions have formally excluded women from membership (Hartmann 1976; Maupin 1974; Falk 1973); others have admitted women but excluded them from union politics and leadership positions (Huber 1976; Wertheimer 1984); still other unions have supported protective labor legislation that effectively eliminated female competition for men's jobs (Abbott 1969). When women sought jobs as guards in men's prisons, however, unions were extremely supportive of their efforts. In both New York and Rhode Island, the guard unions used their seniority provisions to fight administrative attempts to prevent female guards from transferring from female to male prisons.[8] In New York, the union pressured prison officials to establish an integrated seniority list, allowing the seniority accumulated by a female guard at the women's prisons to be used to transfer to one of the male facilities. In Rhode Island, the union fought all departmental denials of women's bids for men's prisons, eventually winning them at arbitration.[9] In both states, then, the union provided an avenue of challenge for female guards already working in the system and eliminated women's need to file lawsuits in the federal courts to gain the jobs to which they were legally entitled.[10]

Women would not have been able to use seniority to gain entrance to men's prisons without the active assistance of union leaders. Although some women complained that a few individual union leaders were not responsive, most female guards in New York and Rhode Island praised the unions' willingness to file seniority grievances on their behalf. This praise was especially surprising because interviews with union leaders revealed that they, like the majority of rank-and-file male guards, feel that women do not belong in men's prisons and that their presence jeopardizes the security of the institutions.

This contradiction between the attitudes and actions of union leaders can be explained by the fact that their foremost goal has been to protect the sanctity of their contracts' seniority provisions. The official union stance is that "a correction officer is a correction officer is a correction officer" and that seniority should be the *only* criterion for determining job assignments. Therefore, when women began to use union seniority rights to bid for jobs in men's prisons, this fundamental principle required union defense of them. Union acceptance of any administrative suggestion to treat sex as a valid factor in post, shift, or facility assignment would have decreased the credibility of the unions' firm conviction that personal characteristics of workers must be excluded from all assignment decisions. Thus, the unions' position was mandated by long-term organizational goals rather than by ideological support for women's right to equal employment opportunity.[11] The logic of unionism prevailed over the personal convictions of union officials, and female guards benefited.

Administrative Acquiescence to Change

Few prison administrators enthusiastically admitted women to the guard forces in male institutions. Before 1972, only two states, Virginia and Idaho, hired women as guards for male prisons (Morton 1979), although male guards were commonly hired in prisons for women (Giallombardo 1966). In both New York and Rhode Island, administrators regularly sent male guards into the female prisons whenever there was a major disturbance or a particularly unruly female inmate who needed to be controlled.

In JoAnn Morton's (1979) survey of prison administrators around the country, 21 out of the 49 respondents reported that their primary reason for hiring women was Title VII's mandate to do so.[12] Their reason for denying employment to women prior to 1972 was concern over the security risk that women would pose for the institutions (Paul, cited in Morton 1979). As was noted in Chapter 1, administrators in some states refused to hire women even after 1972. In attempting to seek an exemption to Title VII, prison officials in *Rawlinson, Gunther*, and *Harden* made one or more of the following claims: women, as a group, are incapable of performing the job adequately; women are in greater danger of being assaulted and thus present a security risk to the institution as a whole; and the presence of women violates the privacy rights of male inmates. In short, administrators claimed that the presence of female guards interfered with their efforts to maintain orderly, secure, and constitutional institutions.

In New York, the administrative decision to comply with Title VII occurred quickly. In 1973, after meeting with representatives from the EEOC to discuss guidelines for Title VII compliance, DOCS officials concluded that they could reserve some positions in male prisons for male guards if having women on them posed a security risk to the institution, if the posts involved potential danger to the women themselves, or if the posts involved an invasion of inmate privacy (Fitzmaurice 1978). The DOCS then ordered supervisors at each male prison to classify all posts as either suitable or unsuitable for women. Female guards had little control over their assignments, and women who were employed during this period report that they were placed almost exclusively in positions that offered little or no direct contact with inmates. They were most commonly assigned to clerical duties and the visiting room (where their main duty was to search female visitors).

Although it is impossible to discern all the motivations behind DOCS administrators' decisions to comply almost immediately with Title VII and employ females as guards in men's prisons, there is some indication that they hoped, by assigning women to "noncontact" positions, to free male guards currently on those posts for reassignment to high-risk jobs in with the inmate population.[13] The administration had long been dissatisfied with the seniority system that allowed experienced, skilled guards to bid for low-contact posts in towers and control rooms.[14] Meetings with EEOC representatives had convinced DOCS officials that Title VII did not require identical treatment of males and females once they were on the job; consequently, the DOCS was able to use the women's newly granted rights to redeploy some male guards back into inmate-contact positions, thereby striking a blow at seniority. And whether intended as such or not, this was an especially effective technique for subverting seniority because administrators were able to respond to any complaints by male guards or union leaders with the claim that Title VII was responsible for the change in policy and the matter was entirely outside their control. Male guards and union leaders naturally were unhappy with this unanticipated consequence of sexual integration.

By 1976, the number of women working as guards in men's prisons in New York State had grown substantially, in part because the State Civil Service Commission had mandated that employees from the defunct Office of Drug Abuse Services (ODAS) be assimilated into the DOCS system. Many of these employees were women who wished to remain in state employment, had considerable seniority with the state, and asked for assignment in the male prison nearest their homes. The New York prison guard union, the American Federation of State, County and Municipal Employees (AFSCME) Council 82, already unhappy with the removal of male guards from noncontact posts, became even more discontented as the number of female guards continued to grow, forcing more and more male guards to give up preferred positions.

As the number of women guards at some facilities increased, the system of differential assignment also began to cause administrative problems. It became increasingly difficult to place all female guards in low-risk, protected areas, and it was anticipated that these difficulties would multiply as time went on because although EEOC guidelines seemed to allow differential treatment of male and female guards once on the job, they prevented the DOCS from limiting the number of women entering the system. It looked as if a growing number of women would have to be accommodated with a finite number of noncontact posts. Thus, when the union demanded in 1976 that the DOCS establish a single, integrated seniority list to be used for all transfers and job assignments, prison administrators quickly agreed. In the few months following this change in policy, supervisors in New York's prisons could and did assign female guards to posts in all areas of the prison, including cell blocks and shower areas.

Several months after the DOCS had agreed to the union demand to assign guards without regard to sex, the state, under pressure of a lawsuit filed by female inmates in the one women's prison claiming that the use of male guards violated their privacy,[15] issued new guidelines for the proper deployment of opposite-sex guards in all state prisons. To "maximize full employment opportunities regardless of sex" and at the same time to "minimize intrusion on individual privacy," the guidelines prohibited the use of opposite-sex guards for strip frisks, shower supervision, escort duty outside the prison, or the guarding of housing units unless a same-sex officer was also on duty. (In those male prisons where housing units are one-person posts, women were automatically excluded.) The guidelines also stated that when entering a housing area, opposite-sex guards were to announce their presence in all but emergency situations. Finally, opposite-sex guards were not to exceed one-third of the total security staff at medium- or maximum-security units.[16] These guidelines, established in 1976, were in effect while this research was being conducted, although in 1981 the policy was changed once again to open up many more posts to men and women working in prisons of the opposite sex.[17]

The entrance of female guards into Rhode Island's male prisons occurred much later than in New York. It was not until 1977 that an experienced female guard at the state's one female unit sought transfer to the male medium-security prison. Her request was denied because of the department's unwritten policy against having women guards in men's institutions. She immediately filed complaints with the local union (the Rhode Island Brotherhood of Correctional Officers), the State of Rhode Island Commission for Human Rights, and the Office of Civil Rights Compliance of the Law Enforcement Assistance Administration (LEAA). Although LEAA had no power to enforce Title VII, it was obligated by the 1973 Crime Control Act to withhold federal funds from any agency engaged in employment discrimination.[18] At the time the complaint was filed, the Rhode Island Department of Corrections was scheduled to receive approximately $500,000 in federal monies through LEAA.

About one year after the transfer had been denied, LEAA sent a team of investigators from its office of Civil Rights Compliance to determine whether discrimination had occurred. LEAA investigators found in favor of the female guard and ordered the Rhode Island Department of Corrections to grant her transfer request and immediately end all sex discrimination in hiring and job assignments. When the administration refused, LEAA announced its intention to withdraw all federal funds, as it had already done with other potential funding recipients found discriminating (Civil Rights Technical Assistance Bulletin 1978).

Rhode Island correctional administrators, with advice from the legal staff, decided to contest LEAA's decision to withdraw federal funds. The Department of Corrections asked for a preliminary hearing before an administrative law judge from the United States Justice Department to determine whether or not the department had a sufficient case to forestall the funding cut-off until the full case could be heard in federal court. At this preliminary hearing, prison administrators claimed that LEAA did not use qualified correction experts in determining noncompliance, that the environment at the men's medium security unit was violent and dangerous, and that the "essence of the business operation at [the] Medium [Security Prison] would be disrupted by the presence of a female correction officer there."[19] The department cited *Dothard* v. *Rawlinson*, claiming that conditions in Rhode Island were analogous to those in Alabama. It also claimed that because "prisoners retain all those rights enjoyed by free citizens, except those necessarily lost as an incident of confinement,"[20] inmates had a fundamental right to freedom from being in the view of females while performing personal bodily functions. Correctional department lawyers argued that because the particular female guard seeking transfer would be in a supervisory position (and therefore required to inspect the entire structure as part of her duties), her presence would automatically violate this fundamental prisoner right. In December 1978, administrative law judge Francis Young determined that because "it is likely that the State Government, i.e., the Rhode Island Department of Corrections, would prevail at a full hearing on the merits," federal funds be continued until that full hearing could be held and a final determination made.

Because the Department of Corrections had prevailed at the preliminary hearing, LEAA was required to continue funding, but in a letter to the department's chief counsel, LEAA reaffirmed its intention to pursue the matter further and notified the Rhode Island Department of Corrections that it was still responsible for requesting the full hearing by May 1979.[21] The letter went on to say that if no such request were made, LEAA was legally freed from accepting the judgment of the preliminary hearing and was, in fact, prepared to accept the report of its own Office of Civil Rights Compliance that discrimination had occurred.

Before the deadline for request for a full hearing, the Rhode Island Department of Corrections suddenly reversed its original position and assigned the female guard to the position she requested. LEAA accepted this action as a suitable remedy and agreed to drop all charges against the department.[22] Thus, after a very long struggle (and after women had worked in male prisons in almost every other state prison system as well as the Federal Bureau of Prisons), the first woman guard entered a Rhode Island men's prison and began work.

Exactly why the department reversed itself after prevailing at the preliminary hearing is still unclear. There is some indication that the department's legal experts felt that the case was not as strong as Judge Young had thought it to be. Most other states using the same defense against introducing women guards had eventually failed, and no federal court had found *Rawlinson* controlling in a subsequent sex discrimination case. The decision to admit women may also have been influenced by the state's involvement in an additional legal battle. The Department of Corrections was, at the time, under federal court order to improve prison conditions,[23] and a claim in the sex discrimination case that Rhode Island prisons were too chaotic to accommodate women's presence might have undermined their claims of compliance in that prison conditions case. Whatever the reasons for the policy reversal with regard to women, the department's decision was neither totally voluntary nor enthusiastic. One administrator told me:

> The handwriting was on the wall; it was just a matter of time before we lost so it seemed foolish to keep putting energy into the battle. Besides, other states had already used women for many years and the reports we were getting from them indicated that maybe it wasn't as bad as we thought at first.

Even though the Department had seemingly acquiesced to Title VII requirements, the entrance of additional women into Rhode Island's male prisons did not occur smoothly. Throughout 1979, other requests by female guards to transfer into male facilities were denied by administrators, and the denials were upheld by the department's Review Committee.[24] This committee is convened only when a transfer request is officially protested by the warden of the facility involved. In one female guard case, the warden of the men's prison, in requesting a hearing by the Review Committee, stated:

> I believe the state has a moral, if not legal, obligation not to subject inmates to the moral degradation of being strip searched by a female. This function is part of the daily duties of a minimum security officer and as such would be part of her duties. In addition, quarters supervision would also be a routine part of her duties. Again, inmates would be subjected to moral degradation, in that the dormitory areas and showers are open and inmates would be supervised in all forms of undress. This situation would create undue discomfort for most men, as even the smallest amount of privacy would be violated.
>
> In addition to the above, the very real potential of allegations of sexual misconduct will sooner or later arise. This situation would not only be embarrassing to the employee, but to the Department itself.
>
> Assigning a female to regular duties in a male facility makes no more sense than housing male and female inmates in the same

unit. These objections may not technically be constitutional grounds for barring appointment, however, appointment above these objections would not only be morally wrong, but in conflict with good common sense.[25]

Union representatives were notified of all Review Committee hearings involving female guards, but they refused to participate on the grounds that the committee was meant to be used only in extreme circumstances (when the highest bidder is for some reason unsuitable for the requested position) and was being improperly used as a vehicle for denying women all job bids in men's facilities. The union filed contract grievances against the department on this point, but before they reached arbitration, the department again reversed its policy and began to grant a few of the women's bids. Some women also withdrew their bids, because they changed their minds about working in a men's prison, a better post in the woman's prison became available in the interim, or because they simply preferred not to engage in a long struggle with the department. By the spring of 1980, the Rhode Island Department of Corrections employed only four female guards in men's prisons. All of them had formerly worked in the state's one female unit and had voluntarily sought transfer into a male unit.

During the summer of 1980, in the next major policy decision concerning female guards, the Rhode Island Department of Corrections decided to assign all new trainees, male and female, directly to the men's maximum-security prison. The five women immediately affected were faced with a difficult decision because they had all entered the training academy believing they would always work in the system's one female unit. One of the five women chose to give up the job; the others accepted their assignments. A year later, two of these women had left prison employment, one had transferred to the female prison, and one continued to work in a male facility. New female recruits in Rhode Island are now told of the "unisex" pattern of assignment and are therefore able to consider this aspect of the job before entering the prison training academy. By the summer of 1981, one year after institution of this policy, only two additional women had entered the Rhode Island training program.

Prison administrators in Rhode Island have ceased to deny jobs automatically to women who seek transfer from the female facility to one of the male units. In 1981, eight women sought and received posts in a new high-security unit for male offenders. Today, the bids of male and female guards seem to be handled in a uniform manner, and Rhode Island has no sex-specific posts in any facility. Female guards perform pat-down frisks of male inmates but do not perform strip frisks, even when it is part of the job for a male officer on that post. In both male and female facilities, guards of the same sex as inmates are called from other posts to perform this function, although the department's general policy is that opposite-sex guards can perform strip searches when there is an emergency and no same-sex guards are available.

At some point, then, high-level prison administrators in New York and Rhode Island, like most others around the country, eventually chose to comply with Title VII. They remain unenthusiastic about the change, however, and fear that serious problems still lie ahead. Neither New York nor Rhode Island has faced a major disturbance or riot in any institution with a large proportion of female guards, and administrators continue to be apprehensive about women's ability to perform adequately under such conditions. The commissioner of the Rhode Island Department of Corrections, John Moran, summed up this general pessimism by the statement, "We haven't had any real problems *yet*."[26] Of most concern to administrators in Rhode Island is the possibility that the number of women who want to work in the men's prisons will increase to the point that women predominate on some shifts. In the minimum-security prison, for example, only seven guards work the afternoon shift; at one point three were female. According to Assistant Director Matthew Gill, there are "psychological drawbacks" in having a guard force that is predominantly female because inmates might be more "tempted to try something" than they would with a predominantly male work force.[27]

High-level administrators in New York are much more cautious in their evaluation of the wisdom of assigning female guards to male prisons. When asked whether the system as a whole would be better off without this change, one administrator responded: "What's the use of answering that question? The law says we have no choice." The feelings of New York Commissioner Thomas Coughlin were revealed, however, after a female guard was killed in a New York male prison in 1981: "I don't think there should be women in maximum security prisons . . . I think it's extremely dangerous."[28] In spite of this statement, New York's policy of assigning women to men's maximum-security prisons has not changed.[29]

The administrators at each local prison—the wardens—have had little opportunity, over the years, to influence policy concerning the use of female guards. When administrators at the central office level in New York and Rhode Island decided to comply with Title VII (rather than seek a BFOQ), wardens were required to immediately

implement this major policy change. They have also had to implement each new modification in the female guard policy, a task that
has been particularly burdensome in New York where from 1973 to
1981, DOCS administrators developed at least three different plans
for the deployment of female guards in male prisons. First, wardens
were given total discretion in assigning female guards; next, for a
very short time, they were required to make all assignments on the
basis of seniority; and, while this research was conducted, assignments on the basis of seniority were to be within the rather severe
restrictions set by the guidelines for guaranteeing inmate privacy.
According to one warden who was managing a prison through the
latter two of these phases, the directive that severely limited equal
deployment of male and female guards caused the most problems:

> When I came here, females were running units effectively. Then
> the directive arrived and I had to pull them off all posts in the
> housing unit. Now there are only so many places I can put them
> . . . It's not the females that cause the problem, but the directive.

Although this warden admitted that he did not necessarily favor the
use of female guards in men's prisons, he found that his greatest
administrative problem was not managing the prison with women,
but finding enough "suitable" places (under the guidelines) for the
women assigned there.

Wardens are especially concerned about the number of women
assigned to their prisons. The warden who blamed the directive, not
the women, for his problems in effectively using his personnel
claimed that even without the directive, a guard force that was
one-third female could not run a men's prison. Another warden
claimed that two females per shift should be the limit. This general
sentiment was unanimous among wardens in both New York and
Rhode Island. Like many male guards, they reached this conclusion
because of women's perceived physical and psychological weaknesses:

> As long as inmates are on their best behavior, the women have no
> trouble. But what if another Attica occurs? Women wouldn't be
> able to handle it—those guys literally went days without sleep.

Another warden remarked:

> There are a few women who can handle a physical confrontation,
> but most of them can't. I can send in two men and a woman to
> break up a fight, but there's no way I could send in three women.
> Most women don't have the strength or guts to break up a fight.

Only one warden enthusiastically welcomed the entrance of women into the male prison.[30] He affirmed the predictions of prison scholars Norval Morris and Gordon Hawkins (1970) that female guards make the prison environment "calmer" and more "normal." He claimed that female guards could successfully use nonaggressive techniques and calm inmates whom male guards would normally confront with physical force. Although he maintained that the proportion of "bad" female guards is no greater than that of "bad" male guards in his prison, he also thought the number of women employed in each male prison should be limited.

In spite of the reservations of most wardens concerning the wisdom of fully integrating the guard forces in men's prisons, wardens are obligated to accept and deploy as many female guards as are sent from the training academy or bid in from another facility. Neither in New York nor in Rhode Island do wardens have any mechanisms for limiting the number of women employees, although in New York one-third on each shift was the maximum allowed under the guidelines. Several wardens claimed that they were already at the "saturation point"—meaning that there were no more posts on which they could (or would want to) place female guards. They continue to worry about the ultimate impact of women's presence but also continue to comply with the legal mandate to deploy female guards in the prison.

Conclusion

Before passage of the 1972 amendments to Title VII, men's prisons were, by and large, all-male environments. A few women were employed as support personnel, but they were not allowed into the "heart" of the prison. The job of guarding violent male offenders was reserved for men, whose assumed aggressiveness, fearlessness, and physical strength made them ideal candidates.

Female guards were intruders into this male world. Their presence threatened the homogeneity of the guard force and the belief that masculinity was a necessary requirement for the job. Male guards responded to these threats with adamant opposition to women's presence—opposition that was justified by claims that their personal security and the security of the prisons were being compromised. Today, a decade after the first women were hired as guards for men's prisons, male guard opposition remains strong.

Although union leaders shared this basic belief in women's unsuitability for the job of guarding male inmates, they helped women gain employment in men's prisons. Their assistance was especially useful in filing the seniority grievances that allowed female guards to transfer from women's to men's prisons. Such union actions, however, were primarily motivated by the desire to preserve the integrity of the seniority system. They opposed any concessions to the firm union stance that seniority—and not the individual characteristics of guards—should be the basis for all assignment decisions.

The male administrators who manage the prisons were also concerned about women's ability to guard male inmates. In many states, administrators initially resisted Title VII's mandate to hire women; nonetheless, by 1980, administrators in all states had begun to comply with the law. Very few of them, however, favored this change in policy or believed that the few advantages to women's presence outweighed the disadvantages. At every level of the administration there is still concern that security problems emanating from women's presence will inevitably occur.

The members of the prison community who reacted most favorably to the hiring of female guards were the male inmates whom women were required to control. Although they had to accommodate women's presence by making some adjustments in their own behavior—most notably, taking precautions to protect their own privacy—most inmates did not consider these adjustments difficult or unreasonable. A few prisoners, however, resent being guarded by women. They join male guards in claiming that "a prison is no place for a woman." Some inmates have filed lawsuits against correctional departments, claiming that the use of female guards violates their constitutional right to privacy. The opinions of male inmates depend a great deal on their attitudes toward women's "proper" role in society and their evaluation of the few female guards they have encountered. But whatever their attitudes, male inmates, like male prison personnel, have no choice but ultimately to accommodate women's presence.

Prisons are institutions especially resistant to change, a phenomenon that was intensified during the 1970s; Title VII's mandate to hire women was among the most dramatic and all-encompassing changes forced upon prisons during this period. It was a change that was contrary to long-standing prison tradition, to shared assumptions about the nature of the occupational role of prison guard, and to stereotypic beliefs about the capabilities of women. It was a change, therefore, not favored or easily accepted by most members of the prison community. The following chapter will examine the various forms that this opposition to women takes and the way in which this opposition shapes the working lives of the women who work as guards in men's prisons.

Female Guards on the Job: Coping with Discrimination and Overcoming Obstacles

In spite of minimal requirements for obtaining the job of prison guard,[1] becoming and remaining effective on the job is difficult, even under the best of circumstances. All guards must learn the prison rules regarding both their own and inmate behavior, develop working relationships with co-workers and superiors, learn to cope with the fear and danger inherent in the job, and design personal strategies for gaining inmate compliance that do not rely primarily on the use of force. The high turnover rate among prison guards[2] attests to the failure of many guards to either make these personal adjustments or meet the minimal performance standards established by their superiors.

The female guard must learn the job and adjust to the working environment of the prison in the face of a set of problems which male guards need not confront. If she works directly with inmates, she may have to deal with their verbal abuse and sexual misconduct. She must develop techniques for obtaining inmate compliance to prison rules with little help from her male co-workers. She will face opposition and/or harassment from male guards, who will continually remind her that she is not only different but inferior. A few male guards will treat her well and give her assistance, but most will be openly hostile. Because she is female, she will be harassed, shunned, ignored, teased, commented on, joked about, snickered at, and excluded from informal social interaction—on as well as off the job. She will be denied access to some jobs in the prison. She will receive conflicting messages about the roles she should play and the duties she is expected to perform. Co-workers, supervisors, and inmates will have different expectations concerning the "proper" behavior of a female guard. Nothing she does will go unnoticed, and any mistakes she makes will become part of local folklore about female guards. In spite of these obstacles, she will be expected to be a "good sport," refrain from complaining about her treatment, and, above all, perform the job as well as or better than her male counterparts. Her failure to meet any of these expectations will increase male guards' negative response to her presence and to the presence of female guards in general.

Continuing Discrimination against Female Guards

Although there continues to be legal confusion over the way female guards can be deployed in men's prisons, the law clearly requires that prison officials, like other employers in the public and private sectors, refrain from all discriminatory hiring practices. Today, in both New York and Rhode Island, if women meet the minimum requirements[3] and pass all entrance examinations, they are probably as likely as male applicants to be hired.[4] Of course, equality in hiring does not always get translated into equal treatment for women, and numerous researchers have shown that, once hired, men and women are often assigned to different positions within organizations and given different internal mobility opportunities (Kanter 1977; Doeringer and Piore 1971; Blau and Jusenius 1976; Harlan and O'Farrell 1982; Epstein 1980). Such discriminatory treatment at the "port of entry" is not apparent in the prison. Once hired, male and female recruits attend a sexually integrated training academy where they receive identical training and are subject to the same examination standards. Once training has been completed, they are assigned to a prison, not on the basis of sex, but on the basis of departmental need; because most job openings occur in men's maximum-security prisons, most new male and female trainees are sent there for their first temporary assignment. Once in the prison, all new guards are on probation while they receive on-the-job training designed to familiarize them with actual prison operations and teach them the subtleties of the job that cannot be taught in a classroom setting. Official policy in both New York and Rhode Island is that male and female trainees receive identical on-the-job training during the probationary period.[5]

Female guards report virtually no discriminatory treatment by prison administrators with regard to hiring, academy training, or first facility assignment, but many of the women who go directly from the academy to a men's prison claim that they are the victims of serious discrimination during their on-the-job training.[6] Not all women report identical forms of discrimination, and the form it takes seems to depend primarily on the particular supervisor under whom each woman works.

It is the responsibility of middle-level managers at each prison (captains or lieutenants) to make assignments and supervise new guards' on-the-job training experience; all trainees should be assigned to a variety of posts so that they become acquainted with all aspects of the job and learn how to perform most typical guard duties. During this probationary period (six months in Rhode Island and one year in New York), trainees are not covered by the unions' seniority provisions and have virtually no control over their daily assignments. Instead, their supervisors have the discretionary power to place them wherever they see fit, taking into consideration both the needs of the facility for staff coverage and the training needs of each guard. Many female guards feel that male supervisors use their discretion in a discriminatory manner, resulting in quite different on-the-job training experiences for men and women.

Many women reported that their training experiences were less diverse than those of their male peers:

> I didn't get the same kind of assignments that male trainees got. In fact, I spent a lot of time doing nothing while the guys were learning how to run a cell block. A few times they let me run a company to chow, but I very seldom got "out back." I guess they figured I'd be leaving here anyway once the training period was over.

Some women who reported this kind of "preferential treatment" were happy to receive it, but others complained that it left them unprepared to take on full guard duties after the official training period had been completed:

> During probation, I worked a lot of different posts, but most of them were in the administration building so I had contact with only "the best" inmates, under the best of circumstances. The year went by quickly and I learned a lot but, by the end, I wouldn't say I was prepared to work on most posts. But you don't stop along the way and say "hey, give me some harder assignments" and you don't tell them at the end of your year that you're not ready to become "permanent." You figure they must know what they're doing.

In contrast to the lenient treatment given these women, others felt they received harsher assignments than men during the probationary period:[7]

My first six months, I got all the worst jobs. I knew if it was raining or snowing outside, I'd get an outside job. One day I was assigned to patrol the perimeter, which usually involves riding in a car. But the day I got it the car was broken down and I had to do it on foot, carrying a rifle and a walkie-talkie.

These women believe that the motive behind such treatment was to force them to quit:

I know he [her immediate supervisor] was trying to break me, but the worse my assignments got, the more determined I became. I figured if I could get through the probationary period, there would be nothing in the job itself to stop me. Every day I finished a particularly tough assignment, I knew I was that much closer to making it.

This woman's effort to turn discrimination into an asset was atypical, and most women who felt they received particularly difficult assignments during the probationary period were angry and resentful about it.[8]

Very few workers (in the prison or elsewhere) ever feel they are being treated fairly by superiors, and it is possible that some of the discriminatory treatment reported by female guards is perceived rather than real. However, at least with regard to the claims of "preferential treatment," the women's stories were substantiated by many male guards and a few male supervisors.[9] One supervisor admitted that he sheltered women from certain "inappropriate" posts:

I would be a fool if I put a woman where I know she can't perform. Some of these women don't weigh 100 pounds. How are they suppose to handle a 250 pound inmate? It just doesn't make any sense to put them in the kind of situation where they might get hurt.

Another supervisor claimed that female guards should receive less training in direct contact with inmates because they will not be on the job long:

These girls didn't know what they got themselves in for when they took this job. Most of them won't last. They'll quit or transfer to one of the "easier" units—the woman's prison or a minimum–security joint. They're only here in "max" because the department sent them here temporarily.

One supervisor explained that he based his assignment decisions on ability rather than sex, although the effect was often the same:

I obviously can't treat everyone exactly the same. If I have a male guard who isn't good in emergencies, and everyone's afraid to work with him, then I look for a place to put him where he won't be a danger to anyone else. It's the same with women. If the men don't want them around on the cell blocks, then it's not doing anyone any good to have them back there.

Other supervisors denied having different policies for male and female trainees, but many were quite open about their opposition to women's presence in men's prisons. Like the majority of rank-and-file guards, male supervisors generally believe that women are unable to fulfill the requirements of the occupational role; it would not be surprising if such attitudes were to affect—either consciously or unconsciously—their assignment decisions.[10]

When female trainees feel they have been discriminated against,[11] there is little they can do short of filing a complaint with the EEOC or the State Human Rights Commission. It is highly unlikely that high-level administrators might detect sex discrimination below because there is no detailed review of each guard's training record before permanent status is granted. The union has no power to act on complaints with regard to assignments during the probationary period, and there are no institutional grievance channels for trainees, male or female. Trainees conceivably could make complaints directly to their supervisors' supervisors (usually the warden or deputy warden), but most trainees probably are reluctant to do so for fear of being labeled as troublemakers early in their careers. Furthermore, many administrators discourage such complaints because they might otherwise be inundated with requests to solve disputes between trainees and their supervisors. One warden told me:

I get complaints of discrimination every now and then from women and minorities, but it usually turns out to be that someone just didn't like the way their particular supervisor makes decisions. There are only so many jobs to go around, and not everyone gets the assignments they want all the time. In the end, I'm sure it evens out.

At this point, there is no way to know for sure whether assignments eventually "even out" for male and female trainees, although the evidence from this study suggests they do not. Male supervisors who wish to use their discretionary power to discriminate against women remain almost entirely free to do so, with little chance of either detection or sanction.

Once assigned to specific posts by their supervisors, female trainees may be discriminated against further by the male guards responsible for providing their on-the-job training. Women report that some of their "trainers" virtually ignored them and failed to teach them how to perform the duties of their assigned post:

> My first assignment was in the library with a male officer. He barely said a word to me and never told me what to do. Finally, I asked him what I should be doing and he said, "nothing." That was it. He answered the phone. He checked out books. He wrote inmate passes. Whenever I tried to do anything he told me to sit back down, that he'd handle it. This went on for weeks. Finally, he asked for a transfer and the next guy in there started to show me the ropes. He came just in the nick of time because the boredom was really starting to get to me.

Because male guards often prevent female trainees from responding to emergency calls, women may finish their probationary period with no training in this aspect of the job. One woman explained:

> The first time I heard the emergency code, I asked my partner what I should do—you know, what was the proper procedure? He told me to wait by the phone in case someone called for information. I didn't see how I could give information since I never knew what had happened, but I just waited there. Later I asked him if someone always waits by the phone and he says, "No, only if there's a woman around."

By withholding the information and training women need to learn the intricacies of performing the job, male guards deny women the full socialization experience that is necessary for adjustment to any new work environment (Van Maanen and Schein 1979; Feldman 1976; Terborg et al. 1982). Delhert Miller and William Form (1980) point out the breadth of information workers pass on to new recruits:

> New employees must learn many things about the social behavior in their work situation. They must learn who's who (the informal status pattern or pecking order), what's what (the "ropes" or how things are done), and what's up (the current situation in their work area). But most important of all they must learn how to fit in. They must learn to play an acceptable role and no formal organizational chart or manual will help very much. They must know how role boundaries are established by their associates. The definition of roles by work groups is a surprisingly complex matter. [Pp. 365–66]

Women breaking into traditionally male occupations seem to be especially likely to encounter insufficient training and socialization from male co-workers. In her study of the first women to enter craft jobs, Bridget O'Farrell (1975) observed:

> [I]t was estimated that as much as 80 % of the job was learned informally from other workers on the job. Because of strong group norms, cliques, status, job satisfaction, and generally negative attitudes, women were excluded from the informal peer group training. Consequently they did not learn the job as well as men thus reinforcing negative attitudes about women not being able to do craft work. . . . In general, men agreed that it was fine for women to work there but they would not get any help. [Pp. 6–7]

Similar experiences of inadequate socialization have been reported by female professionals (Epstein 1971; White 1975), coal miners (Vaught and Smith 1980), police officers (Martin 1980), and steel-workers (Deaux and Ullman 1982).

Adequate on-the-job socialization is especially important for new prison guards to adapt successfully because the formal rules cannot cover even a modest sample of the situations that might arise (Crouch and Marquart 1980). Male guards sometimes complain of inadequate socialization as well (Lombardo 1981), but many women named it as a serious obstacle to their adjustment to the job. The situation is probably exacerbated for women by the fact that they are also excluded from the after-hours socializing that many guards engage in and the information sharing that occurs in such situations.[12]

Once on-the-job training has been completed and women have passed through the probationary period, they are less subject to discriminatory treatment from co-workers and supervisors. For one thing, permanent status means that women can bid for a specific post rather than receive daily assignments from the shift supervisor. This protects some women from discrimination, but a large number of women remain on what is called "miscellaneous status" even after the probationary period and therefore continue to have their assignments controlled by male supervisors whom many women claim engage in discriminatory policies. That discrimination, again, may involve the assignment of women to either the most or the least desirable posts in the prison.

There are several reasons why women might remain on miscellaneous status even after they have gained the right to bid for a specific post. First, for guards with little seniority, few desirable posts may be available for bidding. One woman explained:

A few good jobs have come up since I became permanent, but I knew I would be outbid so I didn't even try for them. I could have gotten Cell Block C on the evening shift but I like working days and so far—on miscellaneous—they've kept me on days. Besides, once you bid for something, you've got to stay there six months and, my luck, the perfect job would come along right after I bid for one I didn't really want.

Some women stay on miscellaneous because they expect the preferential treatment they received from supervisors during the probationary period to continue:

Why should I bid for a post when, right now, I get the best assignments in the prison? I'd never have enough seniority to bid for a job in the administration building and that's where I get assigned nearly every day. For me, a bid post would be worse.

Other women feel unprepared for a large proportion of the openings that are posted:

Most of the jobs I could bid for are right in population where there are apt to be fights and confrontations with inmates. I just don't think I could handle that. I'd rather take my chances on miscellaneous, at least for the time being. I'll eventually bid if I get enough seniority for a control room or something like that.

Some number of women, then, are unable or unwilling to work on direct-contact posts. They prefer to stay on miscellaneous status because they know male supervisors will shield them from the most dangerous and unpleasant aspects of guard work. Should these supervisors fail to do so, these women would presumably obtain the most acceptable bid post available or, if no posts met their standards, terminate their employment.

In New York State, at the time this research was conducted, many women were forced to remain on miscellaneous status because there was a shortage of posts classified as appropriate for opposite-sex guards. The guidelines issued by the DOCS central office in 1976 excluded women from posts involving an invasion of inmate privacy and specifically named, for example, posts that required the supervision of showering inmates. This particular mandate was quite explicit, but for many other posts in the prison the guidelines were difficult to apply and local administrators were forced to make judgments whether or not women needed to be excluded. For example, one guideline stated that "no assignment is to be made requiring an officer to conduct strip frisks of inmates of the opposite sex."[13] Almost all posts in the prison could, on occasion, require the performing of strip searches, especially during emergencies. Another guideline stated that "at least one officer of the same sex as the inmate population at a facility must be assigned to each housing block."[14] On all two-person posts on housing units, it is occasionally necessary for one person to remain alone for a short period of time while the other takes a break or responds to an emergency elsewhere in the prison. The guidelines did not specifically state whether opposite-sex guards had to be excluded from these posts, where there was only the occasional opportunity for invasion of inmate privacy. Local administrators interpreted identical guidelines in very different ways, resulting in considerable variation in the way women were deployed in each male prison in the New York system. The warden at one New York prison claimed that, according to his interpretation of the guidelines, women could bid for only about 10 percent of the posts; another warden claimed that the same guidelines *precluded* women from only 10 percent of the posts.[15]

Although the guidelines themselves put some constraints on a supervisor's ability to indiscriminately assign male and female miscellaneous guards, several factors were operating to encourage a more narrow interpretation of the guidelines than was required. First, male supervisors, like most male guards, do not feel that women are capable of performing the job of prison guard, especially during emergencies. To protect prison security, many supervisors preferred to assign female guards to low-risk areas (e.g., control booths, administrative offices) whenever possible. Male supervisors were also guided by feelings of paternalism and concern for the female guard's safety; they felt that female guards should be protected whether they liked it or not. Finally, supervisors were pressured into a narrow interpretation of the guidelines out of fear that they would be held responsible for problems that might develop from the assignment of females to high-risk posts. The administrative directive on deploying opposite-sex guards included a clause stating that "sound managerial judgement must be used in the assignment of any personnel" because "certain assignments may be wholly inappropriate or improper and therefore detrimental to a well-run facility."[16] From a supervisor's perspective, the best way to avoid future problems was to interpret the guidelines narrowly and assign female guards only to safe, noncontact positions whenever possible.[17]

At some New York facilities women were left with very few options, and always fewer than their male counterparts. To make matters worse, many of the posts classified as acceptable for female guards were already held by male guards with more seniority; most unbid positions were those considered undesirable by all guards. Thus, many female guards in New York, because of a lack of other good options, remained on miscellaneous status, receiving daily assignments on an "as needed" basis from the shift commander.

Supervisors have considerable discretion in assigning guards who remain on miscellaneous status. They often use this discretion to assign women to noncontact jobs, a fact substantiated by male guards who oppose women's presence on these grounds. In fact, the men claimed that when the guidelines were in effect, if the vacant posts for any particular day were defined as unacceptable for opposite-sex guards, supervisors would "pull" male guards from their normal noncontact posts to fill the vacancies and then assign women to take their places. In other cases, supervisors solved the problem of "too many women" by assigning miscellaneous females to jobs not on the roster at all (e.g., third person on a post that normally operates with two, or unscheduled clerical and administrative duties). Some miscellaneous women appreciate this differential treatment and others resent it. A female guard in the latter group relayed her feelings as follows:

> When I found out that no one has my post when I'm not on duty, I was furious. It's humiliating! It means all my work adds up to zero—it doesn't matter one iota if I'm on duty or not. My supervisor was shocked that I would even complain. But how can I ever expect to be taken seriously on the job if my job isn't serious enough to be filled when I'm gone?

Women on miscellaneous status who feel they receive harsher treatment than miscellaneous males are also resentful:

> There's an outside gate that everyone hates to work, especially in the winter, because it has to be opened manually for every truck coming in. Nobody ever bids for it, so miscellaneous guards are always stuck with it. I had it all winter, with temperatures below zero; it was miserable! Come March, my supervisor gave it to a male guard, but then put me back on it whenever it rained. When I complained, he said it was a "coincidence." There's no way I can ever believe that.

The wardens and supervisors who had to administer the guidelines at each New York prison had mixed feelings about them. Since many of these men did not favor equal deployment of male and female guards, the guidelines offered a justification for unequal treatment. On the other hand, the guidelines clearly inhibited supervisors' ability to utilize female staff effectively because the prison sometimes had more women assigned there than could be deployed efficiently, especially when the guidelines were interpreted narrowly. One supervisor summed up his feelings by saying, "I don't want the women here, but if I have to have them, I want to be able to assign them the same as men; otherwise, it's just a headache finding places to put them." Almost identical sentiments have been expressed by military leaders who must accept an ever-increasing number of women but cannot deploy them on an equal basis with male soldiers (Quester 1982; Tuten 1982). Both the military and corrections situations highlight the problems associated with a policy of near equality for men and women. It fosters resentment both among women who want the full range of opportunities and men who dislike the preferential treatment given to women; and, by requiring that supervisors treat the sexes differently, it reduces the flexibility that is necessary for efficient management and deployment of personnel.

Although the New York guidelines for deploying opposite-sex guards presented problems for all participants in the prison work force, they have been most harmful to female guards themselves.[18] And even though DOCS officials had some legal justification for these specific guidelines, they represent a clear example of institutional discrimination against women because other, less discriminatory options were available. The guidelines were promulgated in 1976 while the department was defending against a privacy suit filed by inmates in the state's one women's prison.[19] The judge in that case accepted the guidelines as a remedy for the women's privacy claims, and when guards later complained about discriminatory assignment policies, the DOCS was able to claim, with some justification, that its restrictive policy was not an administrative choice but a requirement imposed by the federal judiciary.

Although satisfying the court's concern over the privacy of female inmates, it is clear that these guidelines were not the only possible solution to the problems raised in the lawsuit. In all cases where the courts have upheld inmates' right to privacy, they have required administrators to develop procedures for guaranteeing this right but have not suggested how it must be accomplished; the New York guidelines were but one possible solution. An alternate one would have been to install curtains, opaque glass, or partial barriers in front of all shower areas. In Rhode Island's newest male prison (with a high-security classification), for example, barriers approximately three feet high were installed in front of each shower, with an open space below and above so that guards can see the heads and feet of showering inmates at all times. If a female guard is on duty, inmates can dry off behind the barrier and cover themselves before leaving the shower area and returning to their cells. Although it would have been more difficult and costly to install protective barriers in the shower and toilet areas of many of New York's older prisons, it was an option that would have permitted maximum employment rights for all guards.[20]

A second possible alternative to the guidelines was for prison administrators to reorganize prison posts so that most of the duties involving invasion of inmate privacy would be concentrated in a few. At one New York prison, for example, women complained that many posts on which they should have been able to work (such as industry or work detail posts) included one shift per week on a housing unit or relief of a housing unit guard for coffee breaks, which made them unavailable for bidding by opposite-sex guards. The post descriptions were not necessarily created to exclude women (they may have been so designed even before women's arrival), but the result was that women were precluded from bidding on them. If the duties associated with each post had been reorganized, many fewer posts would have been forbidden to female guards.

A third strategy would have been for prison administrators to appeal the court decision that mandated protection of inmates' privacy. Of the privacy cases won by inmates in the lower federal courts, none has been appealed by the correctional departments of any state, although the granting of privacy rights to inmates adds a serious constraint on administrators' freedom to deploy workers. In few other cases have prison administrators so quickly accepted a newly defined prisoner right. In fact, inmates normally have to pursue such claims to the Supreme Court, against the vehement opposition of prison administrators. In contrast, administrators have left unchallenged all lower court decisions granting privacy rights to inmates, even though there may be sufficient grounds for a successful challenge. As James Jacobs (1979) points out in his analysis of the important *Dothard* v. *Rawlinson* case, there is no clearly defined constitutional right to privacy for free citizens that encompasses protection from being seen naked or partially clothed, and even if there were, it would not automatically extend to prisoners. Furthermore, any privacy rights of inmates might be mitigated when balanced against the employment rights of women. Only in one court case, *Fesel* v. *Masonic Hospital*,[21] has this balance been attempted; here the court determined that sex could be used as a BFOQ in a nursing home where residents preferred that nurses' aides of the same sex perform intimate body care functions on a regular basis. In the prisons the subjects are inmates, not patients, and the issue is occasional nudity, not regular physical contact. The *Fesel* reasoning, therefore, may not directly apply to the prison context.

It is, of course, impossible to predict the final outcome of an administrative challenge to these lower court privacy decisions. What is more important at this point, however, is that administrators all around the country, including those in New York, did not challenge these decisions but instead chose to limit opposite-sex guards' access to many prison posts. In New York, prison officials could have challenged the *Forts* case before developing the guidelines which, in some prisons, denied female guards access to 90 percent of the posts.[22] The decision to comply immediately with the court's mandate to protect inmate privacy, and the decision to limit women's access to posts rather than develop some other means of compliance, indicates if not a clear desire by high-level administrators to discriminate against women at least the lack of a clear desire to avoid discrimination. Rodolpho Alvarez's (1979) work on discrimination points out that every organizational problem can be solved in a wide variety of ways and that when decision makers choose a solution that produces a pattern of institutional discrimination against a particular population, we should suspect that they are acting upon their own personal prejudices and biases rather than from necessity. The policy guidelines for deploying opposite-sex guards that were established by New York administrators not only created institutional discrimination but, because they allowed the supervisors at each prison to exercise considerable discretion, provided an avenue for personal discrimination as well.

Thus, although New York quickly opened up guard jobs to women after 1972 and Rhode Island resisted for nearly eight years, day-to-day discrimination against female guards has been more significant in New York than in Rhode Island. Discrimination continues to occur in both states, especially during the probationary period when male supervisors control the assignment of trainees, but because the general policy in Rhode Island has been that male and female guards can bid for all posts in opposite-sex facilities, women there have been less often the victims of institutionalized discrimination.

Coping with Male Opposition and Harassment

For female guards in New York and Rhode Island, the negative attitude and behavior of male guards and supervisors serve as the primary obstacles to a successful and easy adjustment to the job. No woman failed to mention opposition and harassment by male colleagues when discussing the difficulties she encountered upon first entering a men's prison and for many women, negative male behavior has continued to be a problem throughout their period of employment.

Although behavior that constitutes sexual harassment has existed and affected working women[23] for centuries (Goodman 1981), the label itself is fairly new and still undergoing definitional changes.[24] The EEOC guidelines, which explicitly include sexual harassment as a form of discrimination prohibited by Title VII, define harassment as follows:

> Unwelcome sexual advances, requests for sexual favors, and other verbal or physical conduct of a sexual nature constitute sexual harassment when (1) submission to such conduct is made either explicitly or implicitly a term or condition of an individual's employment, (2) submission to or rejection of such conduct by an individual is used as the basis for employment decisions affecting such individual, or (3) such conduct has the purpose or effect of unreasonably interfering with an individual's work performance in creating an intimidating, hostile, or offensive working environment.[25]

The guidelines also serve notice that employers are to be held responsible for acts of sexual harassment by co-workers "where the employer, or its agents or supervisory employees, knows or should have known about the conduct."[26]

Even before the EEOC issued these guidelines in 1980, the courts had been willing to consider sexual harassment as a form of illegal sex discrimination whenever there was clear evidence that women had been threatened or coerced or evidence that they had suffered serious employment consequences (such as demotion or termination) for refusal to grant sexual favors.[27] The court also granted Title VII rights when sexual harassment was severe enough to force women to terminate their own employment.[28] Prior to the EEOC guidelines, however, the courts had rejected claims of sex discrimination when no specific loss of employment benefits followed the objectionable behavior.[29] In effect, this meant that women's male co-workers and supervisors were free to engage in harassment as long as they did not later penalize the victims or force them to quit their jobs.

By including situation 3 in the definition of sexual harassment, the EEOC greatly expanded the kinds of behaviors considered illegal; even if male behavior of a sexual nature merely interferes with a woman's work performance or creates an offensive work environment, it can constitute an illegal form of sex discrimination under Title VII. This EEOC rule was tested in the courts a short time later in a case that, coincidentally, involved a woman employed as a Vocational Rehabilitation Specialist in a men's prison. In *Bundy* v. *Jackson* (1981),[30] the court concluded that Title VII had been violated because Bundy's employer "created or condoned a substantially discriminatory work environment" (p. 943) by failing to stop or even investigate Bundy's complaints of demeaning sexual propositions and stereotyped insults by her male supervisors and co-workers. This case represents a major expansion of the legal definition of sexual harassment (and even an expansion beyond EEOC guidelines) because it suggests that comments made to or about women *because* of their sex might be illegal even if those comments are not of a sexual nature. The court concluded that derogatory comments about women were analogous to racial slurs and, if allowed to go unchecked by employers, violate Title VII by "poisoning the atmosphere of employment" (p. 945).

In spite of legal prohibitions, sexual harassment of women by their male co-workers and supervisors is widespread in the workplace in general (MacKinnon 1979; Backhouse and Cohen 1981; Committee on Post Office and Civil Service 1980; Merit Systems Protection Board 1981) and especially prevalent in traditionally male occupations (Martin 1980; Meyer and Lee 1978; O'Farrell and Harlan 1982; Vaught and Smith 1980; Riemer 1979; Gruber and Bjorn 1982; Walshok 1981; Schreiber 1979; Ayoob 1978; Charles 1977; Sichel 1978). Lin Farley (1978) suggests that the motive behind such behavior is to discourage women's employment in male-dominated fields and ensure a sex-segregated job market:

> The naive belief that male opposition to female workers will eventually disappear from a sexual intermingling of occupations, as is now required by law, is best replaced by a more realistic assessment of the ways men, despite this forced entry, will attempt to ensure their domination and the continuation of job segregation. We don't have far to look. Sexual harassment is regarded as an acceptable means of control so available that it frequently is described as just "part of the job." [P. 53]

The Merit Systems Protection Board (1981) outlines the specific types of male behavior classified as sexual harassment; they range from overt criminal acts (rape and attempted rape) to persistent requests for dates or sexual favors to sexual teasing and remarks.

Since *Bundy*, derogatory remarks about specific women or women in general can also be included in the legal definition of sexual harassment.

Every female guard interviewed in the current study described at least one incident that could be classified as sexual harassment,[31] and although the large majority of cases involved behaviors at the least serious end of the continuum,[32] there were some charges of serious harassment as well. For example, several women claimed that after refusing the advances of superiors they were given unfavorable work assignments or poor performance evaluations. I was also told about women who had "voluntarily" left prison employment because of retaliation that followed their refusal to become sexually involved with superiors.

> Everyone here knows about Captain X. At first he tries his "come on," as if he's God's gift to women. If that doesn't work, he tells you what he can do for you if you're "friendly." If that fails, he threatens you with what he'll do if you don't cooperate. Me, I told him to go fuck himself for all I cared. I'm not afraid of him, but some of the other girls are. Sally did everything she could to avoid him—even went on another shift—but he kept after her 'til finally she quit. Some girls just sleep with him and get it over with, I guess. As long as he leaves me alone, I stay out of it. But Sally— that was too bad. She didn't deserve to go through the changes he put her through.

Unlike the blue-collar women studied by Mary Walshok (1981), of whom almost one-third reported being touched, held down, or forcibly kissed by male co-workers, only a few female guards personally experienced such serious forms of harassment. But especially prevalent in the prisons is a form of harassment many women find annoying and discomforting: male guards' constant reference to their appearance. One woman remarked:

> No matter how I look that day, I know someone will make comments about my appearance. I don't dare change my hairstyle because it will become the major topic of conversation for weeks.

Another woman complained:

> The men are constantly asking me if I've put on weight or asking whether I have to "let out" the shirts that are issued. I don't try to flaunt it, but I am "well-endowed," so to speak. I understand that men automatically notice that sort of thing but you'd think they would have manners enough not to bring it up. It makes me feel very self-conscious and uncomfortable.

The most common forms of harassment by male guards are those that, though not explicitly sexual in nature, revolve around the women's female status. The most overt type of behavior in this category is a clear statement of opposition to the presence of women in the prison. These comments may begin as early as the training academy's orientation:

> The first day we were together—there were three women and thirty-three men—the training director lectured us about equality and nondiscrimination. When we took a break and were standing around getting acquainted, the guy I was talking to said, "You know he doesn't mean that. There's no way you can keep up with me, here or in the prison." Most of the guys thought it was a joke that we were there, training together.

These messages from male co-workers become more prevalent when women begin work in male prisons. Even women who expected such opposition found such blatant displays of hostility shocking:

> I expected a negative reaction and thought I was prepared for it. But on my very first day, before I had even been assigned to a post, this male guard came up to me and asked what I was doing there. He said that women don't belong in men's prisons and told me that he would do anything he could to make my life miserable and force me to leave. It gave me a real eerie feeling.

Some women suspect that male guards have tried to frighten them away from the job. While on the job, one woman received obscene phone calls from an inside line. Another received calls telling her of the alleged sex crimes of inmates with whom she had direct contact. Although neither woman has proof, both believe that male guards made the calls.

Sometimes male guards attempt to undermine female guards' chances of receiving favorable performance evaluations. Several women complained that they were reported to supervisors for actions that were technically against the rules but customarily engaged in by male guards who never reported each other. These actions include using the telephone for personal business, reading a book on the job, or temporarily leaving a post unattended. A few women reported that they were cited for violations that were "invented" by male co-workers.

Another form of harassment involves spreading rumors about female guards. Women complained that gossip linked them romantically with male guards, supervisors, inmates, and each other.[33] It is not uncommon for male guards to charge that particular female guards are lesbian; at one prison, stories circulated quickly about two women who had been seen together in a local bar. The most damaging rumors are those suggesting sexual intimacy between female guards and male inmates. Women at one prison claimed that an unfounded rumor of this nature forced the resignation of a female co-worker; the alleged inmate lover had confessed to officials, but the woman's supporters believe that male guards had threatened or bribed him to cooperate.

A great deal of the men's direct opposition to women is too subtle to be classified as sexual harassment and instead constitutes what Mary Rowe (1981) and Karen Bogart (1981) call "micro-inequities." Male guards may ignore women, even to the point of acting as if they are not present. A few women report that men with whom they have worked daily have never spoken to them. Many say they are ignored by men when in common areas such as the locker and lunch rooms. At such times, conversation often centers around male guards' sexual conquests, hardly a subject to make most women feel comfortable. Consequently, many female guards prefer to arrive at the prison just in time for their shift and prefer to leave the building during lunch so as to avoid all informal interaction with male guards.

Many men choose to voice their opposition to women through "harmless" joking and teasing. One woman claimed that she was given a nickname that referred to a past mistake she had made on the job. She had misinterpreted a code that was sent over the radio; now, whenever she passes a checkpoint or enters a new area, male guards call out, "Here comes number 96." She feels that the "joke" has continued for months because the male guards want to remind her (and each other) that she is incompetent. Other women complained of snickering, giggling, and secretive comments whenever they walk past a group of male officers. This form of harassment is difficult to define, even for victims. One female guard told me:

> I don't know what it is. Most of the guys are basically okay. They don't mean any real harm; they just like to have their fun. Most of their jokes aren't funny to me, but I try to ignore it. They probably do the same thing to each other, so it might not have anything to do with me being a woman.

There is a lot of joking, teasing, and banter among guards and some hazing of all new recruits—male and female—so some women are uncertain whether the treatment they receive is actually related to their female status. A few women even claimed that women themselves "cause" the problem by being too sensitive:

If women would ignore the men, they would stop it. When a guy knows he can get your goat, he'll never let up. I just pretended not to hear the comments—or that I didn't care—so they decided I was no fun to pick on.

So although all female guards report some opposition and harassment, not all view it as a serious problem or as an obstacle to adjustment. The difference in reaction is related not only to individual women's tolerance for such behavior (or their ability to counteract it) but also to the actual amount of harassment they encounter. As the following chapter will show, the particular role women choose to play in men's prisons has an important impact on male guards' reactions to them. Male opposition and harassment is not evenly distributed among the female guard population.

Women victimized by sexual harassment and opposition to their presence have been generally unsuccessful in stopping the behavior themselves or obtaining relief through legal channels. Claims of sex discrimination made through the EEOC are difficult and time-consuming to initiate and seldom result in satisfaction (MacKinnon 1979; Backhouse and Cohen 1980). In neither New York nor Rhode Island have female guards pursued these legal remedies.

Both New York and Rhode Island have specific laws prohibiting sexual harassment in the workplace,[34] and the correctional departments have established official channels for women's complaints of harassment. In Rhode Island, an equal opportunity officer is available in the central administrative office to hear complaints; at the time of this research, none had been received. In New York, the Office of Affirmative Action, through its four regional branches, hears complaints, interviews the parties involved, determines whether harassment has occurred, and makes recommendations for relief. Once a case has been affirmed, the staff might suggest counseling for the "offender," demotion, suspension, termination, or a fine. In June 1981, in order to encourage the reporting of harassment incidents, the DOCS sent all employees a memorandum concerning the department's policy on sexual harassment, outlining inappropriate behavior and proper avenues of redress.[35] In the ten months following this announcement, the Office of Affirmative Action received only a handful of complaints from women, and in only one case did the staff find sufficient evidence to recommend punishment. Because their recommendation was not supported by higher-level administrators, however, no punishment was ever imposed.

Women in both states who complained to me about sexual harassment indicated that they were reluctant, for several reasons, to seek assistance through these formal channels.[36] First, they thought such action would prove fruitless because most of the harassment they suffered was perpetrated by male peers who had no direct power to make decisions concerning women's employment; it therefore was not considered sex discrimination by the federal courts at the time of this research. Women were also uncertain whether such behavior was prohibited by state law, and even if it were, women were concerned about having a factual case sufficient to warrant official action. Proof of the more subtle forms of harassment is difficult to produce; one can hardly prove, for example, that a certain male guard always "undresses me with his eyes," although this was a common complaint by female guards.

Second, women feel that departmental channels established to deal with harassment are not actively supported by administrators at either the local prisons or the central offices. Administrators in both New York and Rhode Island are predominantly male, and female guards do not believe they are committed to solving the problem of harassment. When I asked one administrator about a female guard who had reportedly quit after months of sexual harassment, he answered:

> I can't believe anyone propositioned *her*. Have you ever seen her? She just wishes someone would make an advance at her and is angry because no one did.

Other specific cases I presented to administrators were explained away as women with "severe psychological problems" or with personal vendettas against either particular men or men in general. In none of the cases I had heard about were women's stories taken seriously by administrators. Many female guards obviously sense this attitude and conclude that complaints of sexual harassment will not be vigorously investigated.[37]

A third reason why women are reluctant to initiate formal complaints is the fear of further harassment or losing their job, especially if they are still within their probationary period when trainees can be fired with virtually no justification. But even female guards who have been permanently appointed (and are protected by a union contract that requires "just cause" for termination) are fearful of retaliation; they are afraid that complaints of harassment will lead to poor evaluations by their male supervisors and jeopardize their chances for future advancement. In deciding whether to file a complaint, then, many women attempt a kind of cost-benefit analysis: will the consequences of the formal complaint be more detrimental than the consequences of the harassment itself?[38] Many women evidently believe that the potential benefits associated with filing a complaint are minimal while the negative consequences are likely to be substantial.

The unions in New York and Rhode Island have also been ineffective in providing female guards with any relief from sexual harassment because most harassment is perpetrated by male guards who, like the women, are union members. As basically adversarial organizations, unions are best equipped to fight management, not solve conflicts between union members. In fact, Backhouse and Cohen (1980) present a few cases in which management has supported women's claims of harassment (and has attempted to discipline male workers), but unions have backed the alleged harassers. Unions typically defend members against all types of administrative disciplinary charges, and the implication of this general policy is that unions have had virtually no role in helping women solve the harassment problem.

With little power to stop sexual harassment by their male co-workers, female guards learn to cope with it in a variety of ways. Some develop a strategy of rejection and hostility toward men who harass:

> Anywhere you go there are jerks who think they can get away with anything. I tell them right away, "Don't mess with me." They think I'm crazy, and that suits me fine because they leave me alone. Some of these women are afraid the men won't like them if they speak up. I don't care if they like me; this is a job, not a personality contest.

Some women avoid complaining about harassment because they want to prevent further deterioration in the relationship between male and female guards. They may deny that serious harassment occurs or blame themselves for "reading too much into" the "harmless" behavior of male co-workers:

> They don't really mean any harm. Some girls make a big deal about it, but they [the men] are only trying to have a little fun. Men and women don't always think the same things are funny, that's all. It's best just to ignore it or laugh along with the guys. It doesn't help to get upset anyway.

To some extent, sexual harassment is a pervasive part of every woman's life, off the job as well as on it, and a condition that many women simply learn to tolerate. Besides, complaining may draw even *more* unwanted attention to oneself:

I try to blend in as much as possible around here. That's not easy! But going around complaining about the men will only draw more attention to the fact that we are "different" and can't fit in with the rest of the guards. It's best to keep a low profile and not get a reputation as a complainer. The more trouble we make the harder it will be for us.

In addition to "turning the other cheek," some women opt for a strategy of constant vigilance; they are careful about their appearance and try to convey as little sexuality as possible in their dress or manner. They are also careful about what they say, always trying to avoid the "double entendre," where an innocent remark can be interpreted sexually. These women interact with male guards as little as possible; they avoid all personal conversations and attempt to project an aloof, professional manner that will discourage harassment.

Although women who remain employed have learned to cope with male opposition and harassment, it still has a serious impact on them and on their effort to adjust to the job. Researchers have shown that sexual harassment can have detrimental effects, including decreased job satisfaction (O'Farrell and Harlan 1982; Gruber and Bjorn 1982), lower productivity (Merit Systems Protection Board 1981; Segal 1982), increased turnover and absenteeism (Merit Systems Protection Board 1981; Dunnette and Motowidlo 1982; Westley 1982), and emotional and physical illnesses (Goodman 1981; Lane 1981; Backhouse and Cohen 1981). In the prison context, sexual harassment makes an already unpleasant job considerably more unpleasant because women are unable to feel relaxed and confident with their own co-workers; they must be careful about what they say, what they do, and how they look.

Male opposition also blocks women's entrance into the established prison guard subculture, and as a result, women receive neither the on-the-job socialization nor the supportive psychological benefits of belonging to a subculture. Thus, not only does male opposition worsen already unfavorable working conditions, but at the same time it denies women access to a subculture that emerged to cushion unfavorable conditions. Women do not generally feel integrated into the work group and consequently share little sense of camaraderie with their co-workers.

Some women reported that male opposition and harassment caused them to disrupt their established work patterns. One female guard changed shifts to avoid being propositioned by a male supervisor. Another left a post she liked because her male partner constantly harassed her, talking about her body and "undressing her with his eyes." Still another woman reported that she bid for a control room post with no direct contact with inmates only because she wanted to stop the possibility of rumors that linked her romantically with male inmates. Erving Goffman (1959) has pointed out that women's need to alter their behavior in order to counteract possible wrong assumptions and misperceptions about them is a pervasive part of their lives. For female prison guards, such "impression management" often means altering their behavior and activities in ways that may ultimately hinder their careers.

Male harassment may be so severe that a woman quits the job or seeks transfer to a female prison. I spoke with one woman, fresh out of the training academy, who had been in a male prison for only a few weeks:

> Every day I wake up and ask myself if I can face another day. It's not the work, it's not the danger, it's not the inmates—it's the attitude of the male officers. One day I wanted to quit but took a sick day instead and decided to try it a bit longer. Right now I can't tell you if I'll make it or not. If I can make it through the probationary period I can probably transfer to the woman's prison. I hear it's even more dangerous over there, but nothing could be tougher than this.

The full effects of sexual harassment, and the degree to which it hinders women's employment opportunities in corrections, simply cannot be calculated. It is certain, however, that learning to cope with male guards' sexual misconduct and blatant opposition to their presence remains a continuing condition of female guards' employment in men's prisons.

Female Guards' Interactions with Inmates

When new guards leave the training academy, most are probably ill prepared to work in a prison and interact with inmates. Guards from rural areas or small towns tend to experience the greatest adjustment difficulties because they often have had little or no prior contact with the urban (and most likely minority) males who predominate in many American prisons. The cultural differences (in particular, the language differences) between these two groups present real barriers to interaction and mutual understanding. For all new guards, the first few days and weeks are filled with confusion and apprehension, as they adjust not only to a new work environment but also to their first face-to-face contacts with inmates.

Contacts between female guards and male inmates are always sex-bound. Even if corrections officials were to develop policies of equality for male and female guards, male inmates would not treat them identically. Sex remains a "master status" in our society and influences the interactions between people of the opposite sex despite the other statuses they possess. Thus, although "guard" and "inmate" are powerful statuses, the interactions between female guards and male inmates are strongly influenced by the sex of each.

As was noted in Chapter 4, most inmates approached their first contact with female guards with a combination of amusement, amazement, and apprehension. Female guards felt equally apprehensive when they first entered men's prisons. Women were aware that they would be closely watched by inmates; they expected inmates to "test" them more intensely than they do male guards:

> I knew that inmates would right away be wondering if they could get over on me because I'm a woman. I knew I would have to be tough at first to show them I was ready and willing to enforce the rules.

Female guards do feel that they were initially tested more severely than male guards. A few inmates refused to obey any orders until the women followed through with disciplinary action.

In spite of a longer and more intense testing period, many women claimed that, all things considered, their reception by inmates was overwhelmingly positive, especially compared to their expectations:

> Only a few inmates gave me a hard time. The rest stared a lot, but were very polite. A few were downright helpful. They told me who to watch out for and how to do things that other officers had never told me about.

Many women claimed that the inmates were kinder, more helpful, and more accepting of their presence than were male guards.

The most negative experiences female guards have had with inmates were of a sexual nature. A small minority of inmates, in their effort to discourage women's continuation on the job (or merely to rebel against the system as a whole), engaged in verbal and physical sexual harassment. Some men used extremely vulgar language in the women's presence or used obscenities when referring to them. A fairly common experience was for inmates to expose themselves or masturbate in the sight of women guards. Although these inmates often claimed that such behavior was accidentally witnessed by female guards, most women thought it was performed explicitly to shock them and perhaps to force them to resign.

Learning how to handle abusive behavior by inmates has been a problem for many women, in part because of the lack of a clear prison policy.[39] In their effort to treat male and female guards equally, the departments in both New York and Rhode Island have avoided giving women special training on problems which they, as women, are most likely to confront. Female guards are not specifically instructed on the appropriate remedies for inmate sexual misconduct. A Rhode Island rule forbids "indecent exposure" by an inmate,[40] but many women were unsure precisely what this meant. Because of the lack of inmate privacy, it was obvious that mere nudity did not constitute indecent exposure. Also, at least at first, many women preferred to give inmates the benefit of the doubt, trying to believe that the behavior accidentally occurred in their presence. One woman who repeatedly "caught" a particular inmate masturbating said:

> At first I was embarrassed as much for him as for me. Everyone knows that a lot of these guys have to do something to relieve the tension. Inmates shouldn't be doubly punished just because I'm a woman and am offended by the behavior. I tried to turn my head and pretend not to notice. Then I finally realized, after a week or so on the cell block, that he *was* doing it for my benefit. It just couldn't be an accident that many times in a row. Once I told him I would write him up, he stopped. In fact, he is now a model inmate; he gives me no trouble at all.

At some point, most women learn when it is appropriate to write a disciplinary action for overt sexual behavior, but individual female guards may have very different standards. As I stood talking to a female guard in a control room, an inmate stepped out of the shower to dry himself in our full view. Neither of us looked directly at him, but we were aware of his presence and his nudity. The guard explained that she would write him up only if he stayed there an unnecessarily long period of time or if he approached the glass booth to get our attention. Another woman might have reacted differently by immediately writing up a disciplinary action.

Even though only a minority of inmates engage in sexual misconduct, it is something every female guard must learn to deal with if she is to work on a direct-contact post. Many women eventually develop standards they feel comfortable with and convey them to inmates, either directly or through use of the disciplinary system. Other women rely on a few friendly male guards to intervene and "teach the inmates a lesson" in proper conduct. Some women are aided by sympathetic inmates who inform other inmates that their verbal abuse and sexual misconduct will not be tolerated.

Some portion of female guards, however, are unable to develop any techniques for coping with this behavior or for bringing it within the general disciplinary system. They either quit the job or retreat from the situation by removing themselves, as much as possible, from direct contact with inmates. This latter strategy of escape is most easily accomplished by women who have transferred from female units and have accumulated enough seniority to bid for noncontact posts. Another method is to become aligned with male co-workers, especially supervisors, and receive noncontact assignments. The following chapter will identify in more detail the way in which this alignment process operates.

Female guards, like their male counterparts, must develop strategies for gaining day-to-day inmate compliance to prison rules; the primary options available for accomplishing this task are physical force, persuasion, threats of punishment, and forfeiture of their authority. Most female guards feel that their ability to use physical force against inmates is limited, especially as compared to male guards. Some women also believe that the other methods for controlling inmates are predicated on their ability to back up those methods with force; they conclude, therefore, that women are at a serious disadvantage in performing order and control functions. These women try to avoid situations in which they have to enforce prison rules or exert direct control over inmates.

Many other female guards, however, feel that they are as capable as their male counterparts of using noncoercive methods for gaining inmate compliance. These women reported few problems in performing their main function of maintaining order and control among inmates:

It wasn't nearly as hard as I thought it would be. Most of the inmates here know the rules as well as I do. When they break a rule and get caught they expect to get written up and don't even bother to complain. Only once did an inmate refuse to go to his cell. I put in a call for help but before reinforcements arrived he decided it wasn't worth the trouble and just went in of his own accord. Other than that, I've had no problems.

Some female guards believe the problems they experience with inmates are inherent to the job rather than related to their female status:

One day in the Rec Room, an inmate picked up a pool ball and threw it. It barely missed my head and smashed into the wall. He wasn't mad at *me* for anything; I just happened to be in the way. He got locked up for a while, and unfortunately, everyone lost the privilege of having a pool table . . . . The biggest danger in this job is being in the way of an inmate who is mad or frustrated.

Many female guards feel that their female status is an advantage in gaining inmate compliance. Some attribute this to the tendency of many inmates to be "softer" on female officers:

> Some people probably think that it's harder for women to do this job, but for me, I think it's easier. Most of the inmates are glad we're here and don't want to spoil it by being tough and forcing us out. They probably could if they wanted to. . . . Inmates are still men, and they treat us like ladies. As long as it helps me do the job, I won't knock it.

Other women feel that they receive more respectful treatment from inmates because they treat them better than do male guards:

> I didn't come in here like a tough guy. I couldn't. I figured that if I treated the inmates fairly, they'd treat me fairly in return. That's pretty much how it's gone.

There is wide variation, then, in the way female guards interact with inmates, maintain control over them, and deal with the abusive behavior of a few. Some women consider their female status an advantage; others consider it a handicap. Only a few maintain that their gender does not affect their interactions with inmates. In general, inmates do not interact with female guards on a sex-neutral basis, and women's female status and how they use it remain important factors in their ultimate adjustment to the job.

Coping with the Effects of Tokenism

Many of the difficult conditions female guards face on the job result from male opposition to them as women in a man's world. Co-worker harassment, testing by inmates, and discrimination by superiors all occur because of male opposition to the presence of women in this highly nontraditional occupation. Additional problems, however, may result simply from women's numerical scarcity in the guard force. There are, according to Rosabeth Kanter (1977), certain problems that accompany the condition of being "the few" in a group that is dominated by a different type of person. In the prison the dominant group is male and "the few" are female, but it is numerical distribution rather than sex per se that creates the condition Kanter refers to as "tokenism." Many of the special pressures that tokenism created for the female managers Kanter studied can be found among female prison guards.

First, because tokens are highly visible members of a work group, they receive more attention and scrutiny from both co-workers and superiors. Although high visibility may have some advantages, its consequences are more likely to be negative because, according to Kanter, mistakes generally receive more publicity than accomplishments. This is clearly the case in the prison. Female guards are highly visible; in some prisons, guards and inmates alike can recite the name, post assignment, and employment history of every female guard. Their actions and behavior are a constant topic of conversation. Inmates continually discuss women's physical appearance; male guards continually discuss their performance. The details of any mistake they make quickly spread throughout the prison and are talked about for months or even years. As a consequence, many female guards are reluctant to take risks and prefer instead to follow standard procedures whenever possible. As one woman explained:

> I see male guards bending the rules, but if I try to do it, someone is bound to notice and report me. If you make it a habit to follow the rules exactly—even the stupid ones—then you've always got yourself covered.

Following the rules can shelter women from making blatant mistakes that could be used as grounds for dismissal.

A second consequence of tokenism is that observers tend to exaggerate the differences between tokens and the dominant population, thus making it difficult for tokens to become fully assimilated into the work group. This condition is very apparent in the prisons. Aside from sex, probably the greatest difference between male and female guards is their size and physical strength. Male guards and supervisors continually cite this difference as "proof" of women's unsuitability for the job. The similarities between male and female guards are generally overlooked.

A third tendency is for observers to ignore differences among tokens and, instead, to view all members as part of a unified and homogeneous group. According to Kanter (1977), "this load[s] all of their acts with extra symbolic consequences and [gives] them the burden of representing their category, not just themselves" (p. 214). In the prison, the behavior and actions of any one female guard are often attributed to female guards in general. Women realize that their actions will have consequences for all other female guards and often respond to this pressure with increased self-consciousness.[40] One female guard revealed:

> I try not to make any slip-ups. I know that whatever I do, it will reflect on all the other women here. There are times when I'm ready to explode and tell these men about themselves, but I stop and remember how many people would be hurt if I did that. You know, they wouldn't just say *I'm* a bitch, but would say *these women* are bitches.

Because the behavior of a few is attributed to all, women who strive for male co-worker acceptance often resent women whose performance receives unfavorable evaluation:

> I'm here trying to prove myself, and everyone treats me as if I was one of those "sissy" women who run every time there's the slightest hint of danger. One day there were rumors of a riot set for the next day and do you know, a bunch of women called in sick. Now all I hear is "you girls were afraid to be here and get hurt." *I* was here, but whatever one woman does affects all of us.

Some female guards, however, are hopeful that their good performance will reflect favorably on others:

> I think about quitting sometimes, but I want to show that women can do this job. I think I'm in a good position to do that. A lot of the men here are starting to respect me—I've showed them that I am willing and able to do every job in here. Once they get it into their heads that one woman can do the job, maybe they'll go a little bit easier on the other women.

The good performance of tokens, however, is never given the same weight as bad performance, and the few female guards who receive praise from male co-workers are defined as exceptions rather than as representative of women in general.

Judith Long Laws (1975) points out that because tokens are engaging in an activity not "normal" for members of their group, they are often labeled as deviants and are made to suffer the same psychological consequences as other types of deviants. In the prisons, male guards often claim that "no normal woman would even want this job." Thus, even the woman who succeeds in gaining respect for her occupational performance cannot receive respect as a person. By making such a nontraditional occupational choice, she becomes defined at best as "unusual" and at worst as "sick."

As a deviant, the female guard can never be completely trusted or assimilated into the work group. She cannot merely join the guard force, perform the job adequately, and be accepted on the basis of her own accomplishments. Instead, she must cope with the effects of tokenism which, like male opposition, inmate testing, and employer discrimination, increase the difficulties of adjustment in an already difficult occupation.

Conclusion

Nearly all members of the prison community initially opposed the hiring of women to guard male inmates. A great deal of this opposition has been translated into actions that create obstacles to women's adjustment. For female guards, remaining on the job means coping with continual opposition and harassment from male co-workers, discriminatory assignment policies of male supervisors, and some explicit sexual misconduct by inmates. As a consequence, their work environment is substantially more unpleasant than that experienced by male guards and their adjustment difficulties are more severe.

Although high-level administrators in New York and Rhode Island have acquiesced to Title VII's mandate to hire women, they have not fought against either male harassment or the informal discrimination that continues at the local level. There are, of course, no easy solutions to these problems, but at this point even a commitment to search for them seems lacking. This is perhaps because most male administrators also continue to oppose women's presence; while not engaging in direct actions to harm women, they do tend to overlook or minimize the harm of others.

Ten years after women first gained employment as guards in men's prisons, many of the original obstacles to their adjustment remain. The opposition of inmates has decreased but the opposition of male guards remains a major force in the working lives of these women. The following chapter will explore the different ways in which female guards have adjusted to the job, learned to meet the formal requirements of guard work, and managed to cope with the special problems and obstacles encountered by women.

How Female Guards Adapt to the Job

In just the last decade or so, the literature on nontraditional working women has been greatly expanded to include impressive studies from nearly every occupational category, ranging from white-collar professionals to blue-collar hard hats. This literature continues to be lacking, however, in the examination of differences among women who work on the same nontraditional jobs. Kay Deaux and Joseph Ullman's (1982) cursory statement of differences among female steelworkers is fairly typical:

> Some women are muscular, some are slight; some look tough and some have carefully coiffed hair and fingernail polish; some are college-educated and others have only completed high school; some like their jobs and others hate them. [P. 38]

What Deaux and Ullman fail to do is examine the way in which differences among women affect their orientation toward the job, their occupational performance, and their relationships with others in the workplace.

A few researchers have given a little more attention to differences among nontraditional women workers (Kanter 1977; Epstein 1975; Forisha 1981b; McDowell 1978), but only Susan Martin's (1980) study of female police officers includes this as a major research issue. She finds that policewomen are "forced to choose between two polar patterns of behavior"—"defeminization," in which occupational role obligations are stressed, and "deprofessionalization," in which typically female sex-role norms are given priority (p. 185). Martin found examples of each: she describes the *police*woman as one who over-achieves, is ambitious, denies discrimination, and seeks to prove herself as the exception; the police*woman*, on the other hand, is unassertive, has limited expectations for the future, emphasizes the physical limitations of women, and, above all, tries to maintain a ladylike demeanor on the job. Martin goes on to explain the different ways in which female police officers in these two categories make job-related decisions and interact with citizens and co-workers.

Interviews with female guards quickly revealed that there were critical differences among these women, making it impossible to present a composite picture of the female guard, her occupational experiences, and her job performance strategies. There are, of course, important commonalities among these women as well, particularly in the opposition, harassment, and discrimination they face on the job. Those common experiences were outlined in previous chapters; this chapter will focus on the differences among female prison guards, with special attention to the strategies they use to adjust to this highly nontraditional occupation.

Three Adjustment Strategies Used by Women

There is no single way to perform successfully as a prison guard and survive on the job. All guards must eventually develop a personal style of guarding that reflects their individual solutions to job-related problems. At a minimum, they must create mechanisms for coping with fear and danger, develop techniques for gaining inmate compliance, and build adequate working relationships with peers and supervisors. The female guard, however, must adopt a personal style that solves not only these problems basic to the job, but also those specific to women. Her style must also include mechanisms for coping with discrimination, harassment, testing by inmates, and tokenism. In addition, if she is to feel comfortable in her occupational role, she must develop a style that does not conflict with her own sex-role orientation.

Although each female guard adapts to the job in her own way, I have identified three general patterns of adaptation by women working in men's prisons. Some of the dimensions of each pattern coincide with aspects of typical male strategies for performing the job, but others appear to be peculiar to women. Because this study did not include in-depth examination of men's strategies for performing the job, definitive comparisons between male and female guards cannot be made.[1] All three female patterns of adapting seem fairly stable, as examples of each can be found among women who have been on the job for a substantial period of time. As is typical of "ideal types," no single woman fits every dimension in the general pattern that best describes her. Nevertheless, all of the women interviewed for this study fit into one of the three general categories.

Each of the three following categories was arrived at inductively after conducting interviews with female guards, male guards, inmates, and prison administrators. Once the categories were constructed, additional interviews were conducted to confirm their validity. Because these roles are not participant-designated (i.e., are not defined as such by any members of the prison community) but are observer-constructed (i.e., discerned and articulated by the researcher), it was necessary to test the categories against the perceptions of the daily participants. According to John Lofland (1971),

> the best and most stringent test of observer constructions is their recognizability to the participants themselves. When participants say "Yes, that is there, I had simply never noticed it before," the observer can be reasonably confident that he has tapped into exant patterns of participation. [P. 34]

The three separate occupational roles for female guards were refined and formalized through use of this technique in the later interviews with all participants.

A small percentage of female guards (11 percent of my sample) have chosen an adaptive strategy I call the *institutional role*. They try to adhere to all the institutional norms governing the behavior of prison guards by following as closely as possible the formal rules established by the administration and stressed during the academy training. Because women who choose this role want to perform the job on an equal basis with men, they attempt to downplay the importance of their female status in interactions with inmates, co-workers, and supervisors. They generally ignore male guards who oppose the presence of women and try to maintain professional relationships with all persons in the prison environment.

Another group of women (43 percent of my sample) chose the *modified role*. They generally feel that women, including themselves, are unable to perform the job of guarding on an equal basis with men. These women are fearful of inmates and avoid direct inmate contact whenever possible. They are sympathetic to male co-worker opposition to the presence of women and join them in opposing "women's libbers" who think they can do the whole job. Either because they have accumulated a great deal of seniority (usually while working at a woman's prison) or because they have cultivated close relationships with male co-workers and supervisors, they are almost always able to remain on safe, noncontact post assignments. When they must come into contact with inmates, they rely on male co-workers to back them up and provide support. They see their female status as detrimental to full performance of the job.

In contrast, women in the *inventive role* (46 percent of my sample) view their female status as a distinct advantage. These women often work in direct-contact jobs, expecting and receiving the support and assistance of male inmates. They have little fear of inmates, not only because they have developed close relationships with many of them, but also because they expect the majority of inmates to monitor the negative behavior of the few troublemakers. These women receive the most harassment from male guards and are, in turn, most openly resentful about it. Women in the inventive role claim that women's disadvantage in physical strength is compensated for by their intuition, their superior communication skills, and their ability to win the respect of inmates. Although many women in the inventive role believe they are physically weaker than their male counterparts, they are willing to enter dangerous situations and engage in physical confrontations with inmates simply because the job requires them to do so.

The job of prison guard in a men's prison is different for women in each of these three roles. Each offers special ways of solving occupational problems but also generates problems and dilemmas of its own. In the following sections I will examine each strategy in more detail and outline some of the reasons particular women seem to choose a particular adaptive strategy.

Women in the Institutional Role

> When I put on this uniform and this badge, I'm a prison guard and that's all the inmate needs to know. If he does what he's supposed to do, we'll have no trouble. If he decides to break the rules, then I'm here to enforce them—just the same as any other officer. Once the inmate understands that, there's no problem.

Women in the institutional role begin employment in men's prisons expecting to perform the same tasks and duties as male guards. They are willing to work on all posts, including those requiring direct contact with male inmates. In emergencies, such as inmate fights or disturbances, these women respond and use physical force when necessary. Some began guard work already trained in the martial arts of karate or judo, but all describe themselves as physically fit; they stress the importance of physical conditioning as a prerequisite for adequate performance on the job. These women suggest that more physical training is needed for male as well as female guards and would like to see physical fitness classes instituted as part of a continuing on-the-job training program.

Female guards in the institutional role gain and maintain inmate compliance to prison rules by following the established system of rewards and punishments. Most feel this system works well, especially if implemented correctly:

> Most inmates are willing to follow the rules. What gets them upset is unfairness and inconsistency. If a rule is in the book, I'm going to enforce it today and enforce it tomorrow. If I enforce it for one inmate, I'll enforce it for the next one. That way, everyone knows what they're supposed to do and there are no surprises. An inmate's got to know that the rules will be taken seriously every time.

For these women, a major obstacle to performing the job properly—by the book—is the inconsistent rule-enforcement policies of many of their male colleagues:

> It took quite a while for inmates to get used to following all the rules. Most of the male officers are willing to "look the other way" at times. When I came on the cell block, I started enforcing the dress code. First I gave warnings, then starting writing inmates up for not buttoning their top button. It caused quite a stir at first. Now I only have trouble when a new inmate moves over from another block. I've got to "train" him. Pretty soon he figures out that I'll leave him alone as long as he obeys all the rules.

Because these women accept all the rules, no violation is considered more worthy of attention than another. Other guards may sometimes ignore "petty" violations, especially those concerning dress and grooming codes; women in the institutional role generally do not:

> I think some of the rules are pretty stupid and outdated, but it's not my job to make the rules, only enforce them. If I don't do it, an inmate won't know where he stands from one day to the next. He'll always be "testing" to see what he can get away with. With me, he knows what he can get away with—nothing.

Inmates are aware that many female guards' enforcement policies differ from those of most male guards. An inmate said about a female guard working on his housing unit:

> Officer Garrett is okay. She's really nice to have around but she is one of the toughest officers in the place. She will write you up for

anything. I guess she figures that she has to do that or no one will respect her. It's sort of a hassle, but I just get used to "watching myself" whenever she's on duty.

Most inmates found such strict rule enforcement to be tolerable as long as the women themselves were fair and likable.

Despite their inflexibility about rule violations, institutional role women do not generally have negative attitudes toward inmates themselves. They remain professional and "distant" (avoiding personal conversations with inmates) but express compassion about the conditions under which prisoners must exist:

This is a terrible place to live. It brings out the worst in everyone. I've got to give a lot of credit to any inmate who can rehabilitate himself in here.

Inmates are not automatically viewed as either "victims" or "animals"; instead, each is judged as an individual:

Some of these guys are decent men; others, I wouldn't trust for a minute out on the street. I give every inmate a chance to prove himself. If he acts like a man, I'll treat him like a man. If he acts like an "animal," I'll throw the book at him. If he decides to change his attitude, I'll give him another chance. For some of these guys it just takes a while to settle down.

Again, inmates were well aware of this attitude:

I don't know too many of the women in here, but I do know Officer Smith. She treats everybody decent. Most of the male guards are ready to jump in your face even before you do anything wrong. If they decide they don't like you, there's nothing you can do. With Smith, she'll jump on your case, and even throw you in the hole, but when you come back, she'll treat you nice, just the same.

Women in the institutional role recognize that the job of guarding in today's male prison is inherently dangerous. Some of these women believe that female guards are more vulnerable to attack by inmates than are male guards, but all accept the risk of injury or death as an occupational hazard that cannot be eliminated. The danger associated with guard work is, however, best ignored:

Sure, I thought a lot about getting hurt before I took the job. Now, I just don't think about it. It's still there, in the back of my mind, but if I were going to dwell on it, I couldn't be effective on the job.

Female guards who adopt the institutional role try to reduce the chances of an inmate attack by staying in peak physical condition, avoiding angering inmates unnecessarily, and attempting to enforce the rules consistently and fairly. One female guard expressed awareness that attitude and behavior while enforcing prison rules can reduce the likelihood of a direct inmate attack:

> You never know when an inmate might go crazy and just start attacking the first officer he sees—it happens every once in a while. But *usually* when an inmate goes after an officer it is because that officer instigated it. An inmate will just take so much. I can tell you right now which officers will get it eventually. I may get hurt, but I'm sure not going to ask for it. If you treat inmates fairly, they just don't attack you for no reason—they have too much to lose.

Prison guards are less able to control the possibility of injury during emergency situations than at any other time, and several female guards have been injured while helping to break up fights between inmates or between inmates and other guards. In spite of the danger, women who have adopted the institutional role insist on responding to any emergency call in which a similar response would be expected of male guards in their position. On some prison posts (such as main control areas), guards are required to remain stationary during emergencies. On others (such as a mail room or administrative post), guards are instructed to respond to all emergency calls elsewhere in the prison.

Some women feel that because of their peak physical condition they are better prepared to cope with inmate violence than are many of their male colleagues. Others are less sure of their physical qualifications but are willing to put forth their best effort:

> I may not be able to do as much damage as a man, but I'll let my presence be known. The day I run the other way during trouble is the day it's time for me to quit.

These women are willing to enter dangerous situations primarily because such action is a basic requirement of the job.[2] Some women, however, are additionally motivated by their desire to reduce male co-worker opposition:

> If I didn't respond when an emergency was being sounded, they [the male guards] would never let me forget it. There's no way I would set myself up for that kind of harassment.

A few women in the institutional role have gained the respect of male guards and supervisors. Women with superior physical training, especially in some form of the martial arts, have the most self-confidence about their abilities and are most likely to impress male guards as being capable of performing the job. These women are the exception, however, and are often referred to as "extraordinary" or "superwomen" by male co-workers. A male supervisor said about one female guard who had adopted the institutional role:

> Most of these women, I wouldn't give you two cents for, but you can give me as many Jane Maxwells as you can find. Unfortunately, she seems to be one of a kind.

Other women in the institutional role fail to win the men's respect and admiration even though they meet all basic requirements of the job and have proved their willingness to respond to prison emergencies. For them, the institutional role offers no escape from male opposition and harassment. Indeed, male guards are especially hostile to women who attempt to perform the job on an equal basis with men but, according to the men, fall short. One woman claimed:

> There's nothing else I can do to prove myself. I passed the academy with flying colors. I took every job they ever gave me without complaining. I've broken up fights and been in the hospital with injuries. After four years here, most of these guys still don't want to work with me.

The opposition of some men to the presence of women is so strong that no accomplishment by a woman could diminish their belief in female inferiority; they do not accept even the women referred to by others as extraordinary. One male guard said:

> Everyone probably told you about Angela Pointer—how she can do everything a man can do. Well, she may know karate, but she's still no match for a 250-pound inmate. If she ever gets punched, she'll be down on her back before she knows what hit her. I'd take any man here for a partner before I'd take her.

Those male guards who are opposed to women's presence primarily because it invades inmate privacy are also unimpressed with the expertise and accomplishments of the few "exceptional" women:

> You've got a few women in here who can handle the job okay. But what about the inmates? They don't want a woman gawking at them while they're taking a shower or using the john. What kind of woman would even want such a job?

Although women in the institutional role *can* win the approval of male co-workers, this approval neither extends to all women in this role nor represents the view of the majority of male guards in the prison. Thus women in the institutional role, like those who have adopted other roles, must learn to cope with the opposition and harassment of their male co-workers. Their strategy for doing this generally is one of silent tolerance, although they are willing to complain to prison administrators (and have done so) when the behavior of male co-workers becomes intolerable or interferes with their ability to perform the job.

Several women who adopted the institutional role credited a few male co-workers or supervisors with easing their initial adjustment. Male support of female guards is seldom overt, but in every prison there is a small corps of men who either favor the introduction of women or support the few women guards who impress them as especially capable. Although valuing these few good working relationships with men, women rarely allow them to become close friendships or romantic involvements:

> When I first came here, a few of the men asked me out. Some of them I liked, but I knew it would be a mistake to date male officers. I've seen other women do it and it always leads to trouble—they end up playing flirting games on the job. You can't flirt with a man one minute and then work with him as an equal the next.

Women in the institutional role generally refrain from informal socializing with male guards, although at least one "inadvertently" became involved with a supportive male colleague:

> I tried to avoid it—so did he—but eventually we just gave in. It's been harder on him than on me because he has to take all the flak from the other guys on the shift. Right now I have a bid in for another facility because everyone is afraid that he'll leave his post to protect me if I'm in danger. He would never do that, but it will make it easier for everyone if we work in different facilities.

Most women described their relationship with male co-workers as "aloof," "professional," or "nonexistent." One female guard reported that she approaches all but a few select male guards with an "attitude":

> Everyone here tells me I have an "attitude problem." Well, it's my attitude that has saved me—you need an attitude to survive on this job. When these 18 and 19 year old kids [new male guards] come in and get a taste of my attitude, they know I won't take any shit from them. We get that out of the way real quick.

Women who have adopted the institutional role believe that there should be few, if any, limitations on the jobs they perform in male prisons. They recognize that other female guards do not want to perform all duties and actively try to avoid inmate contact, but they want the opportunity to do every job done by men. They recognize the problem of inmate privacy, but most feel it should not be a factor in post assignments:

> As far as I'm concerned, this job is the same as a doctor or a nurse. I don't want to see any inmate naked, but it's no big deal if I do. If some guy is sitting on the toilet as I take the count, I just keep walking. I won't even remember which inmate it was.

Women in the institutional role resent attempts to limit their access to prison jobs. In New York, it was those women who continually challenged the interpretation of the guidelines for deployment of opposite-sex guards; some were able to use the union grievance procedure to gain bid jobs that were initially denied them.

In both New York and Rhode Island it was women who had adopted the institutional role who first sought assignment to prison "emergency squads." These specially trained teams are called upon when an inmate must be restrained or when an inmate disturbance is anticipated. Some women in the institutional role aspire to administrative positions and view service on these riot squads as necessary for future advancement:

> If you want to get ahead in this job, you've got to make yourself look a little bit better than everyone else. You have to show you're committed to the job. It's even more necessary if you're a woman. When I asked for a chance to try out for the squad, the lieutenant in charge said, "over my dead body." Finally, the warden gave his approval and he had to let me on. Now I'm just waiting to get called so I can show my stuff.

The desire of women in the institutional role to be treated as equal members of the guard force reflects their attitude toward the appropriate role of women in the work force as a whole. A typical comment was:

> Women should be allowed to do any job they're capable of doing and as far as I'm concerned, that's every job. It's a real shame we need laws to make sure women get the chance to work where they want to work.

Although some women in the institutional role extend this notion of equality to all realms of women's lives—not just work force participation—not all do. Most women voiced support for the Equal Rights Amendment, but a few adamantly opposed it. None of the women in the institutional role were actively involved in any feminist or women's rights organizations, and they did not become guards because of any desire to exemplify the capabilities of women. Instead, they sought prison employment for a wide variety of personal reasons, ranging from financial considerations to a life-long desire to work in law enforcement. Many of these women are pleased that their performance provides an example of the breadth of women's capabilities, but this did not motivate their decision to take the job.

Women in the institutional role seldom view their accomplishments as extraordinary. One female guard who received the praise of nearly every male co-worker and supervisor in the prison said:

> Any woman can do what I do if she gets herself ready, mentally and physically. Unfortunately, many of the women here aren't ready and don't care about getting ready. It would take a little time, but there's no doubt they could do it.

Thus, even those women who want to perform the job on an equal basis with men fail to see themselves as "pioneers" or "trailblazers." They only want the opportunity to perform the job without special treatment or special privileges. They are frustrated, however, over the continuing need to prove themselves:

> It gets discouraging at times. I've thought about going into police work where a lot of the battles have already been won by women. I talked with the police chief over in town and he assured me that I would be treated just like the men. But every time I think about quitting, I decide to wait a while—just until my latest grievance has been settled. But by the time that one gets settled, I've got another one in the works. Now I've decided to stay at least until another woman makes it onto the riot squad. If I quit now, they'll never let another woman on without another fight.

So, although women in the institutional role do not generally seek prison employment as part of a "crusade" for women's rights, some unwittingly become crusaders because, in fighting for their right to equal employment opportunities, they win this right for other women as well.

Although women who have adopted the institutional role generally are effective on the job, there are some problems and dilemmas inherent in the role itself. These women are often "loners" in the male prison. At some prisons, only a very few women use this strategy, and they may have little contact with each other. Female guards in the prison who have adopted different strategies are often hostile toward women in the institutional role and toward their desire for equal treatment on the job. Unless women in the institutional role develop strong ties with male supervisors or co-workers, they will have few allies in the prison. And because many of these women feel they must avoid close relationships with male co-workers, they end up with no one to turn to for friendly conversation and advice. They must face problems on the job alone. One such woman reported that her husband, who was not employed in the prison, was the only person with whom she could share her work problems:

> Every day I came home with a new story. After a month he "knew" everyone who worked here. I would ask him "did I do this right?" or "should I have said that?" I don't know what I would have done without him. He kept reassuring me that I had always done anything I set my mind to do and that this would work out, too.

When women in the institutional role decide to fight discrimination, they receive little support from other women:

> When I complained about female guards being assigned to "non-posts" such as third person on a two-person post, all the other women here jumped all over me. I find it humiliating to work on a post that doesn't even exist when I'm not on duty. But as far as the other women were concerned, I was trying to spoil a good thing.

Because women in the institutional role have not developed close bonds with any of their co-workers, they miss many of the occupational "tips" that are passed around during informal conversations between guards. These women are also reluctant to ask for advice from other guards because they fear that their ignorance will be interpreted as incompetence. Consequently, they must try to learn, pretty much on their own, all the rules concerning inmate conduct as well as all the rules for their own behavior. By following the rules precisely, they hope to be insulated from the criticism of male co-workers, supervisors, and administrators.

It is largely fear of negative evaluations and the desire to avoid making decisions that could be challenged later that prompts these women to perform the job strictly "by the book." This strategy can create problems, however, because by always following the rules, these women may fail to develop any sense of the circumstances under which the rules should be bent or even broken. For example, a female guard who had adopted the institutional role was working on a gate post when an inmate who was bleeding profusely approached the gate and demanded to be let through to seek medical attention. She refused to open the gate because the inmate had no pass; instead, she waited until a supervisor arrived to give official approval for the gate to be opened. Although she had followed the rules, she was later criticized by co-workers and supervisors for her action. In recalling the incident, she claimed:

> I know a lot of people thought I did the wrong thing—the Captain called me into his office and said he wanted me to bid for a different post where this sort of thing wouldn't come up. As far as I'm concerned, I did the right thing.

She remains resentful of the criticism that followed this incident, claiming that she only did what she was "supposed to do," according to the rules.

This lack of flexibility presents continual problems for women in the institutional role. No job can be performed entirely according to a set of predetermined rules and regulations. In the job of prison guard, flexibility and discretion are especially important to long-term success and personal safety. Another woman in the institutional role attributes an inmate attack to her failure to grant a request that was clearly against the rules. An extremely agitated inmate wanted to retrieve "his property" from the cell of another inmate before returning to his own cell for the night. She refused, ordered the inmate into his cell, and was attacked. She was later told by male guards that because of the inmate's "mental condition," she should have granted the request, then immediately called for reinforcements to restore the status quo. Such an option had never occurred to her.

Women in the institutional role often develop this near compulsion for following the rules because they believe the rules will provide automatic justification for their actions in the face of any criticism. They can be faulted for not following the "best" course of action but never for following the "wrong" course of action. By always obeying the rules, they always have an explanation for their behavior.

The tendency for women breaking into new jobs to follow a rigid set of rules has been found by other investigators. In his study of newly appointed female factory supervisors, Burleigh Gardner (1945) found that subordinate workers complained of female bosses being "too bossy" in their enforcement of the rules. Gardner claims that new and insecure supervisors, male as well as female, often develop authoritarian-controlling leadership styles:

> A new supervisor who feels unsure of himself, who feels that his boss is watching him critically, is likely to demand perfect behavior and performance from his people, to be critical of minor mistakes, and to try too hard to please his boss. A woman super-

visor, responding to the insecurity and uncertainty of her position as a woman, knowing that she is being watched both critically and doubtfully, feels obliged to try even harder. [Pp. 270–71]

More recently, Rosabeth Kanter (1977) found the same phenomenon among women who had just moved into corporate management positions:

> Without the experience or confidence to permit the minor deviations from the rules that in fact make the system work and without enough knowledge and faith in outcomes to loosen control, new managers may be prone to be too directive, controlling, and details-oriented. [P. 204]

Kanter maintains that this leadership style results from women's powerlessness in the organization as a whole:

> The problem of power thus is critical to the effective behavior of people in organizations. Power issues occupy center stage not because individuals are greedy for more, but because some people are incapacitated without it. [P. 205]

Female guards in the institutional role try to compensate for their lack of power by stressing strict adherence to administrative rules. Even though this style insulates them from the constant evaluation and criticism of male co-workers and supervisors, following the rules in an ambiguous situation does sometimes lead to separate problems as well as to the male criticism they are trying so hard to avoid.

The tendency toward inflexibility is least likely to be a problem for women who have confidence in their own abilities and receive some positive reinforcement from co-workers. The few women who are referred to as the "exceptions" have less reason to fear that a single mistake in judgment will result in a barrage of criticism. For women clinging to the institutional role in the face of continual harassment and criticism, however, strict adherence to the rules, and the inflexibility it entails, offers a way to survive. Although the institutional role is the one of the three strategies used by women that most closely resembles the "ideal" occupational role—the role presented in the academy and in the guard rule books—it does not closely resemble a typical male adaptation to the job. The institutional role is also the adaptive strategy that has the most obstacles and dilemmas for women themselves. These women must be willing to cope with the opposition of female as well as male co-workers, must be fully committed to performing all aspects of the job, and must be especially capable. Use of this strategy requires strict adherence to a set of rules that, too often, does not provide effective solutions to the wide range of occupational problems prison guards face.

Women in the Modified Role

> I'll work anywhere they tell me to work. So far, I've been in the visiting room and up front, doing typing. Some of the girls here would complain about that—they'd say "You put me here because you don't think I'm capable." Sure, I've gotten the less trouble-some assignments, but that's where they need me the most. It would be foolish for me to complain.

Female guards who have adopted the modified role believe that women are incapable of performing the job of guard in men's prisons on an equal basis with men. They not only recognize their own personal limitations but believe these limitations extend to all women. The existence of "natural" differences between males and females—differences that are important to one's ability to perform this job—is taken for granted:

> Any woman who starts to believe that she can compete with the men here is in serious trouble. Women aren't built the same as men—we're not built to fight. If an inmate decides to make trouble, there's just no way he's going to be stopped by a woman.

Female guards in the modified role believe that prison security would be jeopardized by giving women equal assignments:

> If you tried to run this place with women on a lot of the contact jobs it would fall within a week. These inmates are not dumb. They know enough to look for the weakest link.

And if such a crisis were to occur, there is the fear that female guards would be more likely than males to be raped, injured, or taken hostage by inmates:

> It just makes sense that if an inmate wants to grab someone, the first one he'll go for is a woman. And you know if they've got a woman, they're going to rape her—and not just once, either.

Women who have adopted the modified role also view women as incapable of tolerating the vulgar language and the sexual miscon-duct of some male inmates. One female guard remarked, "A woman can't take that kind of abuse and still come out of here a woman."

Women in the modified role often voice concern for inmate rights and feel that only male guards can properly protect inmates from each other. They also explain that inmates deserve to have their personal privacy protected and are, in fact, skeptical of the motives of female guards who do not seem to share this concern:

> All men need their privacy and men in prison are no different. Women don't belong in the cell blocks where inmates have to use toilets right out in the open. What kind of woman would even *want* to put herself in that position? What is she trying to prove? Maybe some women get a thrill out of seeing naked men. I think it's disgusting.

Women who hold either or both of these two sets of beliefs—the first regarding women's physical limitations and the second concerning the impropriety of having female guards see naked male inmates—prefer to work on posts that entail little or no direct contact with prisoners. Some of them have enough seniority in the system (usually accumulated at a women's prison) to allow them to bid for noncontact jobs. Other women who prefer the modified role, but do not have enough seniority to obtain a permanent noncontact post, stay on "utility" or "miscellaneous status" and receive noncontact assignments on a daily basis from the supervisor on duty. There are a couple of reasons why some supervisors are willing to comply with the desire of these women to work away from inmates. First, male supervisors may believe that female guards "belong" only on noncontact posts and are relieved when women voluntarily accept a limited role. Second, some supervisors were acquainted with women who chose the modified role even before becoming guards and, because of this friendship, agree to place these women only on safe, noncontact posts. This is especially likely to be the case when women are recruited from the community in which the prison is located and have close ties—often family ties—with men already working in the prison. In fact, some women report that they decided to become guards in men's prisons only because they were assured beforehand that they would receive special treatment and be saved from the most unpleasant and dangerous aspects of the job.

Few women in the modified role, whether obtained through seniority or through male supervisor agreement, can be guaranteed exclusion from all direct contact with inmates. Modified women on miscellaneous status are, in fact, sometimes assigned to contact jobs, although rarely the most dangerous ones in the prison. Carol Talbert, for example, is on miscellaneous status and works a wide variety of contact jobs. She relieves other officers from their day room posts, supervises inmates in the yard, and works in the prison library. According to Carol, she has an "agreement" with her supervisor that he will not assign her to either of the two housing units where the institution's most troublesome inmates are confined.

When women on miscellaneous status are assigned to contact jobs, they often work directly with male guards who are willing to assist and protect a woman who adopts the modified role. One female guard who was married to a male guard reported that she was only "putting in her time" in a men's prison until there was an opening in the female unit; she found that male guards were willing to protect her during her temporary duty in the men's prison:

> The guys know I don't want to be here—they think it's as stupid as I do. But the way the department runs things now, there's no way to get into the woman's unit unless you work here first. So, they watch my back for me.

Some male guards, however, are willing to provide protection over an even longer period of time. Donna Bell is on miscellaneous status in a large maximum-security prison where one of her usual daily assignments is to "run companies to chow" with a male guard. She told how he "straightened out" an inmate who had gotten out of line:

> I was at the end of the line and Charlie was at the beginning. When I came through the door into the mess hall he could tell that something had happened. I told him it was nothing—just one of the inmates mouthing off—but he wanted to know who it was. Well, Charlie and another guard went to visit him later in his cell and explained to him about the proper way to speak to a lady. Since then, I've had no trouble.

Another woman in the modified role said:

> I don't worry too much about the inmates. They know if anything happens to me, I have friends here who will make sure something worse happens to them.

Women in the modified role, then, especialy those who have some direct contact with inmates, rely on male guards to provide protection and support. At the extreme, this help includes the provision of an extra "incentive" for inmates to act cautiously in their contacts with women.

It is general prison policy that when "shakedowns" or emergencies occur, guards will be "pulled" from some noncontact posts (especially those in the administrative offices) to provide additional assistance. At such times, women in the modified role may have little choice but to comply. Occasionally, however, friendly male guards have warned women that such emergencies are imminent and have urged them to "go home sick." This occurred while I was conducting interviews at one prison. A female guard on miscellaneous status on the day shift was normally assigned to clerical duties. She left the prison about 11 A.M. after reporting to her supervisor that she was not feeling well. When I interviewed her the next day, she confided that a male guard had warned her that a major shakedown was scheduled for two cell blocks that afternoon. He suggested that she leave the prison to avoid being assigned there. Another woman in the modified role claimed that in her three years as a guard, she had never been required to respond to an emergency because her supervisor "understands that he should assign people where they can do the most good." Thus some women in the modified role have been able to avoid virtually all potentially dangerous situations.

Because many female guards in the modified role rely on male supervisors to assign them to the least threatening posts and rely on male guards to provide protection when they do have direct contact with inmates, they tend to be more accepting of men's treatment of them than are other female guards. These women do admit that most male guards oppose the hiring of women, and even report some personal incidents of harassment by male guards, but they generally attribute extreme negative treatment to a few "troublemakers." Their overall evaluation of male co-worker reaction to them personally is favorable:

> Most of the guys here are all right. They didn't really like the idea of women coming in here, but once they got used to it, they've accepted it okay.

The overt harassment and opposition reported by other women is viewed as an exaggeration by women in the modified role:

> A lot of these women are just complainers. The men are only trying to have a little fun. They give all new guards a hard time—it's just part of the initiation. If they [the women] would take it as a joke—the way it is meant—the guys would stop it. They don't bother me anymore.

In fact, one female guard who had adopted the modified role admitted to me that her sole reason for agreeing to talk to me was to counteract the "bad-mouthing" of male guards that she suspected other women of engaging in during our interviews. She stressed how well her male co-workers had adjusted to the presence of women.

Female guards in the modified role probably do receive better treatment from their male co-workers than do other women in the prison. Muriel Lembright and Jeffrey Riemer (1982) found that female truckers who were associated closely with specific male truckers were insulated from the opposition and harassment typical of women in male-dominated occupations:

> Our research suggests that women in nontraditional work careers will experience undesirable conditions to the extent that they lack the continual support from established males. [P. 485]

Just as the majority of women studied by Lembright and Riemer became truckers because of their association with male truckers, so did many women in the modified role become prison guards because of their prior relationships with male guards. These close ties buffer women in the modified role from the severe harassment experienced by others and undoubtedly make them less sensitive to the teasing and hazing that do occur. But it should also be remembered that these women are in no position to complain of male treatment of them, no matter how negative it might be, because they often depend on male assistance for their personal safety and continued employment.

Women in the modified role cannot risk the withdrawal of male friendship and support. Therefore, they tend not only to minimize male opposition and harassment but also to maximize the positive qualities of their male colleagues:

> Most of the men here are really good at their job—they know how to handle inmates and they know how to handle administrators. Women are intuitive, but men are instinctual—and that's what it takes to do this job right. It takes me too long to figure out what I should do; the men just react—like it's second nature to them.

A female coal miner interviewed by Judith Hammond and Constance Mahoney (1983) similarly found that deference to male co-workers can be an effective survival mechanism:

> They can't stand the thought of a woman being smarter than them, or doing better than them; that's just typical man. So you have to let them know that you think they're still the best. That's the only way to get along in the mines. . . . They won't like you if you don't treat them that way. [P. 25]

Women in the modified role must be liked by male guards in order to receive their assistance and support. And to be liked, they must accept the view that males are suited and females unsuited to the job and remain good-humored about the gender-related comments and jokes that are made in their presence.

Female guards in the modified role tend to share with many male guards in the prison an extremely negative attitude toward inmates. One woman remarked:

> I never was sympathetic to inmates. Most of them are cry babies—they won't stand up and do something for themselves. The public thinks they're bad guys when they're out on the street, but as soon as they get in here, it's "poor inmates." They eat better than you and I do, and we're the ones paying for it.

When asked whether she thought inmates would protect her during a prison emergency, this woman answered:

> No way in hell! If you start to rely on inmates around here you might as well call it quits. They've committed violent and serious crimes—you can't trust an inmate.

Some women in the modified role plan to bid for a position in a female prison once they have accumulated enough seniority, but others intend to make a career in the male prison. Like other female guards, they claim to have taken the job because the wages and benefits are good, especially when compared with other jobs in their communities. They are not particularly attracted to prison work, and find the job acceptable only if they adopt the modified role. If they were required to work on direct-contact jobs, in the most dangerous areas of the prison, many women in the modified role admit they would terminate their employment.

Although they perform a limited range of duties, women in the modified role feel that they contribute to the overall functioning of the prison:

> There are some things women can do better. For example, before we came, female visitors brought in a lot of contraband because there was no one here to search them thoroughly. We catch a lot more stuff now, and even the male guards are glad about that. I think it's also better to have a woman on the front desk. When visitors come in, female guards are a lot friendlier and more courteous. Women can also work in the control booths and free up the men for other kinds of jobs.

Because they perceive themselves as valuable additions to the male prison, they feel justified in earning the same wages as male guards:

> I may not do everything a man does around here, but I earn my paycheck. I've never spent a day just standing around, and lots of

guys do that. One day I'll be in the mail room, another day at the front desk, answering the phone. If they don't need me on a regular post, there is always typing and filing to get done. Someone has to do it and there is never enough clerical help around here. At least I do it a lot faster than the male guards who used to do it. My supervisor is glad to have me.

Thus, even women who want differential treatment and only a limited range of assignments believe that their presence contributes to the prison's operation. They generally recognize, however, that male prisons can accommodate only a limited number of women. Consequently, they favor restrictions on the number of women employed at each male facility:

Right now, we've got just about enough women here. Once you get too many, they're going to be all over the prison. That would be a real problem. That's what the men are afraid of now. They like having a few women, but know women can't work but on so many posts.

Women in the modified role resent other women who seek and demand equal treatment on the job, calling them "radicals," "troublemakers," and "women's libbers." Fear was expressed that these other women might instigate changes in administrative policy that could alter the arrangements women in the modified role had established with supervisors:

I've been here nearly two years now and everything has worked out fine. Now you've got these radicals coming in. They always want to change things, no matter how good they are now. They make such a fuss that the administrators have to listen to them. If you're just here, doing your job, minding your own business, nobody asks you what you want.

Fear of future changes is one of the major sources of tension for women in the modified role, especially those who do not have the security of a noncontact bid post. Their position is always precarious. Because their arrangements with males in the prison are informal, they cannot demand compliance, and it may take years before some women in the modified role have enough seniority to bid for a noncontact post:

There are lots of posts I could bid for now, but I don't really want any of them. I'm waiting until I have enough seniority to get something good. A control room would be nice, but that would probably take another few years. I'd rather stay on miscellaneous than bid for a post I don't really want.

Another problem for women in the modified role is that new supervisors and new male guards coming into the prison cannot automatically be counted on for support. In fact, these women's only serious criticism of male guards was voiced against the young ones who had been hired after them. Some of them are accused of being as "radical" about sexual integration of the guard force as are the female guards they dislike.

A final source of tension for women in the modified role is the possibility of having to face a dangerous situation that they will not be able to handle. Although these women have the least contact with inmates, they are especially fearful of an inmate attack. And because they have not developed skills for interacting with inmates or mechanisms for controlling them, every potential face-to-face contact produces fear and apprehension. One woman recalls her probationary period at a men's prison away from her home town:

> I'm not sure how I made it through those first six months. It was touch-and-go for a while there. One supervisor put me on all the worst jobs—almost every day I was on a cell block. The inmates were really tough. I just kept telling myself that once I got back here—where I know everyone—things would be different.

Because few women in the modified role are able to avoid all contact with male inmates, however, even a hometown prison staffed by protective male co-workers cannot offer an absolute guarantee of safety. Women in the modified role, therefore, remain constantly fearful of their inevitable contacts with inmates.

Women in the Inventive Role

> The department wants me to act like a man, but I'm a woman and I want to use that to my advantage. I can get an inmate to do lots of things a male guard can't because I'm his mother, sister, daughter, and friend. I took this job because I thought I could do some good. Have I? Well, you'll have to ask the inmates that. I think I've helped some of them.

Women in the inventive role often work on posts that require daily face-to-face contact with inmates. Many of them prefer posts on housing units or on work details where there is the opportunity for sustained relationships with a small group of inmates. In this setting, women are able to become acquainted with the inmates, their backgrounds, and their problems. Women in the inventive role often stress the importance of knowing each prisoner as an individual:

> I know the guys on this unit so well that when I come on duty I can tell right away who is mad at whom, who is upset, who got a bad letter from home, etc. Instead of letting them go at each other, I can usually stop trouble before it begins by giving them a chance to talk these things out.

By integrating counseling into the guard's job, women in the inventive role claim they are able to discover information that helps them to perform their control functions better. For others, however, personal information about inmates is important because it creates the opportunity to help inmates:

> There's no use trying to kid myself—I'm no social worker. But I can offer a helping hand now and then. At least I can listen, and most of the time, that's all inmates need. You can't really solve their problems, but they're grateful that someone cares enough to listen to them.

Another woman claimed that this job was preparing her for an eventual career in social work:

> I've always been interested in working with people. Someday I hope to get my degree and come back here as a counselor. Being a guard is good training for that because I have gotten to see exactly what it's like to live in here. I'll be able to understand inmates' problems better than someone who just popped in here after college.

Although some female guards who have adopted the inventive role claim that male guards could make more use of these counseling techniques, others view them as especially appropriate for female guards. One woman claimed that females have a "second sense" with which they can read the moods of others. Another said:

> To survive on the job, women have to do what they know best. Women know how to listen, how to be understanding, how to soothe wounds. When male guards try it, it doesn't come off right. An inmate just doesn't want to tell his problems to another man.

Thus, although women in the inventive role will usually admit that they are unable to compete with male guards in terms of physical strength, they believe that this one "shortcoming" is more than compensated for by women's positive attributes. In their view, the job can be successfully performed in many different ways; the smart female guard does not try to "act like a man" but uses compassion, understanding, persuasion, and at times manipulation to gain inmate compliance to prison rules. One female guard explains:

A woman can usually get a man to do what she wants without letting him know she wanted it. With inmates, you've got to let them think it's their idea. You plant the seed, but you let them make the decision. Later you tell them, "It was really smart the way you handled that."

Women in the inventive role, then, interact with inmates according to some rather traditional sex-role patterns; for them to be successful, inmates must conform to traditional male sex-role expectations as well. Female guards who use the inventive role find that most male inmates are willing to do so:

These guys may be locked up, but they're still men. You get a few troublemakers, of course, but not too many, really. Just because someone has committed a crime, doesn't mean he's forgotten how to act around a lady.

One sex-role expectation that male inmates generally meet is to refrain from the use of vulgar language in front of women. Almost all female guards report that inmates avoid swearing in their presence; and when they do swear, they usually follow it with an apology. Although women who have adopted the institutional role often claim that such gentlemanly conduct is unnecessary, most women in the inventive role appreciate inmate displays of good manners. They are not necessarily offended by vulgar language, but they are pleased because they view such inmate concern as symbolic of their willingness to treat male and female guards differently.

The second way in which inmates follow male sex-role expectations is in their willingness to protect female guards both from immediate physical danger and from the offensive behavior of other inmates. One woman in the inventive role explains how the majority of male inmates monitor the behavior of the few troublemakers:

Every once in a while a new inmate comes on the block who thinks it's cute to see if he can get me riled up. I don't have to say a thing. The other inmates have a talk with him, and before you know it, he's sweet as can be.

Another woman adds:

Most of the guys cover up when they're coming out of the shower and when they go to bed at night. Last year this inmate claimed that he couldn't sleep with pajamas on. The other inmates told him that he had better learn because I didn't want to see his naked body when I was on duty. Next day, he was wearing pajamas.

Female guards in the inventive role believe that the chivalrous tendencies of male inmates will apply even in emergency situations. Several women claimed that inmates had already protected them from attack by other inmates; one woman said that inmates had urged her to leave a particular area of the prison where trouble was expected. Even in a riot situation, many women believe they will receive the protection of inmates:

> A lot of people think that women don't belong in the prison because they would be more easily raped or killed during a riot. First of all, male guards get raped. Second, I think most inmates in here would hurt the male guards before they'd hurt me. Even if some of them wanted to go after me, the rest would stop them.

Because women in the inventive role trust that most inmates won't hurt them (and that the few who might will be controlled by the remainder), they are generally not fearful about working in a male prison. One woman claims:

> This job is more dangerous than some others I might have, but I don't really feel like I'm in that much danger. I have a lot of friends in here and most of them wouldn't let anything heppen to me. I do get afraid sometimes, but I feel a lot safer here than walking the streets of New York City.

When asked why inmates might be willing to protect them, women in the inventive role give several explanations. Some claim that it is part of the natural male instinct for men to protect women and that men in prison are not different from other men in this regard.[3] Other women suggest that protecting them gives men in prison a rare opportunity to "prove their manhood." One woman presented the following hypothesis concerning why inmates protect rather than attack "the weaker sex":

> No inmate wants to go after a woman. What does it prove if he beats her? You see, if he beats a woman in a fight, it's no big deal—any man could do that. On the other hand, if he should happen to lose in a fight with a woman, his reputation is completely ruined in here. So all around, it's just to his advantage to avoid physical confrontations with women.

Some women also feel that men protect them merely because they want to guarantee the continued presence of female guards:

> Inmates know that if women can't handle the job, the administration is going to pull them out of here. They don't want that. They like to hear a soft voice every now and then. They don't want to spoil it.

Because many women in the inventive role believe that inmates are capable of driving them out of male prisons if they so desire, they are motivated to develop good relationships with the men under their charge. Their dependency on inmates also motivates women in the inventive role to overlook some of the more petty rule violations:

> If an inmate does something wrong in front of my face, I've got to call him on it—otherwise, I would quickly lose my authority and everyone would start to take advantage of me. But I don't go out of my way to look for things. If I did, I could spend my entire shift writing tickets. A lot of the rules don't make much sense anyway. Why should I hassle an inmate for having his shirt untucked— what difference does it make?

The good relationships women in the inventive role have with inmates contrast with the antagonistic relationships they have with their male co-workers. Women who utilize this strategy for performing the job report that most male guards oppose their presence and constantly engage in acts of sexual harassment against them. One woman explains why she avoids almost all contact with her male peers:

> When I first arrived, I tried to be friendly. I knew the men didn't really want us here, but I figured that after a while, they would wear down. Well, I did everything I could to be tolerant, but after a while you decide you've had enough. Now I just leave them alone. If I have to talk to them in the line of duty, I'll do it, but other than that, I've got nothing to say. And neither do any of them, so it works out fine.

Another woman in the inventive role explains that male guards are especially hostile to her because of her good relationships with inmates:

> The men get all nervous when they see me talking to an inmate. Their attitude is that you don't talk to an inmate unless you have to, and then, only to answer questions. They ask me what it is we're talking about, as if a guard and an inmate could never have anything in common. One day a male guard walked by while I was talking to an inmate in Spanish. That really got him—he figured it must be a big secret. The guy just didn't speak very good English, that's all.

Although women in the inventive role generally have poor relationships with male co-workers, black and Hispanic women are, to some extent, an exception. They often develop friendly relationships with minority male guards, a common bond being their mutual hostility toward the white male guards who, they believe, oppose and harass both minorities and women. Minority women, then, are more likely than white women in the inventive role to have some peer friendships to call upon during difficult periods. Because there are few minority supervisors, however, minority women cannot use these friendships to obtain easy, noncontact posts. This probably accounts for the fact that women in the modified role are predominantly white while those in the inventive role are more likely to be black or Hispanic.

The concern that women in the inventive role have for inmates' conditions of confinement extends to a concern for their privacy. But instead of believing that privacy should be used as a criterion for limiting women's access to certain jobs, women in the inventive role prefer to protect inmate privacy themselves. One woman explains:

> Privacy can be a problem, but I do my best to make sure that inmates have as much as possible, given the set-up of this place. Before I take the count, I give everyone warning that I'm on my way down. If someone happens to be on the john, I try not to let him see that I've noticed. If you act professionally, it doesn't have to be a problem.

Many women in the inventive role favor the use of curtains or barriers in the shower areas so that inmates would be protected from exposure to both male and female guards.

One thing that differentiates women in the inventive role from women in both the institutional and modified roles is that their strategy for performing the job emerged entirely while they were learning the job. Many women using the other roles had anticipated their general job performance strategy before entering the male prison. When asked whether they had expected male inmates to be willing to help and protect them, women in the inventive role unanimously claimed that it was an unanticipated occurrence:

> When I first started, I figured that I had to watch out for the inmates—that they were all out to get me. Who would have thought that they would be the ones helping me out, teaching me the job, and offering to protect me? It's a good thing they felt that way because there's no way I could count on male guards for support. They want the women out of here—why should they do anything to help us?

Because the inventive role is built around traditional sex-role patterns, it is a strategy not easily used by male guards; it is clearly an innovation created by women. In addition, it is an innovation that emerges under adverse circumstances. Women in the inventive role continually stressed that male co-workers gave them little assistance in learning the job. Many also felt that male guards would not come to their assistance during an emergency. Dependence on male inmates, then, provided them with an alternate way to remain on the job, work on the direct contact posts they were unable to avoid, and reduce the danger associated with guard work.

In many ways, the inventive role resembles Gresham Sykes's (1958) description of corruption of the guards' authority through friendship. These women must depend on inmates' voluntary compliance with prison rules; although this compliance has so far been forthcoming, female guards cannot be absolutely sure that it will continue. In addition, as the use of the term "corruption" implies, inmate compliance comes at a price. Women in the inventive role claim that the price they pay is the fair and friendly treatment of inmates. But even friendliness may violate rules governing the relationship between guards and inmates.[4] Some women in the inventive role admit that friendship also entails overlooking some petty rule violations; it may be the case that these women overlook more serious ones as well, perhaps even to the point of creating decreased security and order in the institution. This is, in fact, a common complaint of male guards. They claim that when working a shift following a female guard, it is often necessary to regain the control which she has "thrown away":

> Every day I have to follow Keller. When I come on duty, she has given the place away: everything is a mess, inmates haven't gone to their work details, they're hanging around jiving with each other. . . . I have to come down hard and then everyone thinks I'm the bad guy for enforcing the rules.

Because women in the inventive role have a more lenient attitude toward the rules and because they are friendly to inmates, male co-worker opposition to them is especially intense. Lee Bowker (1980) found that prison staff members do sometimes victimize fellow workers who are considered friendly toward inmates:

> Anyone who dares to be too friendly with prisoners is suspect in a rigid caste system, and correctional officers and administrators are quick to apply informal and perhaps even formal sanctions against the offender. [P. 130]

According to women in the inventive role, the most common sanction applied by male co-workers is the withdrawal of their help and support. This eventually becomes a cycle in which lack of support by peers and dependence on inmates reinforce each other. At some point, a strong alliance between female guards and male inmates develops; it is an alliance that is functional for women trying to perform the job in adverse circumstances, but it is one in which inmates hold a great deal of power. If inmates withdrew their voluntary support and cooperation, women in the inventive role would find it extremely difficult to establish their authority.

Although women using this strategy believe that inmate support will extend to emergency situations, few women have evidence to support this belief. There have been cases of inmates protecting women from the attack of other inmates,[5] and cases of inmates assisting women when they are breaking up fights, but there have been no major disturbances or riots in New York or Rhode Island in which the limits of inmate support might be tested. If the day-to-day cooperation of inmates results from feelings of paternalism and chivalry, inmate protection of women might continue during a riot. If, on the other hand, daily cooperation results purely from reciprocity (inmate protection of women in trade for their willingness to overlook petty rule violations) inmate cooperation might evaporate during a crisis. If inmates gain control over some section of the prison, as often occurs during a riot, the pragmatic reasons for protecting women would be removed. Female guards themselves are not absolutely sure why inmates give them compliance and protection. Thus, although they generally believe that inmates will continue to protect them during a prison riot, there is always a shadow of a doubt:

> It's hard to say. I know the guys here pretty well, and I feel like I can trust them. But then again, you can't help but wonder what they would do if they really had the opportunity to take control. I just hope it never gets to that point.

Concern over the conditions under which inmates might withdraw their protection and support remains a major problem, then, for women in the inventive role.

A final dilemma for female guards using this strategy is that inmates sometimes interpret friendliness as romantic interest and women must be careful not to encourage such an interpretation:

> It takes a while to develop just the right attitudes. I like to be friendly and talk to the inmates, but I have to stay a little bit aloof. I make it a habit never to tell them anything about my personal life—they can share their problems with me, but it wouldn't be wise for me to share mine with them.

Another woman explains that she is cautious about her appearance on the job:

> I never wear any makeup to work and seldom any jewelry, except my wedding ring. I make sure my uniform is baggy. There's no sense asking for trouble by letting inmates think you're coming on to them.

There are a few women in the inventive role, however, who seem to have adopted a "seductress" orientation toward the job. They are very concerned with their appearance and seem to encourage the admiration and advances of inmates. Other women in the inventive role join their co-workers in opposing this small group of women:

> It may be a fine line between being friendly and being sexy, but I know where that line is. There are a few women who take this job because they love the attention they get from inmates. And believe me, they get it. But they never last long. Before you know it, inmates are fighting over their attention and they're afraid to come to work. I've seen it before—they keep coming but they don't stay very long.

This extreme use of "femaleness," then, may be a very unstable variation of the inventive role. Many inmates are themselves angered by the presence of these women:

> You have these women all dolled up, walking down the hall, shaking their ass. They're asking for trouble. They won't get it from me, though—I don't want their kind of trouble. I stay out of their way.

Although many inmates are as careful as female guards to avoid romantic relationships, others do develop "crushes" on the women who guard them. Female guards in the inventive role, because they are friendlier to inmates, are more likely than other women to receive love letters from them. They must, then, be careful to act more distant in their future interactions with the particular inmate or with inmates in general. At the same time, becoming too distant would destroy the personal ties necessary for inmate support. Developing a sense of how friendly might be too friendly is an ongoing issue for women who have settled into the inventive role.

Choosing a Strategy

No female guard is forced into one of the three occupational roles outlined above. At various stages of employment in a men's prison, each woman makes some active, conscious decisions about the occupational role she intends to play. Her final choice of the institutional, the modified, or the inventive role will depend on her predispositions (the attitudes, beliefs, and personality chracteristics she brings to the job with her), certain situational contingencies (the type of training she receives and her interactions with inmates, male guards, and supervisors), and her subjective response to her own set of on-the-job experiences. At the same time, however, her options will be limited and her choices inhibited by the particular structural and organizational constraints she faces in the prison, especially the formal and informal policies and practices concerning female guards.

Although women do not begin employment in a men's prison with a clear idea of how they will adapt to their occupational role, they are generally predisposed toward either performing the job on an equal basis with men or assuming a more limited role in the prison. These predispositions are probably closely tied to women's general sex-role attitudes, especially those regarding women's innate capabilities and "proper" role in society.

Women with traditional sex-role attitudes are more likely to believe that female guards should have a very limited occupational role in men's prisons. Because they believe that males and females are innately different, with females lacking the strength, aggressiveness, and fearlessness necessary for successful performance of the job, they favor differential treatment of male and female guards. They are predisposed to assume a modified version of the occupational role of prison guard.

Women with more liberal sex-role attitudes generally attribute any noticeable differences between men and women to differential socialization and training rather than to innate differences. In their view, at least some women (including themselves) are capable of performing the job on an equal basis with men. They, therefore, favor hiring and deployment policies that treat male and female guards identically and are predisposed to assume an occupational role similar to that of their male colleagues.

There seems to be, then, a great deal of congruence between women's sex-role attitudes and their initial expectations for an occupational role in men's prisons. Women who have liberal ideas and describe themselves as "liberated" generally seek equal treatment and equal opportunities on the job. Women who have more conservative views and favor the continuation of traditional female sex-role patterns in society generally seek a more limited role. It is often the case, however, that women with either predisposition fail to adopt an occupational role that coincides with their expectations. On-the-job experiences and interactions with others in the prison lead them to compromise their preferences and gradually define an alternative occupational role for themselves.

The option of adopting the modified role is not available to all women who prefer to perform a narrow range of duties in the male prison. Instead, women must meet one of two necessary criteria. They must either have enough seniority to bid for a safe, low-contact post or they must have strong alliances with male co-workers (who agree to protect them when necessary) and male supervisors (who agree to assign them away from direct inmate contact as much as possible).

In both New York and Rhode Island a number of women currently working as guards in men's prisons previously worked in female facilities where they had accumulated seniority; when transferring to a male prison, many were immediately able to bid for safe posts away from the cell blocks and other areas of inmate activity. Without this option, many would not have transferred to a male prison:

> I wouldn't want to work directly with male inmates; any of them here could over-power me in a minute. I came here because I knew I had enough seniority to get almost any post I wanted. Over at the woman's prison there are only a few noncontact jobs. You have to wait for someone to retire or die before you can bid on them.

Because women obtained these posts through the seniority system, the same system used by senior male guards who want to avoid direct inmate contact, their adoption of the modified role is legitimated. Some male guards complain that women's seniority was not earned in the same way as theirs (working in direct contact with *male* inmates), but these women are able to insulate themselves from male co-worker opposition by choosing posts that are far removed from co-worker as well as inmate contact and do not require dependency on male guards. These women are largely free to choose a modified role, and they need the support and approval of no one in the prison for their occupational role preference. One woman who bid a control room in a male prison after twelve years in the state's female prison summed it up:

> I did my time, and I don't care what anyone says—it was hard time. The inmates over at the woman's unit are really tough; they'll attack you before you even know why they're angry. I was

injured many times, but I kept going back. When this job opened up, I grabbed it; it's completely safe and it's closer to home so I only have to drive fifteen minutes. I got this post because I earned it—same as the men.

The other avenue through which women might successfully implement their preference for the modified role is the establishment of strong alliances with male guards and supervisors. In most cases, such alliances were established well before women sought prison employment. These women often live in a community in which a prison is located; oftentimes they are the wives, girl friends, daughters, and nieces of male guards. In a few cases, these women worked in the prison as secretaries or clericals before entering the guard training academy. It was often the promise of protection or preferred assignments that convinced these women to apply for the job:

I know almost everyone in here and their mother and father. My dad worked here before he retired; two of my uncles still do. They kept telling me to apply. At first I was hesitant—I'm not at all the "macho" type—but eventually they convinced me. I've never regretted it. There have been no problems; all the guys know me and watch out for me.

Women who succeed in adopting the modified role through alliances with male workers are almost always white. Some minority women would prefer to play a limited occupational role, but most lack strong local ties with male supervisors who, in spite of considerable racial integration at the rank-and-file level, are still predominantly white. Consequently, even those minority women who have strong ties with rank-and-file male guards who are willing to protect them are unlikely to have the necessary alliances with supervisors. Black women who are blocked from adopting the modified role often accuse white male supervisors of racial prejudice:

There's no doubt that white women get the softest assignments around here. Did you see the women "up front"? They're all white. You have to go back, on the blocks, to find the black women.

While there is undoubtedly some racial discrimination involved in differential assignment of black and white women, it is primarily the lack of "connections" that prevents black women from implementing their preference for the modified role. White women from urban areas also tend to lack established ties with male supervisors and will likely be prevented from adoption of the modified role as well. The necessary approval of male co-workers seems to be available only to a select group of women—primarily those whose associations with the men working in the prisons preceded their employment there.

When the preferential treatment that many women want is not forthcoming and they are thrown into direct contact with inmates, they will have to either terminate their employment or adopt a different strategy for performing the job.[6] Because of rather traditional sex-role attitudes and patterns of behavior, these women are ill suited to adopt the institutional role. The inventive role, however, is a viable alternative because it allows for—and even depends on—the establishment of some traditional sex-role interactions between female guards and male inmates. Thus, women who wanted to play a modified role because of their female status discovered that they can actually use their female status to perform a much wider range of guard duties than they originally expected. By using the traditional female qualities of intuition, nurturance, understanding, compassion, and even femininity, they are able to perform an occupation that is highly sex-typed masculine. Women in the inventive role end up doing nearly everything male guards do, including the maintenance of basic order and control in direct-contact jobs, but they do so using entirely different techniques. And they do it not necessarily because they believe it is a better way to perform the job, but rather because it works for them and allows them to remain employed in spite of their inability and unwillingness to perform the occupational role as defined by men.

In direct contrast to women who began employment expecting to play a modified occupational role are those women who wanted and expected to perform the job on an equal basis with the men. Equality was never really possible for these women because they were, from the very beginning, treated differently by inmates as well as by their male co-workers and supervisors. The closest these women could come to equality was to adopt the institutional role—a job performance strategy similar to that used by males, but more controlled by formal administrative rules than by the informal techniques and accommodations of male guards. New male guards, with the help of their colleagues, learn how and when to bend the rules. Denied this informal socialization and denied what they feel is the necessary leeway for making a few mistakes along the way, women wanting equality created the institutional role. It allows them to compete with males for all jobs in the prison and provides them with the self-satisfaction associated with doing the full job; unfortunately, it leaves them ill equipped to deal with those situations for which the rules are inadequate.

Not all women who initially want equality are able to settle into the institutional role. Probably the most important thing that happens on the job to deter some women from the adaptive strategy closest to that of their male colleagues is their failure to receive adequate early training in all aspects of the job. The middle-level supervisors in each prison who are responsible for assigning new trainees are almost always male. Because they oppose the presence of female guards, many of these men continue to provide women with a less inclusive training experience than male trainees. When women finish their training period unprepared for many jobs in the prison, a cycle of failure is started. Women lack experience, lose confidence in their own abilities to perform the job, and eventually seek a more modified job role. Some women who began employment expecting equality report that they redefined their role in the prison as these experiences accumulated:

> I came in here like gangbusters. I figured I had had the same training [in the academy] and could do anything a man could do. I guess you might say I got knocked down a few pegs. There was just no way the captain was going to let me on a cell block—he even told me that. After a while, I figured "why fight it?" As it stands now, I earn my paycheck without ever really being in danger. A lot of male guards would jump at the chance, so why should I knock it?

The continual opposition and harassment by the male staff is also responsible for reducing women's belief in their own capacity to perform the entire job. When women exhibit "typically feminine" behavior, particularly crying, male harassment increases, prompting them to question their own suitability for the job of prison guard.

Male opposition to women's attempt to perform the job equally probably has its greatest impact during prison emergencies. When women first respond to emergency calls, male guards may simply tell them to "stay out of the way." If they are still on trainee status, women have no right to question these orders. For women coming directly into a male prison from the training academy this kind of experience is especially devastating. Without the opportunity to "test their wings" in the most dangerous and fear-provoking aspect of the job, these women often reassess their own abilities and begin to agree with the men that they are of little value in emergencies anyway. James Terborg and Daniel Ilgen (1975) found this to be a typical reaction of women who receive differential treatment on the job:

To the extent that women are denied the opportunity to experience psychological success, women may be less likely to set difficult goals for themselves. . . . [This] may lead to actual differences in performance over time due to limitations in self-concept. [P. 372]

Women who lack experience in dealing with prison emergencies sometimes respond by seeking a post (such as a control booth) that does not require the occupant to respond to emergency calls. Or women may continue to respond to emergencies but acquiesce to male guards' demands that they "not get in the way." One woman who initially sought to perform the job on an equal basis with men and had originally bid for a direct-contact job on one of the prison's housing units, reported:

Now when an emergency call goes out, I usually look to relieve a male officer from one of the control rooms. It makes more sense to have him there instead of me if there's going to be trouble.

Another woman said:

At first I thought I should do everything the men do, but I was making them so nervous that I decided I could do more good by staying out of the way during emergencies.

Responding to an emergency is almost always "optional" for female guards and there is, in fact, a great deal of pressure from male guards not to respond. Consequently, many women eventually choose not to perform this aspect of the job. In making this choice, women effectively give up any chance of adopting the institutional role or of winning the respect of their male co-workers.

Early interactions with inmates may also sway women away from their intention to perform all aspects of the job. The initial "testing period," in which inmates often try to determine how strict new guards will be, sometimes turns out to be more difficult than anticipated.Some women find inmate language too vulgar or are frightened by the explicit sexual misconduct of a few prisoners. These women may quickly seek refuge away from inmates and attempt to adopt the modified role. Such a change will be easiest for women who have enough seniority to bid for a noncontact post.

Because of these factors, many women who initially wished to perform the job on an equal basis with men are deterred from carrying through. Some of them may simply quit prison employment in frustration. Others attempt to adopt the modified role, but, as already noted, there are some limitations on the ability of women to do so. Unless women have a lot of seniority, cooperation from the male staff is mandatory but not necessarily forthcoming.

Another group of women who came into the prison expecting equality eventually adopt the inventive role. Because they may not be able to count on male guards for even a "normal" amount of support, they develop close ties with inmates as an alternative way of remaining on the job. The inventive role, then, attracts not only women denied the modified role, but also those who eventually reject the institutional role. It is, in many ways, an ingenious way for women who are committed to remaining on the job, but are denied either the opportunity to perform the job on an equal basis with men or the opportunity to retreat, to adapt to adverse circumstances.

Whereas the institutional role is defined by formal administrative rules and regulations and the modified role is defined by male co-workers and supervisors, the inventive role is created and defined by women themselves as they attempt to find solutions to the situational problems which they alone face. No women in the inventive role report that they began employment expecting the help and cooperation of inmates. Instead, this system of mutual accommodation emerges while women are in the process of learning the job under the adverse conditions of discrimination, opposition, and harassment.[7]

The inventive role, like the others, is not automatically available to any woman who chooses to play it. Just as the modified role requires co-worker approval, the inventive role requires inmate approval. To receive this approval, female guards must, at a minimum, treat inmates with respect and display understanding and sympathy toward their conditions of confinement. It may require as well that female guards compromise their authority by overlooking inmates' violation of minor prison rules. In some cases, the cost of inmate approval may involve overlooking serious rule violations or a corruption as serious as providing contraband to inmates. Neither women in this role nor inmates admitted to this kind of "cooperation," but it may very well exist. In any case, the potential for corruption is ever present for women in the inventive role.

Although personal preferences clearly play a part in women's choice of a job performance strategy, negative on-the-job experiences are more critical factors in most women's choices. At the time of this writing, neither in New York nor in Rhode Island have high-level correctional administrators made much effort to alleviate the special problems that foster women's adoption of these three strategies and encourage even women initially intending to perform all aspects of the job to compromise that position. Middle-level supervisors at each prison continue to have considerable discretion over matters of assignment, especially during on-the-job training. There is no automatic review of these decisions, although female and minority guards have consistently complained that they are discriminated against by local supervisors. Once the probationary period is over, female guards are less vulnerable but, as already noted, the probationary period is especially critical for new guards, and by the time women achieve permanent appointment, much of the damage resulting from discriminatory policies has been done. Once a woman adopts a strategy for performing the job, it becomes very difficult for her to change it because inmates and co-workers begin to relate to her in terms of the occupational role she has adopted. In addition, once women choose a strategy for performing the job, they develop explanations and rationalizations for that choice. In doing so, they become personally committed to the strategy they have adopted even if it is very different from their pre-employment expectations.

Formal and informal policies that discriminate against women have not been fought at the highest levels because most administrators remain personally uncommitted to the sexual integration of the guard force. They were forced to hire women under threat of lawsuits and withdrawal of federal funds. Like administrators in other modern bureaucracies, they follow the letter of the law. They have not accepted its spirit, however, and have not actively sought ways to improve women's conditions of employment.

The continuing ambiguity in the law also plays a role in administrators' failure to confront women's on-the-job problems. There is a belief among administrators (clearly justified given the nature of the case law on this matter) that the legal issues concerning women's employment are not yet settled. Robin Williams (1977) points out that in cases where the law itself is not clear, full compliance cannot be expected. Until administrators are convinced that this change is not temporary, they probably will not devote energy to solving the continuing problems of deploying women in the prisons.

When high-level support for organizational change is lacking, dissatisfaction with the change reverberates throughout the entire organization (Crozier 1964) and sets the tone for discriminatory policies at the lower levels. When middle-level supervisors know that their assignment policies will not be reviewed regularly, they are free to let their own prejudices influence their decisions. Likewise, male guards who receive no negative sanctions for engaging in overt opposition and harassment are unmotivated to curb their behavior.

The lack of high-level policy to eradicate discrimination against women covertly condones the discrimination that results and helps create the situation in which these three strategies emerge and are solidified.

Conclusion

There are some clear contradictions between the traditional female sex role and the occupational role of prison guard. Women in American society differ, however, in their personal acceptance of traditional sex-role definitions, and female prison guards are no exception. Some have very liberal attitudes about the proper role of women in society while others are more traditional. They not only bring these differing attitudes to the job of guarding, but allow these attitudes to influence the manner in which they perform the job. Female guards have some ability to construct a work role that prevents serious conflict between their work lives and their personal attitudes and life-styles.

Although women have the opportunity to create a somewhat personal occupational role, they must exercise their choices in the face of numerous obstacles. Inadequate training, male co-worker opposition and harassment, and inmate testing all serve to make it difficult for women to perform the job similarly to their male counterparts. As a result, women generally adopt one of three "female strategies" for performing the job. In the modified role, women perform only a limited range of normal guard duties, avoiding inmate contact as much as possible. In the institutional role, women work on all posts and attempt to obey all the formal rules and procedures for job performance, but fail to develop the flexibility that is important for guard work. In the inventive role, women ally themselves with male inmates, depending on them for assistance and support.

There are special problems and dilemmas associated with each of these job performance strategies, but each offers women a stable adaptation to the job of guarding in a work environment that includes discrimination and open opposition from co-workers and supervisors. High-level prison administrators have done little to prevent the continuing discrimination and harassment against women that occur at each local prison. Their lack of action can be attributed in part to a lack of concern regarding women's conditions of employment and in part to the continuing legal ambiguity concerning women's role in men's prisons. Without any major catastrophies resulting from women's presence, most prison administrators prefer to obey the law (as they interpret it) and avoid confrontation of the continuing problems associated with the integration process. The following chapter will assess in more detail some of these integration problems (as well as the apparent advantages that result from women's presence) in its analysis of women's overall impact on the male prison.

Impact of Women on the Prison

This study has focused almost exclusively on female guards, their occupational problems, adjustment dilemmas, and strategies for performing the job. In this chapter, attention shifts to the prison itself and the prison's other key participants, all of whom have been critically affected by the introduction of female guards. For inmates, the presence of women has meant the creation of a living environment that more closely resembles the outside world. Male guards have lost their all-male work group and have been forced to question both the nature of the job and its requirement of masculinity. Prison administrators have been confronted with a barrage of legal and practical problems that demand solutions. Although there is no evidence that the hiring of women has led to a decrease in prison security, there are indications that most female guards are less willing and able to use physical force against inmates than are their male colleagues. This difference may have positive as well as negative consequences for the functioning of prisons, depending perhaps on the number of women employed.

Determinants of Occupational Behavior

When public sector organizations such as schools, hospitals, police departments, and prisons are accused of failing to carry out their functions properly, it is often the "line personnel"—teachers, nurses, police officers, and prison guards—who bear the brunt of criticism. It is often suggested that better (or at least different) personnel are needed. Herman Goldstein (1977) suggests, for example, that police departments might improve performance by specifically recruiting persons who appreciate other cultures, understand

148

urban life, are self-disciplined, mature, sensitive, and flexible. Thomas Murton (1979) says that in recruiting prison guards, "the major personnel requirement should be personal integrity, concern for others, and sincere commitment" (p. 34). The investigators of the Attica uprising felt that increasing minority representation on the guard force would decrease racism and improve relationships between inmates and guards (Attica 1972). Each of these suggestions implies that hiring guards with different characteristics will affect the functioning of prisons and the ways in which guards interact with inmates.

Industrial psychologists and sociologists would likely disagree among themselves over the logic of these suggestions as there is continuing debate over whether the occupational role or the people placed in the role are the more critical determinants of occupational behavior (Kohn and Schooler 1982). Richard Hall (1977) claims that because similar occupational role constraints operate on each worker, organizational behavior will not be strongly affected by individual characteristics:

> When a new member enters the organization, he is confronted with a social structure . . . and a set of expectations for . . . behavior. It does not matter who the particular individual is; the organization has established a system of norms and expectations to be followed regardless of who its personnel happen to be. [P. 26]

Some recent studies of prison guards support Hall's views. For example, James Jacobs and Lawrence Kraft (1978) found that race has little bearing on prison guards' attitudes toward prisoners or toward the job; in fact, recently hired blacks have attitudes nearly identical to those of their white co-workers. In the famous experiment involving a simulated prison, Craig Haney and his colleagues (1973) found that individual characteristics have little effect on organizational behavior; college students assigned as guards adapted to the requirements of the role by becoming cynical, hostile, and authoritarian. Finally, in an autobiographical account of his experience as a prison guard, Roger Martin (1980) reports that when he left a career as an airline pilot to become a prison guard, his personality changed substantially to fit his new job. In fact, only one prison study suggests that the occupational behavior of guards might be altered by the hiring of different people. The League of Women Voters' study of a guard strike in Wisconsin found that National Guard personnel— who had not been self-selected for prison work—were friendlier, more compassionate, and more understanding than regular guards

(Ross 1978). These results should be interpreted cautiously, however, because the strike lasted only sixteen days and many guards were assigned to the prison for an even shorter period of time. There is no reason to assume that the positive qualities exhibited by temporary guards would continue indefinitely.

The weight of the evidence suggests, then, that, at least in law enforcement occupations,[1] employees' behavior is shaped by the constraints of the work role and their personalities are, in fact, sometimes changed by the occupational experience itself. Consequently, the recruitment of different personnel would be expected to have little effect on these social control organizations. One might logically conclude that the hiring of women as guards would follow this general pattern and have little impact on the prison. There are some reasons to believe, however, that sex more critically affects occupational behavior than do the characteristics associated with race, class, education, and the like.

Erving Goffman (1959) made the astute observation that because sex is the most basic social division between people, the sex composition of a setting will critically affect people's actions. Alvin Gouldner (1959) likewise stresses the importance of employees' sex for understanding their organizational behavior:

> It is obvious that all people in organizations have a variety of "latent social identities"—that is, identities which are not culturally prescribed as relevant to or within rational organizations—and that these do intrude upon and influence organizational behavior in interesting ways. For example, there is usually something occurring between people of opposite sexes, even though this is prescribed neither by the organization's official rules nor by the societal values deemed appropriate for the setting. Yet many sociologists who study factories, offices, schools, or mental hospitals take little note of the fact that the organizational role-players invariably have a gender around which is built a latent social identity. One does not have to be a Freudian to insist that sex makes a difference, even for organizational behavior. [P. 412]

Although sex-role patterns have changed since 1959, when Gouldner wrote this passage, the current study supports his finding that sex is important to an understanding of organizational behavior. Even in the 1980s, sex remains a "master status" in nearly every social context. In the prisons, many women choose to stress their female status, but even women who prefer that their female status be ignored elicit gender-related responses from inmates, co-workers, and supervisors. No matter how they act, female prison guards are reacted to as women. Their presence, therefore, constitutes a dramatic change for prisons and creates repercussions throughout the prison environment. Additionally, from what we now know about women's strategies for performing the job, their presence should have an impact on the prison. Many of the mechanisms women use for maintaining control and gaining inmate compliance to prison rules are directly related to their female status. Because the entire prison organization is oriented around the control function, the introduction of new control techniques should affect, in some way, the overall operation and functioning of the institution.

Effect of Women on the Inmates' World

Male inmates have never been totally isolated from women. Many receive visits from female friends and relatives. Also, the support staff (clerical workers, teachers, nurses, counselors) of most prisons includes women who come into at least occasional contact with inmates. The entrance of female guards, however, created a major change because, for the first time, prolonged face-to-face contact between inmates and women became the norm. It is merely tautological to claim that the presence of women "normalizes" the prison environment. Any change that makes the prison more closely resemble the world outside can be termed a normalizing condition. The important question is whether or not it is beneficial for prisoners to live in an environment that (like the world outside) is sexually integrated.

Several prison scholars have suggested that deprivation of heterosexual contacts is psychologically damaging to male inmates. Charles Silberman (1978) finds that in the absence of women, male prisoners generate considerable anxiety about their own masculinity. In *Society of Captives* (1958), Gresham Sykes points out that lack of contact with females not only produces sexual frustrations but also threatens the prisoner's maintenance of a healthy self-concept:

> In addition to these problems stemming from sexual frustration per se, the deprivation of heterosexual relationships carries with it another threat to the prisoner's image of himself—more diffuse perhaps, and more difficult to state precisely and yet no less disturbing. The inmate is shut off from the world of women which by its very polarity gives the male world much of its meaning. Like most men, the inmate must search for his identity not simply within himself but also in the picture of himself which he finds reflected in the eyes of others; and since a significant half of his

audience is denied him, the inmate's self image is in danger of becoming half complete, fractured, a monochrome without the hues of reality. The prisoner's looking-glass self, in short—to use Cooley's fine phrase—is only that portion of the prisoner's personality which is recognized or appreciated by men and this partial identity is made hazy by the lack of contrast.

Writing in 1970, John Irwin (1970b) attributed a portion of the reentry problems faced by released felons to their confinement in an all-male world; these men felt awkward and disoriented when faced with the prospect of socializing with females after a long period of near isolation from them. Today, because of the employment of female guards in men's prisons, many prisoners have sustained interactions with women. Most male inmates respond to women's presence by engaging in "female-appropriate" behaviors. They display better manners, reduce their use of vulgar language, and react protectively toward female guards who are threatened. Several inmates I interviewed not only were cognizant of their own behavioral changes but believed that such changes would prove beneficial when they left prison. One inmate explained:

> After a while in here, you really do forget how to act around women. When McBride came on duty, it took some getting used to. I had to remember to cover up coming out of the shower. I had to remember to watch my mouth. I think it's good, though. In six months I should be home and I won't have to break those bad habits around my wife and daughter.

Female guards, then, provide male prisoners with some practical experience interacting with women.

A second problem that Irwin (1970b) found among the released felons he studied was that they had extremely high expectations concerning the women who might be potential sexual partners:

> Their conception of what the average female "on the streets" is like has been distorted, and their standards upgraded, in their isolation from women. This is because female images that are available to them through the mass media are skewed toward glamour and beauty. [P. 139]

By interacting with female guards, inmates may retain less stereotypic and distorted images of women. In addition, because at least some female guards present the image of the "new liberated woman," inmates are given the opportunity to experience first hand some recent changes in female sex-role definitions. This experience, too, may aid their adjustment when they leave the prison.

In addition to the normalizing effect, the presence of female guards may have a calming effect on the male prison. Norval Morris and Gordon Hawkins (1970) suggest that women "bring a softening influence to the prison society, assisting men to strengthen their inner controls through a variety of deeply entrenched processes of psychological growth" (p. 133). Several studies have shown that the introduction of women into the formerly all-male prison environment does result in improved male behavior, whether the women work as therapists (Biemer 1977; Cormier 1975) or guards (Becker 1975; Flynn 1982; Graham 1981). These changes in inmate behavior might be due, in part, to the psychological processes suggested by Morris and Hawkins, but they may also be elicited simply by women's less threatening behavior. In fact, when asked to compare male and female guards, inmates in the current study continually made claims such as, "the men are always trying to prove something," "male guards are on an ego trip," or "male guards get pleasure out of writing you up."[2] In contrast, the descriptions of female guards included, "they don't have anything to prove," "they don't 'woof' in your face," and "they're not looking to put you down." Inmates also claim that female guards are friendlier and more pleasant.[3] Daniel Glaser (1964) points out that friendliness may be the best measure of a good guard because pleasant interactions with guards foster inmates' own self-respect; and, according to Glaser, improvements in self-respect may be the change most critical to prisoners' long-term rehabilitation.

Even administrators who generally oppose the presence of women admit that female guards often have a positive influence on inmates' behavior and help to foster a calmer, more pleasant atmosphere:

> There are some good things about having the women here. I would have to say there is a change in inmates' behavior when there are women on duty—a change for the better. They tone down their language and their aggressiveness toward each other. They keep the dormitory areas cleaner. They treat female guards with more respect.

Edith Flynn's (1982) survey of prison administrators produced remarkably similar comments.

For a very small number of inmates, the presence of female guards provides the opportunity for an intimate heterosexual relationship in prison. Most women carefully avoid any romantic involvements with inmates:

> I've made a lot of mistakes when it comes to men, but believe me, that is one I wouldn't make. Any woman who gets involved with a man in prison is asking for trouble. She can no longer do her job, that's for sure.

A few female guards, however, may encourage or accept romantic relationships with inmates. Although none of the women I interviewed admitted to having intimate relationships with inmates, rumors of such involvements circulate throughout the prisons. Even romances between male and female employees can cause problems in the workplace (Quinn 1977; Mead 1980; Harragan 1980), but intimate relationships between guards and inmates offer unique problems and administrators are understandably concerned about their occurrence. Whether or not actual sexual contact occurs, there is a potential security risk if a guard's primary loyalty shifts from the institution to an individual inmate. While I was conducting this research, administrators mentioned two such incidents; in both cases they were able to halt the relationships by convincing the female guards to resign.

There is also the possibility that female guards will voluntarily engage in sexual intercourse with one or more inmates, perhaps for money, as recently occurred in Delaware prisons (Krajick 1979). The governor's task force in that state concluded that because of such incidents, the employment of women should be severely restricted (Governor's Investigative Corrections Task Force 1980). Again, there is legitimate reason for concern, but it should be remembered that male guards are not free from sexual misconduct at work. Male sexual abuse of female prisoners certainly occurs and, just recently, two male guards in Delaware were arrested on charges of sodomy after they were caught forcing male inmates to commit homosexual acts with them (Krajick 1979). Although the presence of females provides additional opportunity for sexual activity between guards and inmates, most women are unwilling to engage in such behavior, setting a "natural" limit on the potential magnitude of the problem. And, whereas much of sexual misconduct of male guards involves force and coercion over inmates (of either sex), sexual encounters between female guards and male inmates do not. From the male inmate's perspective, then, any sexual contact that does occur is likely to be positive.

Impact of Women on the Male Guard Force

The large majority of male guards are unhappy with the introduction of women into their ranks, fearing that their own safety and the security of the institution are threatened by women's presence. But it is obviously not just the actual performance of female guards that causes so much disapproval, because many men oppose even the few women they admit can outperform a large portion of their male colleagues. What male guards seem additionally to resent is elimination of their all-male world, disturbance of the camaraderie they have enjoyed with co-workers, and destruction of the notion that masculinity is a necessary requirement for the job. The presence of women, then, calls into question not only their assumptions about the nature of men and women, but also their assumptions about the nature of their work.

In many traditionally male occupations, especially those involving risk, overt displays of masculinity among workers are common (Haas 1977). Criminal justice occupations in particular seem to be prone to develop rather "macho" subcultures that stress the necessity of masculinity for successful job performance (Martin 1980; Wilson 1982; Lamber and Streib 1974). Researchers have sometimes supported this view. Thomas Gray (1975), for example, maintains that a police officer's conception of his own masculinity is as important to his performance as are the required skills and values. Ben Crouch (1980) says that the prison guard "who cannot muster some version of this masculine image before both inmates and peers is in for trouble" (p. 217). The presence of women—and, more importantly, the successful performance of women—threatens the long-held assumption that heightened masculinity is necessary for these criminal justice jobs. For some workers (particularly those who need to reinforce their own masculinity through performance of "a man's job"), women's presence may be extremely distressing.[4] But for nearly all male guards, women's presence requires a reassessment of the nature of the job as well as their own personal qualifications for it.

The introduction of female guards into the male prison has also been unsettling to male guards because it requires them to alter their behavior on the job. Regardless of women's wishes with regard to male behavior in their presence, most men (consciously or unconsciously) behave quite differently when women are present. David Bradford and his colleagues (1980) feel that men's discomfort in women's presence accounts for their reluctance to accept female executives:

> The introduction of a woman could activate male-female relationships so that men would feel great consternation not only about how they should act, but also about what subjects and language are appropriate and inappropriate. The bantering among men often has a veiled competitive tone that attempts to score points without hurting feelings or causing retaliation. Many men feel uncomfortable treating women in a similar fashion or even demonstrating such behavior in front of them. [P. 25]

In predominantly male blue-collar jobs, men may be unwilling to give up what Jeffrey Riemer (1978) calls the "army camp atmosphere"—profanity, pornography, girl watching, and generally crude behavior. In the prisons, the all-male world has long been protected by walls, fences, and gates that kept even female administrative workers at a safe distance; today, with the presence of women on the cell blocks of most prisons, the all-male world has been effectively eliminated. For many men, this represents an undesired change in their work environment and requires undesired alterations in their work behavior.

Some researchers have suggested that destruction of the all-male work force might not only be unpleasant for men, but might also hinder their ability to perform the job. Some jobs do seem to require a high level of worker solidarity and cohesion, and to the extent women's presence lessens solidarity, there might be some impact on men's occupational performance. Charles Vaught and David Smith (1980) found that the entrance of women into the coal mines created a "boundary crisis" that threatened the solidarity of the work group. In her study of women's entrance into police work, Susan Martin (1980) claims that "bonds of manhood strengthen the work-related ties among men; the presence of women changes the rules of the group, and threatens its existence" (p. 96). But the most critical view of women's impact on male performance comes from Richard Gabriel's (1980) account of women's integration into the military:

> What evidence is available suggests strongly that the complete integration of women in the military, especially in ground combat roles, may have devastating consequences for the level of cohesion and effectiveness that can be expected of integrated units. [P. 44]

Jeff Tuten (1982) joins Gabriel in placing the blame not directly on women themselves, but on their interference with the "male bonding" process outlined by anthropologist Lionel Tiger (1969). According to Tiger, relationships between men represent the strongest and most basic elements of any society and are as important to human society's survival as they are to the survival of animal species. The intrusion of women into all-male groups decreases solidarity, increases rivalry among the men, and threatens the stability of the entire group. Tuten (1982) and Gabriel (1980) conclude that a work group that benefits from solidarity—such as the combat unit—will have better performance when composed of all men than when composed of men and women. Although a recent study by John Woelfel (1981) finds no evidence of poorer performance in integrated military units, there has been no test of the effects of sexual integration on actual combat troops.[5] Male prison guards complain that the presence of women hinders their ability to perform effectively, but there is as yet no evidence to support or refute those claims.

Although male workers generally discuss only the negative impact of women's presence, there might be positive consequences on their own behavior as well. Jean-Paul Drolet (1976) found that male miners followed the safety precautions more carefully when women workers were present. Male police officers were also found to be more courteous, efficient, and concerned when working with a female partner (Weldy 1976). Having female co-workers might have the same kind of effects on male prison guards, promoting positive behavior and inhibiting some negative behavior.

One female guard I interviewed suspected that some male opposition resulted from men's realization that women could not be counted on to cover up their misconduct:

> These guys are scared to death we'll blow the whistle on them. They sleep on the job; they take bribes from inmates; they have no qualms about beating up some inmate who gives them a hard time. And they all cover up for each other. But they're not sure about us—they're afraid we won't be "loyal." And why should we be after the way they've treated us?

When male guards talk about their belief that women "can't be counted on," then, they may be referring not only to what they perceive as women's lack of ability but also to women's lack of loyalty to the work group. Among the police, such loyalty has long been recognized as detrimental to attempts to rid police forces of abuse and corruption. Although corruption among prison guards has not been studied as extensively, a recent report from New York (State of New York Commission of Investigation 1981) indicates that guards' failure to report each other's wrong-doings hinders investigation and eradication of the problem. Hans Toch (1977) also found that both the union and the guard subculture tend to encourage the covering up of guard violence against inmates. And although there is no evidence to suggest that female guards *are* more willing to report co-workers, their mere presence as "unknown entities" may deter some male guard misconduct. If women become fully integrated into the guard force, this impact may diminish, but for the time being, the presence of women may improve the work behavior of male guards.

At some point, the presence of female guards might also result in a change in the way male guards perform the job. Barbara Forisha (1981a) points out that "women by their very presence pose a threat to those at home in the workplace and . . . their presence calls into question accepted tenets of organizational behavior. . . . Women are thus agents of change—the constructiveness of change, however, is theirs to determine" (p. xvi). Female guards currently use different techniques than men in performing the job, and male guards might eventually incorporate some of them into their own job performance strategies. Male guards are probably least likely to adopt aspects of the institutional role because they are not subjected to the pressures that necessitate strict adherence to prison rules and regulations. Men are also unlikely to adopt the modified role because this strategy involves the cooperation of male co-workers, and there is no motivation for men to protect other men from the dangers of guard work. The inventive role, however, might encompass some strategies that could be used by male guards. It is still not clear how much of inmates' favorable reaction to women in the inventive role is generated by their female status (and inmates' desire to protect women) and how much by these women's special techniques for dealing with inmates. If the latter is the more critical factor, some male guards might eventually adopt these techniques, although at the present time, male hostility toward women in this role probably precludes the possibility of learning from them.

A final consequence of women's presence in increasing numbers is to further break down the homogeneity of the guard force and perhaps ultimately the occupational subculture itself. The literature on occupational subcultures does not reveal the degree to which their emergence and survival might depend on the social-demographic similarities of workers. We do know that all-male occupations are likely to develop subcultures. We also know that workers in one-industry towns are especially likely to develop subcultures. Perhaps the critical variable in both cases is worker homogeneity.

In the prisons, the homogeneity of the guard force has been steadily eroding. Even rural prisons that once recruited mainly from the local community now employ persons who commute from nearby major metropolitan areas. In addition, the number of minority officers working in the prisons has continued to increase. In New York State, for example, more than 20 percent of guards are black or Hispanic, compared to 6 percent less than a decade ago.[6] Racial tension and mutual distrust between black and white guards have accompanied racial integration of prison work forces (Jacobs 1977; Zimmer and Jacobs 1981), and in most cases minorities have not been integrated into guard subcultures.[7] This study shows that female guards have been excluded as well. An increase in the number of women and minorities, then, seems to decrease the number of guards available for assimilation into the subculture. Although occupational subcultures survive without the participation of all workers, their survival may require the support of at least a minimal proportion of employees. The presence of women in increasing numbers, then, offers a threat to survival of the guard subculture as long as that subculture fails to assimilate women.

The entrance of women as guards may also decrease homogeneity by creating a new source of division among the men. Although most male guards oppose the presence of women, the magnitude of their opposition is far from uniform. Many male guards oppose the employment of women altogether, but others admit that a few women do their job well. A few male guards even claim to favor hiring women, although they rarely broadcast such views. The male guards interviewed for this study usually expressed any favorable comments about women in a whisper. A few men asked to speak with me off the prison grounds because they feared others might overhear; they had already been ridiculed and shunned by their male co-workers after making favorable remarks about women's performance. The divisions caused by men's attitudes about women may contribute further to the declining homogeneity of the guard force and a weakening of the guard subculture. Whether a weakened subculture has positive or negative consequences on male guard performance and the functioning of the prisons is yet to be seen.

Impact of Women on the Administration of Prisons

Over the last few decades, the prerogatives of prison administrators have been steadily eroded by legal mandates concerning how they can manage the prisons. The federal courts have defined a body of prisoners' rights that administrators must comply with. State legislatures have established policy guidelines over matters that were once entirely within the administrative domain.[8] Civil Service Law often governs who will be hired and promoted within the prison. And in many states, unionization of guards has forced administrators to share some of their power with rank-and-file workers; in particular, where the unions have bargained successfully for strong seniority systems, administrators have lost much of their independence to deploy guards on the basis of either merit or departmental need.

Title VII has further reduced the power of prison administrators to control the makeup and deployment of their own work forces. As a legal mandate stipulating how administrators must manage the prisons, Title VII is an additional constraint on their ability to make personnel decisions. If nothing else, then, Title VII represents a further loss of administrative power.

It does not automatically follow, of course, that loss of administrative control over personnel decisions leads to a decrease in prison efficiency or security. At one time, many administrators claimed that unionization and the granting of seniority rights to guards would so "tie their hands" that the prisons could not function. Although seniority did decrease administrators' freedom to assign guards to posts on the basis of merit and expertise, no obvious decrease in security could be discerned.[9] A change that did occur, however, was that administrators were required to devote a considerable amount of time and energy to implementation of the seniority system and the solving of seniority-related problems and conflicts. Middle-level supervisors and union officials at each prison often disagree about how the system should operate and administrators at each prison must try to resolve these conflicts. The central administration often becomes involved as well, in some states, with the assistance of legal counsel and labor relations specialists. In short, complying with a contractual seniority system has become a complicated and time-consuming administrative task; continuing management opposition to seniority is probably based as much on the administrative problems it creates as on its actual impact on prison operations.

The mandate to hire women as guards has similarly created new administrative burdens for prison managers at every level. At the highest levels, early decisions about compliance with Title VII had to made. With the advice of their legal staff, administrators in some states concluded that corrections employment was an allowable exception to Title VII—under the Bona Fide Occupational Qualification (BFOQ) Clause—and they refused to hire women without a court order. In these states, the allocation of department resources to a legal defense of this position became necessary because women began almost immediately to make Title VII claims. Throughout the 1970s, many corrections departments devoted considerable administrative time, energy, and money to their effort to keep women out.

Even in states that chose to comply with Title VII, the law's exact requirements had to be determined. Title VII clearly prohibits discrimination against women in matters of employment opportunity, but because it does not explicitly require identical treatment of males and females once they are on the job, decisions about women's deployment had to be made. Especially in states where women were hired shortly after the legal change, high-level administrators had little assistance or guidance in deciding how to legally (and efficiently) use female staff. Nonetheless, policies and guidelines had to be quickly developed and distributed to the local prisons. In some states, few distinctions between males and females were made, but more commonly, guidelines limited the posts to which women could be assigned to those that involved little or no direct contact with prisoners. Local prison administrators then had the task of reassigning male staff to make way for the women.

Virtually none of the early policy decisions for deploying women diminished administrative attention to the "female guard problem" because they were almost immediately attacked from all affected groups. First, policies that limited women to noncontact positions were attacked by male guards on the grounds that such policies discriminated against men by excluding them from those jobs considered the least dangerous (and therefore most desirable) in the prison. There was a considerable amount of complaining by male guards, and in states with strong seniority systems, a barrage of formal challenges to these policies through the unions' grievance procedures.

Policies that limited the assignment possibilities for women were also attacked, in some cases, by female guards who desired a wider range of assignment options. Some women wanted access to more jobs so they would have a better chance of obtaining a desired shift or a transfer to another facility, perhaps one closer to home. Other women, hoping to advance within the organization, wanted to obtain assignments that would broaden their experience. Still others just wanted to be equal members of the guard force, with no special privileges or differential treatment. For a variety of reasons, then, some women also attacked administrative policies that limited their deployment options; they complained, filed union grievances, and in some cases, filed or threatened to file lawsuits claiming illegal sex discrimination.

The final group to attack administrative policies for deploying female guards was inmates. Throughout the 1970s, prisoners filed state and federal lawsuits on a variety of grounds; most successful were those claiming that the use of female guards violated their right to personal privacy. In a series of cases, the courts ruled that female guards could not be assigned to posts at which they could observe inmates while naked or using the toilet,[10] but even these guidelines proved difficult for prison administrators to interpret and implement. The case law did not make explicit whether women needed to be excluded only from those posts where invasion of inmate privacy was a regular occurrence or from all posts where it was possible. Since there are very few posts in the prison on which there is no chance of privacy invasion, a narrow interpretation of these cases required female exclusion from the large majority of posts.

Further complicating matters for administrators, the courts ruled that Title VII could not be violated in order to protect inmate privacy; instead, administrators had to rearrange posts so that women would be guaranteed their right to equal employment opportunity.[11] Thus prison administrators were not allowed to limit the number of women entering the system, but once they were there, had to deploy them to posts that did not violate inmates' privacy. In prison systems with a large number of women guards, like New York, this assignment arrangement proved to be extremely difficult; guidelines were promulgated at the central office, but the local managers at each prison were left to find suitable posts for all the women on their staffs. At prisons with an exceptionally large proportion of women, this task was formidable, if not impossible. In some New York prisons, local supervisors either had to deploy women to posts at which their presence violated inmate privacy or place them on "unnecessary" posts, doing clerical or administrative work. In some prisons, there simply were not enough "proper" places for all the female guards working there.

Throughout the 1970s, prison administrators in many states found it necessary to change their policies for deploying female guards a number of times, either because of lawsuits filed directly against them or because of cases decided elsewhere in the country. Keeping current with and interpreting such cases became, in and of itself, an important administrative task. Policy changes were also sometimes required as a result of union pressure or the complaints and grievances of various parties. Additionally, changes in the number of women employed as guards often affected administrative policies. To make matters worse, in responding to these various pressures and changing their policies, administrators could never feel they had reached a final solution to the "female guard problem." Lawsuits continued to be filed by male guards, female guards, and inmates. Potential lawsuits were always lurking in the background, and prison administrators knew they would have to respond to them. More than a decade after the amendments to Title VII, there was still no formula for complying with the law or pleasing all parties. Regardless of women's effect on prison operations, the requirement to hire women as guards has placed a burden on prison administrators; that burden is likely to continue at least until the legal issues are resolved in a less ambiguous manner than they are currently.

Impact of Women on the Functioning of the Prisons

The most frequent and probably most important questions that are asked about female prison guards are: Can they do the job? Can they control male inmates? Can they perform as effectively as male guards? The answers to such questions must lie at the core of any analysis of women's impact on the functioning of the prisons. Edith Flynn (1982) says that women's assignment to contact positions on the tiers serves as "'prima facie' evidence as to their utility and effectiveness in such settings" (p. 325). Such a conclusion is totally unjustified; definitive conclusions about women's performance must rest on evidence and, unfortunately, very little is currently available. No correctional department has, to my knowledge, undertaken a systematic assessment of women's performance. Nor did this study focus explicitly on women's effectiveness on the job, although supervisors were asked to rate women's performance. Their evaluations were by and large negative,[12] but should be accepted cautiously because there is reason to suspect some degree of bias on their part. A substantial body of research indicates that most evaluators are biased in favor of males and continually devalue women's performance, even when it is identical to that of men.[13] And because most male supervisors are vocally opposed to women's presence, there is additional reason to be skeptical of their negative evaluations of women's performance. We can hope that empirical research on the job performance of both male and female guards will be conducted in the near future;[14] in the meantime, some tentative conclusions can be offered, based on limited evidence from the current study as well as the insights and observations of other researchers.

There is no reason to doubt that women can perform a large

portion of typical guard duties effectively. Guards spend considerable time on routine tasks such as locking and unlocking gates, counting inmates, writing inmate passes, filling out reports, searching for contraband, and ensuring that prisoners follow their daily schedules of work, meals, recreation, visits, and the like. There is no evidence that women cannot do these jobs, and even the male guards and administrators who continue to oppose the hiring of women readily admit that most female guards perform them effectively. Of greater concern is whether women have the authority to enforce the rules and regulations against recalcitrant inmates and whether women can effectively use physical force when necessary.

Most prisoners obey most of the hundreds of prison rules because it is in their own best interest to do so. The prisons operate on a system of rewards and punishments, and although guards often complain that the punishments are not severe enough (or sure enough) to act as serious deterrents to infractions of the rules, most inmates still prefer to avoid disciplinary hearings and the possible loss of privileges. As George Grosser (1968) points out, "The prisoner attempts to make his imprisonment as bearable as possible, and if satisfaction of this kind must be 'purchased' by adherence to some official norms, he will comply" (p. 20). Inmates follow most of the rules, then, because the cost generally is not worth the benefit of breaking them.

Within this general pattern of compliance, of course, many inmates try to break (or bend) an occasional rule, and a few inmates actively engage in extensive rule breaking. Enforcing the rules is therefore an important aspect of the job for any guard who works directly with inmates. How do guards, who are unarmed and greatly outnumbered, gain compliance with the rules, especially from inmates who are willing to risk the possibility of punishment? One option is the physical restraint of an inmate who is breaking a rule and his removal and confinement to a cell. Although such tactics are occasionally useful, Gresham Sykes (1958) pointed out more than two decades ago that "the ability of the officials to physically coerce their captives into the paths of compliance is," given the realities of guard-inmate ratio, "something of an illusion" (p. 50). There simply are not enough guards to enforce compliance and cooperation. On a day-to-day basis, physical force must be used sparingly and only as a last resort.

Fortunately, guards have some useful alternatives to the use of force. Foremost among these is the utilization of interpersonal communication techniques. Clarence Schrag (1961) found that "the officer's control over an inmate depends primarily on his skills of persuasion and leadership" (p. 340). Terrence Morris and Pauline Morris (1980) claim that guards who develop "insight" and persuasive skills are often able to avoid the use of force, even when disciplining or removing refractory prisoners. Many officers, they claim, "go out of their way to handle prisoners in the way which they believe to be the most likely to avert trouble" (p. 252). Women should be as able as men to use the skills of leadership, persuasion, and accommodation. In fact, there is some evidence that current female guards are especially adept at using these techniques, perhaps because of natural talents in these areas or perhaps because they more consciously seek alternatives to the use of force.

Although technically prohibited, another way for guards to obtain inmate compliance to prison rules is to overlook some minor infractions of the rules. Gresham Sykes (1956) referred to this behavior in its most extreme form as "corruption through reciprocity," because it if were allowed to escalate, guards could eventually lose all their authority to enforce rules. Nevertheless, some degree of reciprocity is probably necessary because guards simply cannot enforce all of the rules all the time and such arrangements between guards and inmates at least guarantee compliance with the more serious ones. Thomas Murton (1976) finds that guards must

> strike the delicate balance between enforcing the rules just enough to maintain the fiction of staff supremacy (which is essential for the institution to function) and at the same time not antagonize the inmates to the extent that they refuse to cooperate in the charade. [P. 66]

Such mutual accommodations between inmates and guards should not depend on the sex of the guard. When inmates were asked about differences between male and female guards' approaches to rule enforcement, the answers were equivocal: some women were accused of excessive enforcement (what we would expect from women in the institutional role) while others were reported to be more lenient than male guards about rules related to dress codes and displays of inmate respect (what we would expect from women in the inventive role). There is no evidence of substantial differences in the use of reciprocity between male and female guards (as groups) although it is possible that differences exist. Female guards should be able to make at least as much use of reciprocity, as an alternative to physical force, as do male guards.

A final alternative to coercion, widely used by male guards, is the development of positive, friendly relationships with inmates. Most likely to develop in situations of sustained contact (such as on housing units or work crews), these relationships generally grow out of a guard's willingness to listen to and sympathize with inmates and help them solve personal problems (Morris and Morris 1980). In return for this friendship and assistance, inmates voluntarily comply with prison rules to make sure the guard "looks good" to supervisors. Prisoners in this study report that female guards, in general, are more willing than males to enter friendly relationships that are conducive to inmates' confiding their problems and concerns (both those related to institutional life and those related to their life and relationships outside). Such friendly attitudes on the part of female guards undoubtedly contribute to prisoners' willingness to assist and protect women during emergencies. Although as Sykes (1956) points out, friendly relationships between guards and inmates might ultimately lead to a corruption of the guard's authority, some level of friendship can be useful as an alternative to physical force. Women are at least as able as men, and perhaps are more willing than men, to use this method of obtaining inmate compliance.

I have maintained thus far that the use of physical force over inmates is often impractical and that guards, both male and female, use a variety of alternate techniques for enforcing the rules on a day-to-day basis. In some situations, however, guards' ability to use force may be critical: inmates may physically attack guards, with or without provocation; they may attack each other; and they may engage in collective destruction of the prison. In such situations, alternate techniques of control may be inadequate and guards may find it necessary to use physical force to restrain and control prisoners. How effectively can female guards perform this function? Again, there is no definitive evidence. Women have been involved in physical confrontations with inmates and several have been injured in such situations. Many women (especially those in the institutional and inventive roles) accept the risk associated with physical confrontations as a necessary component of the job. Even women of small stature and limited self-defense skills stressed their willingness and intention to respond quickly and to take whatever action they could to bring these kinds of situations under control.

Male guards claim that most women are reluctant to become involved in physical confrontations and that when they do, they are at best ineffective and at worst a hindrance to the men's efforts. The men tell numerous stories of women who "froze," women who ran away from dangerous situations, and women who were merely "in the way." Some of these stories are undoubtedly true, but it is also true that some proportion of *male* guards are either afraid or ineffective in such emergencies. Very few male guards would voluntarily go "one on one" with a prisoner. When emergencies occur and the use of force seems imminent, reinforcements are immediately called for; if the situation is deemed serious, specially trained tactical teams are called in to restrain inmates. Membership on these teams is very selective and predominantly male, although in both New York and Rhode Island some women have met the requirements and joined the tactical squads at their local prisons.

At least some female guards, then, seem to be capable of performing all aspects of the job, including using force when necessary. But how do the current women guards, as a group, measure up to men as a group, with regard to the use of force? There are, of course, women (especially those in the modified role) who actively avoid all situations that require use of physical force. Disregarding this group, we still might conclude that because of their smaller size and different socialization experiences, the women generally are less capable of using force than are most male guards (especially because current female guards do not appear to be extraordinary in terms of size, strength, or aggressiveness). Without evidence to the contrary, we would expect female guards as a group to be less effective than men in the part of the job that requires the use of physical force. But two important questions remain: Does this difference between male and female guards jeopardize the security of the prisons? And might women bring some additional positive qualities to the job that counterbalance their deficiencies in strength and physical aggressiveness?

Most of the country's large maximum-security prisons experience periodic episodes of inmate fighting, gang warfare, attacks on staff, collective protest, and destruction of prison property; occasionally these disturbances erupt into full-scale riots. One of the major security tasks facing today's prison administrators is the prevention and control of such outbreaks. A 1981 report by the American Correctional Association suggests that successful prevention requires, among other things, a well-trained staff. The three areas of expertise it identifies as most critical are: insight into the causes of criminal behavior; an understanding of the cultural, social, and ethnic differences among prisoners; and knowledge of the legal rights of inmates. Because these characteristics are not sex-linked, female guards should be as likely as males to possess them.

Even when it focuses on the control rather than the prevention of riots, the Association report makes no mention of guards' strength or aggressiveness. It does suggest, however, that because riot control requires unique skills and familiarity with sophisticated equipment, special "reaction teams" be trained for this function. Members would presumably volunteer and be chosen on the basis of strength, agility, stamina, cool-headedness, and whatever other qualities were deemed important. Only guards who were highly qualified (whether male or female) would have direct responsibility for handling riot situations; guards who were less suited to these tasks would provide the necessary support functions. With this division of labor, a guard force that is 10, 20, or 30 percent female might be as capable as an all-male force of handling serious prison emergencies even if female guards, as a group, are less able and willing to use force.

One high-level prison administrator in Rhode Island said that his primary reservation about the employment of women was that inmates would be more likely to "try something" because of female guards' smaller size and less aggressive nature. That is, even if the institution is not less secure, inmates might believe that it is and therefore be less deterred from breaking the rules, trying to escape, or starting a riot. This argument, which rests on the social-psychological attitudes of inmates, may have some merit, but to date there is no indication that it has been a factor in inmate conduct. Security has not appeared to decrease in New York prisons since 1973 or in Rhode Island prisons since 1980. No riots, major disturbances, or escapes have occurred that might be attributed to women's presence. Nor is there evidence that New York's upstate prisons, which have an extremely low percentage of women, are any more stable or secure than the downstate institutions where most of the women are concentrated. Of course, it must be remembered that even in prisons with the largest proportion of women, women remain a rather small minority; no conclusions can be drawn regarding the effect on prison security of a guard force that was, say, 50 percent female.

So far, this section has focused only on the possible shortcomings of female guards by bringing some logic (and evidence, where available) to each of the claims that is made regarding women's performance. An analysis of women's impact on the operation of the prisons, particularly on the control and security functions, also requires a look at any positive contributions made by women.

Female prison guards may be less willing and able to use physical force, even when it is called for. In the long run, however, their unwillingness to use force might decrease the general level of violence in the prisons. Several studies have indicated that the use of force and aggression by agents of social control, especially in marginal situations, promotes and encourages increased aggression and violence by those persons being controlled (Stotland 1976; Toch 1977; Report of the National Advisory Commission on Civil Disorders 1968; Attica 1972; Stark 1972). By choosing to use alternatives to physical force, then, female guards may elicit a more pacific response from inmates and thereby contribute to the security and control of the institutions in which they work.

As Lee Bowker (1980) points out, the occupation of prison guard today is among the most dangerous jobs in the marketplace; personal injury and death at the hands of inmates are constant threats. At this point (although there are no statistics available) it appears that female guards are less vulnerable than males to personal attack by prisoners. Several women have been injured while responding to inmate fights, but female guards are seldom the victims of direct attacks by inmates.[15] This difference is probably due, in part, to traditional sex-role proscriptions and the reluctance of some men to strike a woman. But there is also no status to be gained by attacking and overpowering a female guard, as there might be when an inmate fights a male guard. In addition, it also appears that female guards seldom provoke inmate aggression. Inmates frequently said that female guards do not antagonize and "bait" them. There is, on the other hand, often a high level of tension between male guards and male inmates, related to the desire of both to prove masculinity and superiority. Ben Crouch (1980) claims that "interaction between guards and inmates . . . may be described by employing the analogy of a contest, placing the two parties in rather constant competition" (p. 216). Once the "contest" begins, peer pressure not to back down is exerted on both sides, and violence may result. Women do not get involved in these ego showdowns; they do not threaten inmates and do not provoke them into a fight.[16]

The final contribution of female guards to an overall reduction in prison violence is through their disinclination to victimize inmates. Bowker (1980) claims that although many incidents are undetected or covered up, there continues to be a steady stream of beating and torture by prison guards. Female guards are not automatically immune from such behavior (and are under many of the same pressures that contribute to the violent reactions of some male guards), but I received no reports on any woman working in the prison having been accused of physically victimizing inmates. Their smaller size is undoubtedly a factor, but women in general engage in considerably less violent and aggressive behavior than men.[17] The hiring of women could, then, contribute to a decrease in guard brutalization of inmates.

Conclusion

The hiring of women to work as guards in men's prisons was a change in correctional policy forced on reluctant prison administrators by legal mandate; it is a change that has created new problems for all participants in the prison world. Adjustment has been easiest for inmates because for most of them the advantages of women's presence outweigh the disadvantages. Male guards have been the least successful in adapting to this change; they still view women as "outsiders" who can neither be trusted nor counted on for assistance and support. For prison administrators, women's presence has meant additional work in terms of interpreting and implementing the legal requirements. They are less emotionally involved in the change than are male guards, but do share their concern about the impact of women's presence on prison order and security. While not all of their fears have been assuaged, their early predictions of doom have not been borne out, and there appears to have been no noticeable reduction in the prisons' ability to fulfill their functions since women began working as guards. It is true, however, that most female guards are less able and willing to use physical force than their male counterparts. In some instances, this may decrease their effectiveness in controlling individual prisoners or responding to collective disturbances. On the other hand, their disinclination to use physical force means they may elicit less violent behavior from inmates and engage in less direct aggression against them.

The impact of women on the prison cannot be evaluated merely on the basis of how closely their individual performance approximates that of male guards. Some women do perform the job very similarly to men; most do not. The long-term consequences of these differences are still not known and may be impossible to measure accurately. What we do know, however, is that prisons with all-male guard forces have been plagued with problems ranging from inefficiency to violent riots. Women's presence may aggravate some problems and alleviate others. But no matter how the positive and negative contributions of women balance out—no matter what their overall impact on the prison—their presence and their role in the male prison

will depend, in the future as in the past, primarily on the requirements of the law. The following chapter will examine the future role
of women by focusing on some possible resolutions to the continuing
legal ambiguities; it will also examine the ways in which prison
administrators, and women themselves, might solve the practical
problems generated by various legal outcomes.

The Future of Women in Corrections

This study is, in many ways, a "snapshot" view of female guards' experiences and their impact on prisons for men; women's future in corrections remains uncertain. For one thing, some important legal issues are still unsettled, and new judicial or legislative decisions could alter women's employment opportunities and the tasks they are allowed to perform. Women's future will also depend on the willingness and ability of prison administrators to make the sexual integration process more successful than it has been so far. Women have adapted to the job, and the performance of many has been evaluated as adequate or even superior, but many serious problems remain. Male opposition and harassment remain strong, and differential treatment of male and female guards continues; these conditions present serious obstacles to women's ability to perform the job effectively. As a consequence, the full potential of female guards is not being realized and cannot, in fact, be easily assessed.

There are no easy solutions to what prison administrators often call the "female guard problem." Some changes, however, could be made to promote and facilitate successful sexual integration. After exploring the remaining legal issues and how various decisions might affect women's future, this chapter will suggest some possible efforts to be made by both prison administrators and women themselves to solve the practical problems created by women's presence.

Possible Solutions to the Remaining Legal Issues

The right of women to work as guards in men's prisons was established by federal law, and although the courts have not clearly or consistently defined the precise boundaries of this right, they have

172

generally agreed that prison employment is not an exception to Title VII's mandate of equal employment opportunity. Only the *Rawlinson*[1] decision suggested that there might be grounds for a bona fide occupational qualification (BFOQ) exemption, but even then, only under "deplorable" prison conditions. In the cases that followed, no similar conditions were found,[2] and women's right to prison employment was reaffirmed. At this point that right appears to be secure, although there are possible legal changes that could limit or even remove women from men's prisons.

The Supreme Court might, for example, eventually hear another female guard case, and it could establish an even broader BFOQ than that offered in *Rawlinson*. One weakness in the *Rawlinson* decision is that, although it suggested that women's presence in the prisons might decrease overall prison security, it cited no supporting evidence. If such evidence were to be presented in a future case, the courts might take even more seriously prison administrators' concerns with the effect women have on internal order and security. The likelihood of such evidence emerging is probably slim, because even if prison unrest and escapes were to increase after women were hired, it would be difficult to prove a causal relationship. Nonetheless, the judiciary could possibly be swayed by correlational data and establish a broader BFOQ that would allow prison administrators to deny guard jobs to women. Such a decision would, of course, be a dramatic reversal of the post-*Rawlinson* decisions and remains, it seems, only a very remote possibility.

The second way that women's right to prison employment could be curtailed is through a change in the federal law that granted them that right. Probably few supporters of the original 1964 Civil Rights Act or the 1972 amendments to that act realized that one consequence of the legislation would be the hiring of women to work as guards in men's prisons; they may, in fact, have assumed that traditionally male criminal justice jobs such as prison guard and police officer would be covered automatically by the BFOQ clause. Had women's use of Title VII to gain employment as guards in men's prisons been known, some supporters may have declined to vote for the measure. Even today there is no consensus among the American population with regard to the desirability of unqualified equal employment opportunity for women. Probably many people would support the removal of a few jobs from this general mandate, and the job of prison guard, which brings the emotional privacy issue to the fore, would almost certainly be among those to go.

If there were public support for such a measure, Congress could decide to override the judiciary's support of EEOC's narrow interpretation of the BFOQ exemption by explicitly removing some jobs from Title VII's general prohibition of employment discrimination on the basis of sex. The possibility of such a legislative change is probably remote because organized women's groups undoubtedly would mobilize strong opposition to such a proposal. And because most members of Congress are probably not under direct pressure from specific groups to limit Title VII, they would have no reason to initiate a legal action that would certainly provoke a political battle with women's groups. Therefore, a legislative change in Title VII sufficient to reverse the steady movement of women into guard jobs or remove those women currently working in the prisons is possible but seems, at this point, highly unlikely.

Another possible legal change that would not totally disqualify, but would severely limit the number of women who qualify for the job, is judicial support for height and weight requirements. The justices in *Rawlinson* struck down Alabama's height and weight requirements because those standards disproportionately disqualified women and thus constituted a prima facie violation of Title VII. Not all height and weight standards automatically violate Title VII, however,[3] and as James Jacobs (1979) points out in his analysis of the *Rawlinson* decision, several justices stated that such standards might be allowable if shown to be substantially related either to actual strength or to the appearance of strength. That is, if departments of corrections (or other law enforcement agencies) can show that size is related to efficiency—or even an improved show of authority—minimum size requirements will not violate Title VII, even if they discriminate against women. Depending on the actual standards, a substantial percentage of female applicants could no longer qualify. Such standards could not be used to fire small women (or men) who had already been permanently appointed to guard jobs, but they could result in a gradually decreasing number of women as new applicants were hired.

Whereas any of the above possible legal changes could be used by prison administrators as justification for denying guard employment to some or all women, it is important to understand that none of them would *require* discrimination against women. If some occupations, such as prison guard, were explicitly defined as exceptions to the prohibition of sex discrimination, employers would still be free to hire women if they so desired. If the courts suddenly ruled that the job of prison guard qualifies for a more complete BFOQ exemption, prison administrators could still choose to hire women. And even if the courts were to allow height and weight standards, no corrections department would be compelled to establish them. The effect of these legal changes would be to eliminate or reduce the legal mandate to corrections departments that they hire women. Of course, lacking legal compulsion, many prison administrators would almost certainly either stop hiring women or hire fewer of them; a few prison officials may have decided that women can be useful and effective in this job, but most have hired women only because they are legally required to do so. If the legal mandate were removed, probably very few would continue the practice.

The likelihood of a legal change (legislative or judicial) sufficient to make the hiring of women as guards purely voluntary appears to be remote. Further change regarding the deployment of women within men's prisons, however, is likely. Must male and female guards be used interchangeably, or can prison administrators assign them to posts on the basis of sex? And perhaps more important, *must* prison administrators take workers' sex into account when making assignment decisions? Do inmates have any rights that need to be considered in assigning guards? All of these questions have been confronted by the courts but, to date, the answers remain both confusing and contradictory. Consequently, prison administrators find it almost impossible to follow the rules with regard to the deployment of male and female guards and are, in fact, often able to find legal justification for any particular deployment policy they prefer.

The primary issue on which this confusion rests is prisoners' legal right to privacy. Some prison administrators initially tried to block implementation of Title VII on the grounds that women's presence violates inmate privacy. In all of these cases, the courts disagreed because administrators were unable to present any evidence of inmate complaint or dissatisfaction. In both *Gunther* v. *Iowa State Men's Reformatory*[4] and *Harden* v. *Dayton Human Rehabilitation Center*,[5] the courts ruled that if prison officials were personally concerned with inmate privacy they were free to protect it in ways that did not violate women's employment rights; they even suggested such measures as reorganizing job assignments and installing protective barriers for inmates who were undressing, showering, or using the toilet. The *Gunther* court did rule, however, that a limited BFOQ might be claimed for the few job assignments that involved mainly toilet and shower supervision. Importantly, the decision did not *require* prison officials to use the BFOQ to protect inmate privacy but stated that doing so voluntarily would not violate Title VII. Neither *Gunther* nor *Harden* left room for prison officials to deny guard jobs to women; instead, they were ordered to find ways to accommodate inmates' privacy concerns without infringing on women's Title VII rights.

Although the courts did not seriously consider prison administrators' concern with inmate privacy,[6] they did take seriously privacy claims made by prisoners themselves. In *Forts* v. *Ward*,[7] female prisoners in New York State claimed that the use of male guards violated their privacy. Although the district court agreed, the decision was reversed by the Circuit Court of Appeals after the Department of Correctional Services agreed to issue the women "suitable sleepwear" and grant them the right to cover their cell door windows for fifteen-minute intervals while dressing or using the toilet.

Male prisoners around the country also began to complain and file lawsuits against correctional departments that used female guards in areas that violated their right to personal privacy[8] and two important cases were decided in their favor.[9] In *Hudson* v. *Goodlander*,[10] the court found that an inmate's "privacy rights were violated by assignment of female guards to posts where they could view him while he was totally unclothed"; female guards could render assistance on such posts during prison emergencies, but could not be permanently assigned there. In *Bowling* v. *Enomoto*,[11] in a suit brought by a California inmate, the court ruled that "prisoners in all-male inmate institutions had limited right to privacy which included right to be free from unrestricted observation of their genitals and bodily functions by prison officials of opposite sex under normal prison conditions." California prison officials, who defended their female guard policy by referring to their obligations under Title VII, were ordered to devise policies that maximized equal opportunity for women but did not violate the rights of inmates. In these cases, then, the court is not merely allowing prison officials to deploy female guards in a way that does not violate inmate privacy, but is *requiring* them to do so.

The courts have not, however, been receptive to all inmate claims regarding privacy invasion by female guards and have, in fact, rejected inmates' claims that the use of women to conduct general "pat down" frisks (during which inmates remain fully clothed) violates their privacy. In *Smith* v. *Fairman*,[12] the Circuit Court ruled that an "inmate is not entitled to full protection of the Constitution he would otherwise enjoy, including the right to be free from unwarranted intrusions into personal privacy" and that "if the state is required to hire women as guards in its male prisons, it reasonably seems to follow that it must be allowed to utilize female guards to the fullest extent possible." Even Muslim inmates, claiming that such procedures violate their constitutionally protected right to religious freedom,[13] have not been successful in prohibiting frisks by female staff. In *Sam'i* v. *Mintzes*,[14] for example, the district court ruled that such searches, conducted "in a dignified manner," did not violate inmates' privacy rights and that the defendants' interest in administering the prisons (including their obligation to comply with Title VII) outweighed the prisoners' religious claims. Again, in *Madyun* v. *Franzen*,[15] the Circuit Court of Appeals rejected an inmate's First Amendment claim, saying that "frisk searches of male prisoners by female guards is reasonably adapted to serve the important state interests of providing adequate prison security and equal opportunity for women to serve as prison guards."[16]

None of these cases (either those won or lost by inmates), provide prison administrators with any way to deny guard jobs to women. Some of them, however, do require that women be deployed in a way that will protect inmate privacy. *Smith*, *Sam'i*, and *Madyun* make it clear that women can work on posts that require them to pat-frisk inmates. *Hudson* and *Bowling* indicate that women guards should not work where they might see unclothed inmates. But what these latter cases fail to make clear is whether women must be denied all posts where there is a possibility of a prisoner being unclothed or only those posts where inmates are particularly likely to be naked. There are, in fact, very few prison posts on which a guard can be absolutely assured of not seeing a naked inmate (for example, front desk, mail room, visiting room); any post in a housing area or cell block involves occasional contact between a guard and an unclothed or partially clothed inmate.

Without clear legal guidelines, prison administrators have, over the years, interpreted these privacy decisions in a variety of ways. When they want to limit women's deployment options, they can point to their legal obligation to protect inmate privacy. On the other hand, when they want more flexibility in deploying women, they can point to the lack of clear definition of privacy in these decisions.[17] And, of course, because all of these privacy rulings were made at the District or Circuit Court of Appeals levels, prison administrators in many parts of the country have not been obligated to follow them at all. Only a Supreme Court decision outlining prisoners' right to privacy would establish a single rule of law for all state correctional departments. One reason why there has been no Supreme Court case dealing directly with the issue of prisoner privacy is that none of the correctional departments losing privacy suits to inmates at the lower levels appealed those decisions. Maryland officials did not appeal

Hudson past the district court level; neither did the California officials who lost the *Bowling* case to inmates. The judge in *Hudson* even stated that "the court suspects this is one case the State is prepared to lose." And because these cases do not directly involve female guards (that is, they are not parties in the suits), the courts have not been called on to provide an explicit balance between the employment rights of women and the privacy rights of inmates.

Issues of employment rights have been explicitly considered only in cases filed by *women* against correctional departments. Issues of inmate privacy have been dealt with in cases filed by *inmates* against correctional departments. Which set of rights should take precedent? In spite of the decisions granting prisoners' privacy claims, it is still not clear that inmates have a constitutional right to privacy. The judge in *Fairman* explained that the general right to privacy is implicit in the Fourth Amendment guarantee of freedom from unreasonable searches. But as James Jacobs (1979) points out in his analysis of *Rawlinson* (in which the issue of inmate privacy was considered, although not critical):

> No Supreme Court case decision hints that an individual has a constitutional right not to be placed in a position where while undressed he or she risks observation or physical contact by persons of the opposite sex. . . . The Court has resisted the temptation to expand the constitutional right to privacy beyond the area of contraception and child bearing. [Pp. 407–8]

How the Supreme Court would rule on an inmate privacy claim involving female prison guards is unknown. Only an appeal by correctional administrators to the cases won against them by inmates or a direct Title VII challenge by women to correctional policies that protect inmate privacy would set the stage for settling these issues. Until such a case occurs,[18] the extent to which women's employment rights must be diminished to accommodate inmates' privacy rights will not be clear. And until it is clear, prison administrators will remain confused about their legal obligations to women and inmates and will be able, if they desire, to use the conflicting and ambiguous decisions to justify a wide range of deployment policies.

Even if the courts outline a more definitive balance between the rights of inmates and the rights of women, prison administrators may still have leeway in developing policies that protect whichever set of rights is left with less judicial protection. That is, even if the courts were to find no constitutional right to privacy, prison administrators could seek to protect it in ways that did not violate women's employment rights, such as installing shower curtains and protective barriers. These physical changes could also be used as a way of allowing women's full employment even if the courts were to give preference to inmates' privacy rights.[19] But most critical at this point is for the courts to establish exactly what women's Title VII rights entail when applied to the prisons. Once that is clear, women can either demand compliance with the law or seek the voluntary cooperation of prison administrators in achieving equal employment opportunity. So far, the law has formed the framework for nearly all decisions by prison administrators, and there is every reason to suspect that the future role of women in corrections will depend largely on how the remaining legal issues are resolved. Until that happens, women's future as guards in men's prisons remains uncertain.

Solving the Practical Problems

Prison administrators have been slow to develop policies that both require and allow women's full performance of all aspects of the job of prison guard.[20] At the early stages of sexual integration, most male prisons could easily accommodate some number of women who played only a limited occupational role; there was some male resentment (and the filing of grievances) when women received safe, noncontact job assignments, but overall security and efficiency were probably not affected. In fact, even women who performed a modified role offered some advantages because they often performed necessary clerical and administrative functions more effectively than male guards and were able to search female visitors for contraband more thoroughly. If prison administrators had been able to severely restrict the number of women coming into male prisons, all women might have adopted the modified role without a noticeable reduction in manpower. However, even a guard force that is 5 percent female can probably not function efficiently if women stay only on noncontact positions. In many prisons today the percentage of women is considerably above that figure, and their numbers could very well increase in the years ahead. Therefore, regardless of the preferences of individual women, sound management policy requires that female guards do the full job. Put simply, the best female guard, from the management perspective, is one who is willing and able to perform all guard duties and is, to the extent allowed by the law, interchangeable with male guards.

Only a few currently employed female guards are willing and able to perform all guard functions in the male prison. Of the remainder, some are clearly unwilling, but many others have been discouraged from full participation by discriminatory treatment during on-the-job training, male opposition and harassment, and formal policies that limit women's post assignments. For many women, these structural barriers set in motion a psychological cycle of failure that eventually destroys their desire, motivation, and ability to perform all aspects of the job.[21] Prison administrators must have an affirmative plan if they hope to reverse these trends. Whatever their reasons for failing to do so in the past—hoping females were only there temporarily, hoping the legal guidelines would finally become clarified, hoping time would solve the problems of sexual integration—they cannot afford continual ambivalence if they hope to make full use of their female employees.

Prison administrators are justifiably concerned when some employees—male or female—are not willing or able to perform all aspects of the job. This is not a problem that emerged with the hiring of women, although sexual integration undoubtedly exacerbated the problem because some female guards seem to be substantially protected from the processes that ordinarily "weed out" most unqualified male guards. Male guards who are unable to handle inmate confrontations or their verbal abuse, for example, will not last long on the job—probably not even through the probationary period. On the other hand, this study has shown that at least some female guards are protected from the most negative aspects of the job and are able to achieve permanent appointment without proving (to either themselves or others) that they can handle all of the job's requirements. Without adequate training and experience, they are unable to perform the entire job, regardless of any original intentions to do so.

Policies that require all trainees to perform the wide range of guard duties, including responding to emergencies, conducting shakedowns, and managing large groups of inmates, will ensure that those women (and men) unable or unwilling to perform all aspects of the job are identified during the on-the-job training phase. They might then be offered additional training or counseling and, if such efforts fail, be terminated. Such a plan would require more formal guidelines for guards' on-the-job training than are currently used in most prisons and an automatic review of all new guards' training records before permanent status is granted. There would certainly be resistance to such a proposal by the middle-level supervisors who now have near total discretion over the assignment of trainees, but this study suggests that they cannot be counted on to provide women with the full range of training experiences. Either because they discount the ability of all women or desire to protect specific women, some male supervisors fail to assign female trainees to the posts that require direct, face-to-face contact with inmates. Consequently, many women fail to "test their wings" in the most difficult aspects of the job and management has limited criteria with which to make decisions about permanent appointment.

Efforts might also be made to improve screening procedures at the application stage because it is possible that current devices effectively "screen out" inappropriate male candidates, but not females. For example, certain levels of strength and agility and the ability to physically break up fights might not be important to test for if only male applicants are accepted because the large majority of males in the society probably possess these qualities to the degree required on the job (and, if not, can often acquire the required levels with a minimum of experience and training). Female applicants, however, might vary more substantially among themselves, with a smaller proportion possessing minimum qualifications. Therefore, more formal screening procedures might be needed when some work forces become sexually integrated. Such recommendations have been made with regard to sexual integration of the military (Binkin and Bach 1977; Nabors 1982) as a way of avoiding the arbitrary exclusion of all women from some jobs just because the majority of women may lack certain physical requirements. If prison administrators were to develop job-related requirements for the position of prison guard and appropriate measures of them, they might more effectively screen all applicants. To the extent those requirements are related to strength and the ability to use force, more female than male applicants might be eliminated. However, valid requirements could also include such qualities as empathy, communication ability, and persuasiveness, qualities that might be more prevalent in female applicants. What is needed, then, is some definition of what makes a good guard and the establishment of application procedures that screen for those qualities. As long as the criteria are justifiably job related and not used as a purposeful mechanism for discriminating against any group, they should be legally acceptable even if they do, in fact, discriminate between males and females.

The advantages of screening more successfully at the application and on-the-job training stages are substantial. The prison itself benefits by having a more efficient work force; managers gain flexibility in assigning all employees; women will be assured training on all posts, boosting their self-confidence and ability; female guards who truly qualify for the job will be judged more readily on their own merits;[22] and male resentment toward women because some "don't pull their own weight" should be reduced.

Establishing policies to guarantee that only qualified women receive permanent appointment is only half the battle and will, in fact, be counterproductive and discriminatory if not implemented along with policies that allow and encourage women's full performance of the job. If nothing else changes in the prison, better screening procedures at the on-the-job training phase will eliminate not only women unable or unwilling to do the whole job, but also women who are capable but currently deterred from full performance. Making sure they receive equal training will help, but efforts must also be made to reduce the male opposition and sexual harassment that currently prevent nearly all female guards from achieving their full productive potential.

When women work in traditionally male jobs where they are subjected to substantial male co-worker opposition and sexual harassment, they experience low levels of job commitment (Gutek and Nakamura 1982), low productivity (Merit Systems Protection Board 1981), physical and emotional health problems (Goodman 1978; Rustad 1982), and high rates of absenteeism and turnover (Gutek and Nakamura 1982; Crull 1980). The task force report of the Federal Bureau of Prisons (1980) did find higher turnover rates among female than male guards, although they were unable to attribute this difference to specific causes. The current study did not assess turnover rates, but women were quite articulate about the emotional price they pay as a result of negative male behavior. One woman, for example, who initially hoped to make a career in corrections work said:

> It's like beating my head against the wall—there is no payoff. I thought I could eventually prove to them [the men] that no matter what they thought of most women, that I could do the job. I volunteer for extra duty; I always respond to emergencies; I learned self-defense so I would qualify for the "tactical team"; and still, I'm no different in their eyes than any other woman here. So I'm thinking of going into police work; women seem to be more accepted there. Maybe it will be the same as here, but I've got to try something different. Here, they just wear me down, day by day.

Other women do not take the male opposition quite so seriously but indicate that it does take its toll:

I try not to let it bother me, but you know, you're always waiting for the next remark. You find yourself on guard, hoping one day will pass without someone telling you you don't belong there. I used to try to think up clever comebacks but I've given up on that because it only eggs them on to harass you even more. So mostly I ignore it; I pretend I didn't hear it. If they think you don't care they eventually find someone else to pick on. Now, it's mostly the new men who pick on me; every time a new group comes in it all starts over again. You get used to it, but you never really learn to accept it.

Regardless of whether male opposition and harassment produce higher turnover rates among female guards, they do affect negatively women's attitude toward the job and, undoubtedly, their effectiveness and productivity as well.

One might have hoped that once male guards got used to women's presence in the prisons, opposition and harassment would decrease as in some other recently integrated occupations (McIlwee 1982; Epstein 1980). However, in highly sex-typed male occupations, such as the military (DeFleur et al. 1978; Larwood et al. 1980) and police work (Martin 1980; Price and Gavin 1982), the record has been more bleak, and Cheryl Peterson's (1982) participant observation study of female guards in a men's prison indicates that male hostility has remained strong over time, even though it did become slightly less overt and visible. Some of this male opposition might diminish if those women who are ill-equipped to perform the job—women who, according to Meyer and Lee (1978), "reinforce old stereotypes"—are eliminated, but other research shows that even successful performance by women does not always lead to positive evaluations of them (Feather and Simon 1975; Yarkin et al. 1981; Deaux and Emswiller 1974). It is important, then, for prison administrators to more effectively control male behavior if they wish sexual integration to succeed.

Men's opposition to women's presence in this job, as in others, is often based on their deeply held beliefs that women are overstepping their proper role boundaries; and although prison administrators cannot be expected to completely change the sexist attitudes of their workers, they might make some moderate attempts in that direction. Many businesses and corporations have used educational, consciousness-raising, and role-playing techniques to prepare workers for sexual integration and although the results so far have not been encouraging (Dunnette and Motowidlo 1982), further innovations might improve the effectiveness of such programs.[23] Right now, virtually no efforts in this direction are being made in the prisons, and there is, in fact, some strong opposition to doing so. One high-level administrator, for example, told me that he expected any effort to change men's attitudes to only solidify their opposition to women:

> These guys don't want the women here in the first place. Now if we come in and tell them they have to accept it—they have to change their attitudes—they have to be *nice* to the women—they will probably respond with more hostility toward them. It's best to just leave them alone and let them work things out in their own way. Some men will never accept it; others will. But we can't be in the business of trying to change attitudes.

Attitudes cannot, of course, be changed by force, but there is no reason to believe that nothing can be accomplished. Some workers may be unaware that their attitudes and comments injure others; they may not understand that situations they define as "fun" or "just fooling around" are not fun for those on the receiving end of racist, sexist, or ethnic jokes. Educational and awareness sessions might help male guards become more sensitive to their own attitudes and behavior and might be further useful as a way of notifying lower organizational members that the organization as a whole takes the integration process seriously. Merely holding such sessions indicates that high-level decision makers are concerned about the incoming group and committed to their successful integration into the work force; instituting the process itself, then, may be more important than the messages contained in any awareness sessions.

Although liberalizing male attitudes toward women might be part of a plan for reducing male opposition to their presence, it will be ineffective without additional plans for changing male behavior. Bridget O'Farrell and Sharon Harlan (1982) found that "women do not necessarily need a supportive atmosphere on the job so much as the absence of sexual harassment" (p. 263). So regardless of how men feel, their hostile behavior must not be tolerated.

It is difficult to be optimistic about the potential for reducing sexual harassment in the workplace, but as the Center for Women Policy Studies (1981) points out, the problem of sexual harassment has never been vehemently attacked by management. Prerequisite to a successful antiharassment program in the prisons is the active and visible support of top management. They might want to rely on the expertise of specialists in designing actual programs and policies, although the following principles, borrowed in part from the Merit Systems Protection Board (1981) and Constance Backhouse and Leah Cohen (1978), can serve as a general overview of the most important ingredients of an all-encompassing antiharassment program in the prisons.

Management needs to issue a clear statement condemning sexual harassment and outlining the specific forms of behavior that are prohibited. Some actual examples from the prisons should be included. The illegality of sexual harassment and the possible legal sanctions for both the individual harasser and the organization need to be specified. Short training sessions on sexual harassment could be valuable for all employees but, at a minimum, should be provided for middle-level managers[24] and included in the general orientation for all new guards. In short, knowledge about the harmful effects and illegality of sexual harassment needs to be completely disseminated within the prisons.

Female guards must be informed of their right to a harassment-free work environment and assured that their complaints will be taken seriously. Each prison currently has a reporting procedure, but many women are reluctant to report incidents, not only because they believe investigators are unsympathetic but also because they are sometimes as unsure of which specific behaviors are unacceptable as are the harassers. When a woman reports an incident, investigators should assure her that she will be protected from reprisals. If she works directly with the harasser, one or the other should be temporarily reassigned until the investigation is completed.

Management should establish a clear disciplinary agenda to be followed in all cases, beginning with warning and counseling, progressing to probation, and ending in dismissal (for the recalcitrant harasser). Both the investigation and discipline might be best handled by outside consultants (or arbitrators) rather than existing members of the organizational structure. Both the alleged offender and victim need to feel that their case is handled fairly and objectively in order to avoid resentment and/or disillusionment with the system itself. In addition, top management needs to know that cases will be handled in a way that will best avoid future lawsuits and bad publicity.

Sexual harassment and vocal male opposition are problems that cannot be solved easily, but unless they are vigorously attacked, no progress will be made at all and female guards will have to continue to work in an environment that is not conducive to their full and effective performance of the job. If even modest progress is made, women, the prison organization as a whole, and, perhaps even male guards themselves will benefit substantially.

One final way that prison officials might make the process of sexual integration more successful is by providing special assistance to women. Most prison systems have some special policies for deploying female guards, but in all other areas, administrators have made no official distinctions between male and female guards. Such a position has some ideological advantages, but it ignores the reality that men and women have different occupational problems, not only because they bring different attitudes and skills to the job, but also because their on-the-job experiences may be quite dissimilar. Regardless of the formal policy of equality, women are not treated as equals by male co-workers, supervisors, or inmates, and to ignore the impact of these informal practices is to relegate women to continued inequality. Susan Martin (1980) found this same dilemma in the newly integrated police department she studied. Administrators there had prohibited sex discrimination "but had done little else, hoping that time and experience would eliminate the difficulties faced by the first group of women. Unfortunately such has not been the case" (p. 211). Martin suggests that police departments implement special policies addressed to women's special work-related problems. The same should be done for female prison guards.

Female guards might benefit from some special physical training. Many women feel that the self-defense training they received at the training academy is inadequate; they would like regularly scheduled physical fitness and/or advanced self-defense classes taught at the individual prisons. Such programs might increase women's ability and willingness to use physical force when necessary. Assertiveness training might be beneficial as well. Although ongoing training sessions might be especially oriented toward the needs of female guards, there would be no need to exclude those men who would like to attend.

Another area in which female guards could benefit from special training is in dealing with inmate sexual advances and sexual misconduct. Because male and female guards now receive identical training (which was initially designed for men), it gives little consideration to problems unique to women. And because most on-the-job training is done by male guards, women lose out there as well. In fact, women are sometimes told that the problems they uniquely face are the "cost" of taking the job:

> I asked my partner what I should do about a certain inmate who always seemed to be changing his clothes when I did the count. He would always appear to be "caught" with his pants down. So I asked, "Can I write him up?" and my partner said no because he

wouldn't be doing it if I wasn't there. He seemed to be saying it was really my fault so I just had to take it.

Inmates can, of course, be disciplined for sexual misconduct. The reaction of many women now is ignore the behavior until it gets out of hand and to apply discipline only in extreme cases. The result is that they either tolerate a great deal of unpleasant inmate behavior or rely on inmate peer pressure to halt it. Female guards need explicit instruction in the behaviors considered inappropriate and the possible remedies available to them. Male guard trainers, who have no personal experience with such problems, cannot be relied on to provide this information.

Now that the number of female guards has grown, it might also be possible to assign new female recruits to female trainers for at least part of their on-the-job training experience. The Federal Bureau of Prisons (1980) study found that female guards were often reluctant to ask men for advice or assistance for fear of appearing foolish or weak.[25] Research on policewomen has shown that women perform more effectively (and are more assertive in performing the most "masculine" aspects of the job) when they are assigned together (Sherman 1973). Such results should not be surprising, given the strength of male opposition and the attitudes of paternalism that men often exhibit toward female partners. By teaming women together, new female guards might be more likely to receive the kind of socialization experience that is necessary to the building of self-confidence and ultimately, successful job performance (Van Maanen and Schein 1979; Feldman 1976; Terborg et al. 1982). Furthermore, such a policy would give women the opportunity to establish some lasting, working relationships with other women in the prison.

Women Helping Themselves

Women's future in men's prisons depends not only on the law and administrative efforts to solve their problems, but also on their own willingness to organize themselves and mobilize support for programs and policies that will be beneficial to them. At a minimum, women need to form support groups at each prison and establish a mechanism (such as group meetings or a telephone network) through which they can share work-related problems.[26] The mere process of sharing problems has been therapeutic for women because, as Joan Bowker (1981) found, it "validated their vaguely-perceived feelings that something was wrong, and maybe it wasn't something wrong with them as persons" (p. 224). In addition to preventing excessive self-blame, problem sharing can also serve as the first step toward solution sharing. This is particularly important for new female guards who, more than likely, have just finished their academy training in a class dominated by men. Unless they were able to develop strong alliances with those men, they may feel totally isolated at their first prison assignment where critical on-the-job training will take place and problems and questions will continually arise. Experienced and sympathetic women can help new women through this difficult adjustment period. The creation of such support groups could be facilitated by administrative assistance (in terms of publicity and, perhaps, a meeting space in the prison), but it must be maintained, and probably initiated, by women themselves. In other traditionally male occupations, women have had difficulty forming such support groups (Hammond and Mahoney 1983; Harragan 1980), but where they have been formed, they have successfully eased new women's adjustment problems (Forisha 1981b; Meyer and Lee 1978; Epstein 1981; Candy 1981).

Collectively, women might also successfully lobby prison administrators for programs that respond to their special needs (for example, self-defense, sexual harassment, sexual misconduct by inmates, and the like). They will probably be less successful in influencing female deployment policies simply because women themselves are so divided on this issue, with some women wanting assignments restricted to noncontact positions and others favoring policies of absolute equality with the men. These extreme differences might subside in the coming years, especially if administrative policies both require and encourage women's full participation; in the meantime, women should work toward influencing those policies on which they can present a fairly united front. To the extent women can find a common ground on which to work together, they might more successfully create more common ground of women's interests in the years to come. It is important that women not wait until they agree on all issues before organizing around the problems they currently share.

Finally, women should more actively seek the support of their unions in addressing their special work-related problems. Without union support, women's movement into guard jobs in men's prisons would have been much slower in many states, but these same unions have not become actively involved in improving women's conditions of employment; now that women are themselves union members, they might pressure their unions to take a more active role. The

Women's Labor Project (1980) suggests that union contracts duplicate Title VII's prohibition of sex discrimination. Any changes in that law or in judicial interpretation of it would, then, have minimal impact on women protected by a union contract. Special clauses prohibiting sexual harassment by supervisors might be also included to provide an additional avenue of redress for women who are victimized; such a provision might also, as Backhouse and Cohen (1978) suggest, serve as an illustrative example of proper and improper male conduct for the rank-and-file workers not specifically covered. The Women's Labor Project also suggests that unions negotiate for a clause that guarantees victims of sexual harassment automatic transfer to an equivalent position so they can avoid retaliation. As the number of female guards increases in many states, their ability to pressure union leadership with contract demands such as these should increase as well.

By becoming more actively involved in union affairs women might also begin to break down some of the barriers that now exist between themselves and their male co-workers. As James Fox (1982) pointed out in a recent study of maximum-security prisons, male and female guards share a substantial number of work-related concerns. By focusing on those concerns, and working together toward solutions, the differences between male and female guards might begin to appear to both groups to be of less consequence. And once they become more active in the union, women might find it easier to use the union as a forum for voicing their special concerns. Union newsletters, for example, might include articles aimed toward changing male attitudes about women and educating male members about sexual harassment. In those states with unions, women have still not been innovative in marshaling union power for their own causes. This is, perhaps, something they can do for themselves in the future.

Conclusion

There is still a great deal of uncertainty about women's future role in corrections. The next few years could bring important legal changes either limiting or expanding women's role in men's prisons. At this point, a clarification in any direction would be a positive change because it would establish more uniformity and end the continuing ambiguity that allows prison administrators to maintain a "wait and see" attitude before creating policies that might make sexual integration more successful than it has been.

Each possible legal solution will, to some extent, guide the form of practical solutions. If administrators are required to limit women's deployment opportunities because of prisoners' privacy rights, then the problems of "near equality" that are so prevalent today will undoubtedly continue. However, even then, administrators should make every effort to solve the inmate privacy dilemma in a way that will allow women maximum opportunity, allow managers maximum flexibility, and guarantee minimum discrimination against male as well as female guards. Administrators should also move affirmatively to reduce male opposition, to the extent possible, and strictly enforce laws against sexual harassment. If male and female guards are to work together, it is to everyone's advantage that current tensions and hostilities be alleviated.

To whatever extent ultimately allowed by the law, prison administrators must work to create policies that both allow and require sexual equality on the job. Informal policies that allow some women to remain on the job without performing all duties are just as harmful as those policies which currently prevent even dedicated women from realizing their full potential. The needs of women and the needs of management can both best be met by ending all formal and informal policies that allow either discriminatory or preferential treatment of women.

Regardless of legal solutions, much can be done to improve the success of sexual integration. Still, guarding will undoubtedly remain a predominantly male occupation because it is unlikely that enough women will ever choose to enter corrections work to change the current sex ratio substantially. It is, therefore, probably not necessary to consider whether or not the prisons could operate efficiently with a majority of female guards. But even if the number of female guards remains about the same, there are many unanswered questions concerning their future. The use of women as guards is still in the experimental stage. If some of the pressures that push women into one of the special female roles are eliminated, will women act more like their male counterparts?[27] And if they do, what is the inmate reaction likely to be? If inmates begin to treat male and female guards similarly, will females' lower capacity to use force be more detrimental to prison security than it is now? Or will those women with less capacity to use force be "weeded out" more readily than they are now? Will the job of prison guard itself change, perhaps because of women's presence?[28] Will those women recruited into guard jobs in the future—women socialized into a world with more occupational opportunity for women—be substantially different from current female guards? Answers to these questions cannot be provided at this time. What is clear, however, is that as the conditions under which women work change, so will women's job performance; the three dominant strategies currently adopted by female guards might very well be replaced by others. But there is no doubt that at least some women will perform this job efficiently and effectively, as women do today, even under generally hostile working conditions. Exactly how women perform the job in the future, however, will depend on the law, on the policy decisions of prison officials, and on the actions and interactions of all members of the prison environment.

Building a Theory of Women's Occupational Experiences

As women have begun to enter many occupations formerly open only to men, researchers have examined their experiences and collected insightful descriptive data concerning the special problems and dilemmas women face on these jobs. The results of these studies, which have employed varied research techniques, have been remarkably similar: in entering traditionally male occupations, ranging from lawyer to construction worker to police officer, women must endure such conditions as opposition from male co-workers and supervisors, overt sexual harassment, a lack of sponsorship, and inadequate socialization and training. This study finds that female prison guards face almost identical phenomena when they work in men's prisons. As a consequence, it is virtually impossible for women to achieve equality on the job.

A great deal of the research on women in nontraditional ocupations is purely descriptive in nature (Meyer and Lee 1978; Wetherby 1977; Walshok 1981; Schreiber 1979); it provides rich details of women's experiences but little interpretation or analysis. In fact, the only recent empirical study of women in a nontraditional occupation that uses data to build toward a general theory for understanding women's experiences on the job (and their difficulties in making further occupational advances) is Rosabeth Kanter's *Men and Women of the Corporation* (1977). Other researchers have since utilized Kanter's conceptual formulations in interpreting their own data (Martin 1980; Rustad 1982; Riemer 1979; Stiehm 1982; Harland and Weiss 1982; Deaux and Ullman 1982), but they have generally not used those data to support either reformulations of or additions to Kanter's ground-breaking theory. This chapter examines Kanter's theory in light of the data gathered on female prison guards and explores some avenues for further development of a general theory of women's occupational experiences. In particular, it suggests the addition of individual level variables to Kanter's primarily structural model and an increased focus on the processes of formal and informal sex discrimination in the workplace.

The Gender versus Job Models of Women's Occupational Behavior

Although research and theory development concerning women who work in nontraditional jobs is a relatively new phenomenon, issues related to women and work have long been of interest to researchers. Of particular concern has been the determinants of women's labor force participation (Mahoney 1961; Sweet 1973; Gysbers et al. 1968; Dowdall 1974; Waite and Stolzenberg 1976), determinants of their occupational choice (Psathas 1968; Elder and Rockwell 1976; Nagley 1971; Crawford 1978; Wolkin 1972), and the resolution of conflicts between their work and family lives (Hoffman and Nye 1974; Howell 1973; Safilios-Rothschild 1970; Roscow and Rose 1972; Coser and Rokoff 1970; Hunt and Hunt 1977; Epstein 1980). The major assumption underlying much of this research is that women's relationships to their work (their occupational choices, attitudes toward the job, occupational behavior, commitment, satisfaction, and the like) are determined by factors related directly to their female status rather than factors inherent in the particular jobs they hold. As Roslyn Feldberg and Evelyn Glenn (1979) point out in their critique of this research, it utilizes a "gender model" of women's occupational behavior rather than the "job model" that forms the basis of research into men's occupational experiences.

The job model assumes that occupational choices and work-related attitudes and behaviors are the consequences of the conditions of employment; men's job satisfaction, for example, is assumed to depend on such work-related factors as pay, degree of on-the-job autonomy, and opportunity for advancement. As Feldberg and Glenn point out, even studies examining both male and female workers (e.g., Blauner 1964; Beynon and Blackburn 1972) often employ the job model when examining men and the gender model when examining women, without apparent realization that they are making such distinctions.

In recent years, a small body of research has tried to overcome this major bias in the study of work behavior by applying the job model to women. Joanne Miller and her colleagues (1979), for example, replicated with female workers a study formerly done on men which measures the effects of the job's "structural imperatives" (closeness of supervision, complexity of work tasks, opportunity for self direction, degree of bureaucratization, etc.) on workers' psychological functioning; they found that women react similarly to men. Joan Acker and Donald Van Houten (1974) examined the different forms of supervisor control used on male and female workers and found they critically affected workers' occupational behavior. But most important for present purposes, because it is the only "job model" approach which focuses on women in a traditionally male occupation, is Rosabeth Kanter's (1977) study of women in the corporate setting. It represents a substantial contribution to occupational sociology and an important foundation for a theory of women's experiences in the workplace in general as well as in nontraditional occupations specifically.

Kanter's Structural Model of Organizational Behavior

Kanter breaks from tradition by building a comprehensive theory of women's (and men's) behavior in the corporate world that does not include sex or gender roles as critical variables. Based on her research at "Indsco," Kanter identifies three dimensions of occupational *positions* that determine the behavior of men and women holding those positions. Because the focus is on the positions themselves, rather than the occupants, the job model is clearly being employed. The characteristics that Kanter finds to be most critical to the position of manager (in influencing managers' actual behavior) are opportunity, power, and relative numbers.

"Opportunity" refers to individuals' prospects for future advancement within the organization. Most salient to opportunity in the corporate context is the "career path" associated with each entry-level position. Some positions have low promotion rates, and people placed in those positions are likely to make horizontal rather than vertical moves. According to Kanter, when individuals are employed in "dead-end" positions that offer no chance for upward mobility within the corporation, they lower their aspirations, seek satisfaction in nonwork activities, and become parochial (that is, they become attached to a subunit of the organization rather than to the organization as a whole). People in positions offering greater opportunity have high aspirations, consider their work to be a central interest in their lives, and remain committed to organizational goals.

The behavior and attitudes of individuals in the organization are also affected by their access to power, defined by Kanter as "the capacity to mobilize resources" (p. 247). Again, different positions within the organization afford their occupants differing amounts of power; for persons in similar organizational positions, actual power might also depend on informal alliances with peers and superiors. According to Kanter, the amount of relative power obtained determines organizational behavior. She argues that people who possess little organizational power become rigid and authoritarian and use coercive rather than persuasive authority over subordinates. People with greater amounts of organizational power, on the other hand, are more communicative, cooperative, and allow subordinates greater latitude and discretion.

Finally, individuals' behavior within organizations is shaped by the relative number of "similar types" of people in comparable positions. People whose "type" is represented in a very small proportion will be highly visible, be stereotyped by others, be excluded from informal peer networks, and experience pressure not to make mistakes. In short, Kanter argues that they will suffer from the effects of "tokenism." In contrast, people whose "type" is in high proportion will quickly fit into the group, automatically have credibility, easily form strong peer alliances, and be likely candidates for sponsorship by higher-status members of the organization.

Kanter asserts that the behavior of workers can be traced to such factors as power, opportunity, and relative numbers embedded in the organizational positions they occupy. Their behavior will then often serve to reinforce the belief that these individuals were placed in organizational roles that were proper for them. Because most women at Indsco work in clerical and secretarial jobs that offer little power or opportunity for advancement, they exhibit the behaviors associated with low power and blocked opportunity. Their behavior thus reinforces the belief that women "naturally" exhibit these behaviors and therefore belong in these jobs. Kanter goes on to explain that when women are placed in positions that rank higher in power and opportunity, such as manager, they almost always work among men and, therefore, are affected by the structural conditions of tokenism. As in the case of women working in low-level positions, the behavior of women suffering from tokenism then serves as "proof" that women are not suited to higher-status occupational roles.

In keeping with her use of the job model rather than the gender model, Kanter is careful to explain that the experiences associated with tokenism are not dependent on sex:

> Certain popular conclusions and research findings about male-female relations or role potentials may turn critically on the issues of proportions. One study of mock jury deliberations found that men played proactive, task-oriented leadership roles, whereas women in the same groups tended to take reactive, emotional, and nurturant postures—supposed proof that traditional stereotypes reflect behavioral realities. But, strikingly, men far outnumbered women in all of the groups studied. Perhaps it was the women's scarcity that pushed them into classical positions and the men's numerical superiority that encouraged them to assert task superiority. Similarly, the early kibbutzim, collective villages in Israel that theoretically espoused equality of the sexes but were unable to fully implement it, could push women into traditional service positions because there were more than twice as many men as women. Again, relative numbers interfered with a fair test of what men or women can "naturally" do, as it did in the case of the relatively few women in the upper levels of Indsco. [P. 208]

Kanter's vocabulary for her theory of tokenism is purposefully sex neutral. Although her aim is to explain the organizational behavior of women in the corporate setting, she does not refer to men or women but to "the dominants" and "the few"; she does not talk about male-dominated groups but about groups that are "skewed"; and perhaps most important, she does not focus on sexism but on "tokenism." Kanter's implicit assumption is that men who work in predominantly female work groups will experience the same effects of tokenism as the female managers at Indsco.

Kanter's primary contribution is that she turns our attention away from the behavior of women as a group and directs it toward the behavior associated with the organizational roles women normally fill. She therefore suggests that "what appear to be 'sex differences' in work behavior emerge as responses to structural conditions, to one's place in the organization" (p. 262). Men in dead-end jobs in organizations behave similarly to women because these men are responding to the same structural conditions of powerlessness and blocked opportunity that affect most women.

Kanter concludes that neither the sex-linked behavior of women nor the sexist behavior of men in the corporation accounts for women's lack of advancement. Instead, women fail to achieve equality on the job (remaining in low-level positions and often failing to succeed in high-level ones) becuse of the way corporate positions are organized and filled. For this trend to be reversed, Kanter suggests organizational structures must change, not individual women or men.

Assessing Kanter's Job Model in Light of the Occupational Experiences of Female Prison Guards

Like Kanter's examination of men and women of the corporation, this study of the integrated prison finds important differences between the occupational experiences of male and female guards. Female guards meet opposition from male co-workers, discrimination in training and assignments, and ongoing sexual harassment; they also perform the job differently from most male guards by adopting one of the three strategies outlined in Chapter 6. How well does Kanter's sex-neutral theory of organizational behavior account for these sex differences?

Male and female guards fill identical organizational positions within the prison hierarchy so women do not suffer from the kind of "port of entry" discrimination experienced by Kanter's corporate women. Of course, as Kanter points out, even seemingly identical organizational positions do not necessarily enjoy the same levels of advancement opportunity and power. In the prisons, however, the position of guard itself is practically devoid of power (except vis-à-vis prisoners). Guard unionization, now present in many states, has given more power to guards as a group but has, if anything, limited the ability of individual workers to accumulate power through such informal means as alliances with co-workers and superiors. Many unions, including those in New York and Rhode Island, demand that rational criteria (for example, length of service) be used by management as the basis for making decisions on all employment matters. Differences between males' and females' occupational behavior, then, cannot be attributed to differences in power.

The position of prison guard also offers little opportunity for advancement to either males or females. There are no established career paths leading from security (guards) to treatment (counselors, teachers, and the like), and although guards can move into uniformed supervisory positions (sergeant, lieutenant, captain), the number of available slots remains small. Promotions are made primarily on the basis of written examination scores, and there is no evidence that these tests discriminate against women. In fact, women have been promoted into supervisory positions in many male prisons, although, at this point, primarily at the lower ranks. Nevertheless, most guards, male and female, never move beyond the level of guard. Kanter's variable of advancement opportunity, then, does not differ substantially among males and females and cannot account for differences in their occupational behavior.

Where the opportunities of male and female guards do differ is the opportunity to achieve training and experience on all posts in the male prison. This situation has been due, in part, to formal policies aimed at protecting inmate privacy. Such policies were especially prevalent in New York State while this research was being conducted although many of the restrictions on women's post assignments have since been removed by administrative mandate. In neither New York nor Rhode Island, however, are male and female guards now treated as "interchangeable." Even in Rhode Island, where the formal restrictions are minimal, female guards are prohibited from performing strip searches and must call for male assistance when this task needs to be done. Therefore, differing degrees of "near equality" mark the occupational experiences of female prison guards.

Although formal policies that dictate differential assignments of male and female guards are operative, they are probably less consequential than the informal assignment policies of many middle-level supervisors. When new guards enter the system they are subject to the discretion of superiors, who are virtually all male. As noted in Chapter 5, because of their own personal beliefs concerning women's capabilities, male supervisors often give different assignments to male and female trainees. Some supervisors assign women to difficult posts, hoping to discourage them from continued employment. Others seek to protect women by assigning them only to nondangerous positions. In either case, during their probationary period, women's assignments often are quite different from those of male trainees.

Finally, women's early experiences on the job are affected by the fact that most of their on-the-job training is conducted by more experienced male partners. With only a few exceptions, male guards are adamantly opposed to women's presence in men's prisons, and many of them, either consciously or unconsciously, provide new female trainees with inadequate training and occupational socialization. Many women report that male partners did not teach them the requirements of specific posts and sometimes refused to let them perform job-related tasks at all. In addition, female trainees were regularly told by male partners to "stay out of the way" during all kinds of disturbances or prison emergencies.

Although some differential treatment of female guards may be required by the law, most of it is the result of unsanctioned actions by male guards and male supervisors. Supervisors are given a great deal of discretion in assigning trainees to posts, and there is no automatic review of their decisions. Rank-and-file guards perform on-the-job training functions with very little supervision. As a consequence, any trainee may be subjected to unequal treatment for which there are few avenues of redress. Even individual males may be singled out for differential treatment; new female guards, however, are virtually guaranteed differential treatment. Occasionally they meet individual male co-workers willing to treat them as individuals and judge them on their merits, but they spend most of their time working with men whose actions reflect their belief that women should not work as guards in men's prisons.

Once female guards complete their probationary period (six months in Rhode Island, one year in New York), they are less subject to the discretionary power of male co-workers and supervisors. They can bid for the prison, shift, and assignment of their choice and receive union support if they suspect discriminatory treatment because of their sex. But by the time female guards obtain permanent status, a great deal of damage may already have been done and their ability to perform all aspects of the job will have been severely hampered. Women who receive inadequate on-the-job training and who work only on a limited range of nondangerous assignments will often lack both the self-confidence and the ability to perform many jobs in the prison. They may have finished their probationary period with very little direct, face-to-face contact with inmates and virtually no experience in handling violent situations. At least in part as a result of this limited experience, many women adopt either the modified role, continuing to avoid inmate contact as much as possible, or the inventive role, relying on the support and protection of male inmates. The few women adopting the institutional role will continue to try to perform all aspects of the job with little support from most of their male co-workers. So although Kanter's concept of advancement opportunity probably has little consequence for male and female guards' occupational behavior, their differential opportunity to be trained and gain experience and self-confidence on a wide variety of posts does severely limit women's ability to achieve equality on the job.

The final component of Kanter's structural theory of organizational behavior is what she calls "tokenism": the consequences of being "the few" among "the many." Female prison guards, like the female managers at Indsco, are "the few" within a predominantly male work force. Kanter maintains that tokenism is most prevalent in highly skewed groups, which she defines as having "a preponderance of one type over another, up to a ratio of perhaps 85:15" (p. 208). Although there may be a few exceptions, less than 15 percent of the guard forces of male prisons all around the country is female.

This study indicates that female guards experience the effects of tokenism as outlined by Kanter. Women guards in men's prisons are highly visible. They are not assimilated into the work group. And, at least from the perspective of male guards and administrators, differences between female and male guards are more prominent than are similarities. As a consequence, female guards are watched constantly and put under extraordinary pressure to perform successfully; they often become extremely self-conscious about their role performance and under such pressures find it difficult to perform the job. Deficiencies in their performance, real or perceived, then contribute to male guards' beliefs that women are unsuitable coworkers.

Kanter argues that the experiences associated with tokenism are not dependent on sex and that men working in predominantly female occupations would experience the same general effects as women working in predominantly male occupations. She is able to offer, however, only minimal evidence to support this sex-neutral claim. She interviewed one blind man who said he often felt conspicuous and pressured to succeed when working in a group of sighted people. Kanter also presents the results of an experimental study (Taylor and Fiske 1976) in which subjects who watched a film of group activity were found to pay more attention to a single black man in an otherwise all-white male group than they did to any of the individual white men. Subjects who watched films of integrated groups paid equal attention to blacks and whites. (No film depicted a group with black members and white token.) Finally, Kanter cites a study (Segal 1962) in which male nurses were isolated by their female coworkers. Although they were sometimes treated with deference by the women, they still experienced "role encapsulation" because, as tokens, they were treated as symbols. According to Kanter, "deference can be a patronizing reminder of difference, too" (p. 241).

On the one hand, then, Kanter does recognize that the actual consequences of tokenism differ depending on "the specific kinds of people and their history of relationships with dominants" (p. 212), but in discussing the behavior of female tokens, she virtually ignores the fact that, historically, relationships between men and women in this society are sexist in nature and that male tokens often benefit from token status while women are disadvantaged by it.

Recent studies of men in female-dominated occupations support the assertion that tokenism has different consequences for males than females. Carol Schreiber (1979) reports that both men and women in nontraditional jobs experience opposition, harassment, and teasing from their opposite-sex co-workers, but that these experiences are much more intense for women moving into traditionally male craft jobs than for men entering clerical occupations. Another important difference between the two situations is that men's opposition to their new female co-workers is often based on the males' assessment of women as incapable whereas opposition by women to entering men is based on a fear that these male newcomers will advance quickly in the organization, thereby retarding advancement by women.

Other evidence of the effects of tokenism on males who enter occupations traditionally held by women is equivocal. One study of male nurses finds little evidence of resistance or opposition to them from female co-workers (Fottler 1976). Other studies report that male nurses do experience opposition (Auster 1979; Silver and McAtee 1972), but in none of these cases was the opposition severe enough to be considered a major obstacle to their continued employment or to their occupational adjustment. Male elementary school teachers, according to Patrick Lee (1973), may be perceived as deviant and must be "rather impervious to social innuendo" (p. 85). Kevin Seifert (1973) found that "in the process of disproving children's sex-role stereotypes the male teacher may have to endure a bit more rejection from them than will a female teacher of comparable talent and temperament" (p. 169). And finally, Alfred Kadushin (1976), who began his study of male social workers expecting to find considerable "role strain" and problems with female co-workers, concluded that "most respondents did not find their status to be particularly troublesome" (p. 442). Only 10 percent reported problems with female colleagues, and these problems most often centered around the question of sexuality and the women's misinterpretations of friendly interactions. In fact, the most common problem named by male social workers concerned their interactions with other men outside the work setting; men in the community often perceived them as "odd" because of their occupational choice. Kadushin concludes that "regardless of problems that might exist, it is clear and undeniable that there is a considerable advantage in being a member of the male minority in any female profession" (p. 441).

The most obvious advantage for men moving into the "female professions" is that they have more opportunity to advance than do their female colleagues. In the field of social work, for example, in which women hold more than two-thirds of the positions, men are more likely to hold administrative jobs and are more likely to be elected as officers in professional voluntary organizations (Rosenblatt et al. 1971; Gripton 1974). Eighty-one percent of librarians are women, but males are more likely to be appointed head librarians—and at an earlier age (Blankenship 1971). Only 15 percent of elementary school teachers are male, but 79 percent of principals are male (Gross and Trusk 1976). Male nurses represent 1 percent of the profession but are highly overrepresented as nursing directors and presidents of nursing associations (Robinson 1973). On the other hand, women entering professions traditionally practiced by men receive no such advantage and are, in fact, likely to encounter resistance during their education and training and, once in the profession, opposition, hostility, and rejection from male peers and supervisors (Theodore 1971; Bourne and Winkler 1978; Epstein 1971, 1980; White 1975).

A final example of men's less traumatic experience in entering predominantly female work groups can be found in the sexual integration of the guard forces of women's prisons. Although my research did not focus on this aspect of the integration process, I did have the opportunity to interview several men who had recently begun to work in a female prison. They reported no opposition from female staff or administrators. In fact, the female warden at one women's prison told me that hiring the men guards was "the best thing that could have happened around here." She claimed that female inmates had started to keep the institution cleaner and had started to pay more attention to their personal hygiene. She hoped that the presence of men would lead to a decrease in lesbianism.

These examples of men's experiences as tokens suggest that being "the few" in a highly skewed work group has very different consequences for males and females. It may be that both males and females in nontraditional occupations suffer from the effects of tokenism, but the evidence strongly suggests that for women, the effects of tokenism are overpowered by the effects of sexism. Therefore, only a portion of the negative experiences of female prison guards (as well as those of women in other nontraditional occupations in which they occupy identical positions to men) can be attributed to tokenism itself. The concept is useful, but it provides only a partial explanation for the problems women face on the job and for their behavioral responses to them. Even if the sex ratio of the guard force were to become more balanced and the condition of tokenism eased, it is not at all clear that sexism would disappear.[1] Male guards' belief in female inferiority is often based on deeply ingrained assumptions about "natural" differences between men and women. Being viewed as inferior is not the same as being viewed as different. Therefore, the negative experiences of female guards can probably not be understood without considering the effects of both tokenism and sexism in the workplace.

This research on female guards suggests another important influence on occupational behavior that Kanter virtually omits from her analysis: the predispositions of women workers. Kanter's structural model of occupational behavior includes an explicit rejection of the "individual model," which she claims, locates

> at least some of the causes of injuries in the actions of the injured. . . . Individual models absolve the system of responsibility for manufacturing the psychology of their workers. They assume that organizations take people as they find them; the making and molding has all occurred before the workers enter the door. The slots exist for the kinds of people pre-designed to fit them. This view is highly misleading. Certainly people are prepared beforehand for careers set on tracks, and to some extent even develop the appropriate mind-set in advance. But to a very large degree, organizations make their workers into who they are. Adults change to fit the system. [Pp. 262–63]

Kanter's alternative to the individualistic model is to explain individual differences in occupational behavior in terms of the structural conditions of organizations and of positions within these organizations; because men and women are normally placed into different positions (with different structural constraints), they normally behave differently. By adding into this model the issue of sex stratification and sexism (and the kind of informal discriminatory policies it is likely to generate) we can, perhaps, even better understand why men's and women's occupational behavior tends to be different. What is still unexplained, however, is why women (or men) who work under nearly identical conditions exhibit varied forms of occupational behavior. Kanter, for example, found that women managers reacted to tokenism by adopting one of four "informal role types": the mother, the seductress, the pet, and the iron maiden. Are women forced into one or another "trap" by an additional set of structural constraints, or do women choose whichever role is most comfortable and compatible with their personality? Kanter provides no answer.

This study also finds some distinct differences in the occupational behavior of women working as guards in men's prisons. Each of the three dominant roles identified in Chapter 6 involves different techniques for handling common problems. How can we account for these three different strategies and for any specific woman's adoption of one rather than the others? Certainly occupational experiences (including the degree of male harassment, the depth of early training, and the like) play a role, but it is also clear that women's sex-role orientations (particularly their notions concerning women's ability to perform all aspects of the job of prison guard) were critical factors influencing women's responses to the job. Some women admitted that they began guard work with no intention of performing all aspects of the job and no desire to "behave like men." These women found some flexibility within the boundaries set by their formal organizational position and the constraints erected by male supervisors and co-workers; they were able to develop job performance strategies that, if not coinciding perfectly with their predispositions and desires, at least did not contradict them. They were not forced into a rigid, predetermined occupational role; nor were they forced into a special female guard role. Instead, female guards have molded and created jobs for themselves that are compatible with their individual characteristics and predispositions.

Although I am arguing that individual predispositions and desires are important factors shaping how female prisons guards adapt to the job, I also want to stress that Kanter's criticism of the "individual model" has merit. The individual model clearly would not be supportable if it were used as the primary explanation for occupational behavior; far too often, it has been used exclusively, especially when women workers have been examined. Whenever individual-level variables are included, they should be added with caution, because while they may be a necessary component, they are seldom if ever a sufficient explanation for occupational behavior. Female guards were able to incorporate traditional sex-role attitudes into the modified role, but only because male supervisors and male co-workers allowed and encouraged them to perform a limited range of duties. Without such support, the modified role probably would not be possible (except as female guards, like males, gained enough seniority to bid for noncontact positions). Likewise, the support of male inmates was critical to women's ability to adopt the inventive role; women's own predispositions provided only one component. Perhaps most interesting is the case of women in the institutional role. These women began employment with more liberal sex-role attitudes and were predisposed to perform all aspects of the job, but not all women with these predispositions ultimately adopted the institutional role.

For some women, early on-the-job experience, especially opposition and harassment from male co-workers, prompted them to abandon their efforts at equality in favor of the modified or inventive roles.

In no case, then, can we find a direct, causal relationship between sex-role attitude and occupational behavior. For each of the three job performance strategies adopted by women, structural conditions either facilitated or hindered women's preferred choices. Structural conditions also set the basic context in which special "female strategies" emerged in the first place. However, the fact remains that individual sex-role attitudes were a part of the strategy choice process and, in some cases, a substantial part. No women with traditional sex-role attitudes adopted the institutional role and although some women with more liberal attitudes drifted into the modified or inventive roles, women in the institutional role exhibited the most nontraditional sex-role orientations. Attention to individual-level variables is necessary, then, to understand differences in the occupational behavior of female prison guards.

Toward an Integrated Theory of Women's Occupational Experiences

Feldberg and Glenn (1979), in criticizing exclusive use of the gender model to study women, warn that the mere substitution of the job model could create as much distortion as it eliminates. In fact, they suggest an integration of these two models as a more useful way of studying the occupational behavior of both women and men. The data on female prison guards support this perspective: both job- and gender-related factors are critical to an understanding of women's occupational experiences and their adoption of performance strategies that differ considerably from those of their male co-workers.

Rosabeth Kanter's work provides a necessary foundation for such a theory. She sensitizes us to the necessity of examining how occupational positions are organized and filled. Understanding organizational structure and the constraints associated with each set of positions provides important insight into the occupational behavior of both male and female workers. A critical variable to be included in any theory of women's occupational behavior, then, is the formal organizational structure of the work environment, including the recruitment procedures for different positions and the behaviors encouraged by those positions. Kanter points out the importance of considering power, advancement opportunity, and relative numbers when examining organizational positions. Future research on occupational behavior may suggest additional structural variables that need to be examined as well.

While paying special attention to the kinds of job-related factors that have long been neglected in the study of women workers, an integrated theory of women's occupational behavior must also include issues of gender stratification. As Feldberg and Glenn (1979) point out, even when women workers are in a position to act like men, and in fact do act like men, they are often *treated* differently by others in the work environment. Female assembly line workers who performed their jobs exactly like their male co-workers have been, nonetheless, subjected to closer scrutiny and different forms of social control by male supervisors (Acker and VanHouten 1974). Female executives who successfully "learn the rules of the game" still often fail to move up the corporate ladder because many males will not treat them as credible players (West 1982). In the prisons, even women who achieve organizational positions identical to men's and try to perform all aspects of the job similarly to men are subjected to discriminatory treatment by male employees who are given some discretionary authority to make training decisions that affect them. The structural approach, with its focus on the formal hierarchy, fails to account for what Feldberg and Glenn (1979) call "the less visible forms of stratification that do not appear as formal organizational categories." The data on female prison guards support their suggestion that an "analysis of informal processes is needed to identify norms governing interpersonal relationships between men and women in work organizations" (p. 534).

Some interpersonal relationships between men and women in organizations are undoubtedly governed by the relative numbers of each group as Kanter suggests in her description of tokenism; however, the sexist attitudes and behaviors of men who work in newly integrated occupations must be considered as well. In some occupations—such as the legal profession—male opposition and harassment have decreased considerably in recent years (Epstein 1980), while in others—including that of prison guard—male opposition and harassment remain strong. These differences in male behavior might be attributable to tokenism, to the degree to which male workers in these settings hold sexist attitudes, or to some combination of the two. Sexist attitudes might be further linked to the educational and class backgrounds of male workers in different occupations,[2] or to the nature of different jobs themselves; the job of lawyer, after all, requires verbal and writing skills that are not substantially sex-typed whereas the job of prison guard, especially as currently defined by male guards themselves, requires the traits of strength, aggressiveness, and authoritativeness which are highly sex-typed male. Researchers of women in nontraditional occupations have not tried to untangle these various factors, but have generally followed Kanter's lead in identifying many of women's problems on the job as resulting from tokenism (e.g., Rustad 1982; Hammond and Mahoney 1983; Martin 1980; Stiehm 1982; Deaux and Ullman 1982; Riemer 1979). At this point, there is simply not enough evidence to conclude that tokenism—rather than blatant sexism—is primarily responsible for women's problems on the job, and the evidence on men in token positions strongly suggests the opposite. The sexist attitudes and actions of male co-workers, supervisors, and employers must be included in an integrated theory of women's occupational behavior and the degree to which negative male behavior depends on the relative numbers of male and female employees researched more carefully before it is given such theoretical importance.

Finally, a theory of women's occupational experiences must include individual-level variables such as personality characteristics, attitudes, beliefs, and preferred ways of doing things. Women's occupational behavior differs from men's not only because of differences in their organizational positions, the effects of tokenism, or the sexist actions of others in the organization, but also because, in contemporary American society, female workers often enter the employment setting with skills, attitudes, beliefs, and prior experiences that are different from those of their male co-workers. Differences between male and female workers cannot automatically be assumed to be sex-linked, for as Kanter correctly points out, there is both a wide range of differences among women and a great overlap between the work behavior and attitudes of men and women. However, a theory of women's occupational behavior should not totally ignore the continuing differences between males and females in our society.

Nor should individual differences *between* women be ignored, because only by examining these differences can we begin to understand why women workers within a single organizational setting exhibit such varied occupational behaviors. Several studies have found important differences between women in terms of their orientation toward the job and, like the current study, have found that some women adopt "typically feminine" job performance strategies (Kanter 1977; Epstein 1980; Martin 1980; Rustad 1982). None of these studies, however, explores the reasons for these differences. This study did identify women's sex-role attitudes as a critical variable affecting their behavior on the job and their choice of a job performance strategy. It did not, however, focus on the source of those attitudinal differences and their possible relationship to women's race, social class, age, or urban/rural background. Future research might focus more explicitly on these social characteristic variables and their relationship to differences among women workers. For the time being, however, women's actual sex-role attitudes seem to be an important factor in women's behavior in some jobs, especially jobs like prison guard which offer some flexibility in how the job can be performed. Other jobs may, of course, offer less opportunity (or reason) for "typically feminine" role adaptations.

Conclusion

In comparison to theories of occupational segregation (Hartmann 1976; Glenn and Feldberg 1982; Doeringer and Piore 1975; Bibb and Form 1977; Blau and Jusenius 1976), the theory of women's occupational behavior—particularly in nontraditional jobs—is in its nascent stages. Rosabeth Kanter has proposed a sex-neutral theory that is, in many ways, appealing because it avoids the sex-biased assumptions of the gender model which has, for so long, guided the study of women and work. However, Kanter's theory cannot fully account for the work experiences of female prison guards. Of course, those experiences may very well be unique: the job of prison guard is more highly sex-typed male than most nontraditional jobs into which women have recently moved; the period of integration has been marked by continual legal turmoil; and some degree of male-female inequality on the job has, in fact, been legally sanctioned. But at the same time, a general theory of occupational behavior should at least contain the components necessary for analyzing diverse work settings. And while gender-based theories can be faulted for failing to include work-setting characteristics at all, Kanter's theory can be faulted for its failure to incorporate findings from settings other than the corporation. Data from the prisons suggest that Kanter's theory of organizational behavior cannot stand alone as a general theory for understanding women's experiences on the job. I therefore agree with Feldberg and Glenn that a new paradigm is needed. It not only should include the structural elements found in the job model and individualistic elements from the gender model, but also should focus explicitly on how these factors combine and interact to produce particular outcomes. Because it pays special attention to the rela-

tionship between the individual and the group and the inter-
dependency between the roles of group members, the interactionist
perspective[3] may offer the best framework for analyzing the outcomes as well as the processes through which women's work experiences are created. It is my belief that a general theory of women's
occupational behavior must be developed cautiously and be
grounded in data gathered from a wide range of traditional and
nontraditional work settings over time.[4] I hope the data presented
here on female guards, and my analysis of those data in terms of
existing theory, will prove useful in that pursuit.

Appendix: Research Methodology

This study was undertaken in the ethnographic tradition exemplified by the work of sociologists such as Gerald Suttles (1968), William Foote Whyte (1943, 1948), Elliot Liebow (1967), Herbert Gans (1962), and Howard Becker (1963). The goal of such work is "to make a set of integrated observations on a given topic and place them in an analytic framework" (Schwartz and Jacobs 1979:289). The first step is to describe the phenomenon under study as accurately and with as much detail as possible. The second is to relate observed phenomena to important features of the social context in which they occur.

One can, of course, never account for all features of the social context in which any particular social phenomenon is embedded, but for a study of female prison guards, some aspects of the social context stand out as especially crucial for understanding the experiences of the women themselves as well as other participants in the change. These aspects include the legal framework that prompted and guided women's employment as guards; the specific environment in which this change took place (the American prison in the 1970s); and the sex-role definitions that guide the attitudes and interactions of all participants. A sociological study of female prison guards requires that the events and experiences studied be examined and analyzed within an understanding of these broader social phenomena.

Although this study began with some expectations derived from the recent literature on female guards and the more general literature on occupations, it also follows the view of Barney Glaser and Anselm Straus (1967) that it is not necessarily productive to begin an ethnographic study with a clear set of research questions or hypotheses:

> To be sure, one goes out and studies an area with a particular sociological perspective, and with a focus, a general question, or a problem in mind. But he can (and we believe should) also study an area without any preconceived theory that dictates, prior to the research, "relevancies" in concepts and hypotheses. Indeed, it is presumptuous to assume that one begins to know the relevant categories and hypotheses until the "first few days in the field," at least, are over. [Pp. 33–34]

Soon after the research began, it became apparent that the original questions either were largely irrelevant or did not deal with the most interesting aspects of the experiences of female guards. Therefore, the important research questions were allowed to emerge during the research process. As the research progressed, for example, major distinctions *among* female guards became evident. The existing literature on women in nontraditional occupations, which served as the initial basis for developing tentative research questions, does not suggest that such distinctions would be important. Had this research design not been flexible, the data and analysis presented in the following chapters would have been very different. Glaser and Straus (1967) stress that flexibility is a good reason for virtually ignoring the theoretical literature on a topic:

> An effective strategy is, at first, literally to ignore the literature of theory and fact on the area under study, in order to assure that the emergence of categories will not be contaminated by concepts more suited to different areas. Similarities and convergences with the literature can be established after the analytic core of categories has emerged. [P. 37]

The inductive, grounded-theory approach allowed this project to change and evolve, eventually focusing most intensely on the different strategies female guards use for creating stable occupational roles in a largely hostile work environment.

Information on female guards was gathered from many sources, but the New York and Rhode Island prison systems were chosen as the primary sites for data collection. New York offered a large and diverse correctional system in which women had been working in men's prisons for almost a decade. By 1980, 275 women guards were working in male prisons. Statewide, women held almost 4 percent of such jobs although their distribution was not equal throughout the various facilities. The Rhode Island prison system was chosen primarily because, unlike New York, where administrators began to integrate women into the male guard force shortly after passage of the 1972 amendments to Title VII, administrators in Rhode Island long resisted implementation of this change. When the research began in 1980, the first few women had just begun working in Rhode Island's male prisons. Several high-level administrators in the Rhode Island system encouraged a study of this change while it was occurring. Conducting the research in these two states, then, offered the opportunity to obtain information at two different phases of the integration process.

Just as ethnographic research requires some flexibility in defining the research problem, it also requires flexibility in technique (Bogdon and Taylor 1975). Participant observation is well suited to ethnographic research, but the prison is a difficult environment in which to do this, especially for a female researcher. Some areas of the prison, such as inmate segregation units, may be totally off limits to female visitors. Other areas are potentially dangerous. Only one warden gave me permission to leave the administrative wing of the prison to interview male inmates in their housing areas. At that time I was also able to observe female guards on the job. Most observation, however, was limited to lunch rooms, locker rooms, and administrative offices, the areas where most interviews with male and female guards were conducted. Although limited, these settings did provide valuable opportunities to observe male and female guards in informal interactions. These observations turned out to be an important supplement to the information gained through interviews.

The primary data-gathering technique used was the unstructured, open-ended interview (Lofland 1971; Bogdon and Taylor 1975). This form of interview was chosen because it allows "appropriate or relevant questions . . . to emerge from the research process of interaction that occurs between interviewer and interviewees" (Schwartz and Jacobs 1979:40). The major exception to this unstructured format was a short list of standardized questions that were asked of all female guards to assess their attitudes toward the "proper" roles of males and females in society (see Chap. 3).

Over a period of nearly two years, I conducted in-depth interviews in New York and Rhode Island with female guards, male guards, inmates, and prison administrators at both the central office and local levels. Seventy female guards working in male prisons were interviewed. In Rhode Island, women from all the male prisons were represented (minimum, medium, maximum, and high-security prisons as well as the drug abuse unit). Because only a small number of women work as guards in Rhode Island's male prisons (approximately fifteen at any one time), all female guards there were interviewed. In New York, the women interviewed came from different prisons throughout the state. Most, however, worked in one of three prisons: an upstate, rural, maximum-security prison, a downstate maximum-security prison, or a downstate minimum-security facility. About 20 percent of the female guards working in New York prisons were interviewed. Most of the interviews with women were not scheduled until I had arrived at each prison. In most cases, administrators arranged appointments for me. At times, women approached me and volunteered for interviews. The women I interviewed often suggested names of several other women who might agree to talk with me. Through these various methods I was able, in some prisons, to interview nearly all the female guards.

The length of the interviews varied greatly depending on the stage of research and the characteristics of the women interviewed. Some interviewees were especially verbal and articulate and were eager to share details of their personal lives as well as their experiences on the job. Others were willing to give only brief answers to specific questions about themselves or the job. With such women, probing techniques were used to "draw them out." As the research progressed and the important issues became better defined, the need for lengthy interviews decreased. Glaser and Straus (1967) find this structure typical of the grounded-theory approach to research:

> At the beginning of the research, interviews usually consist of open-ended conversations during which respondents are allowed to talk with no imposed limitations of time. Often the researcher sits back and listens while the respondents tell their stories. Later, when interviews and observations are directed by the emerging theory, he can ask direct questions bearing on these categories. These can be answered sufficiently and fairly quickly. Thus, the time for any one interview grows shorter as the number of interviews increases, because the researcher now questions many people, in different positions and different groups, about the same topics. [Pp. 75–76]

Although interviews with female guards were the most important part of the study, it was also necessary to interview those who shaped policy concerning these guards and those who interacted with them on a daily basis. At each prison I visited, I interviewed as many male guards as possible. I spent considerable time in the employee lounges in each prison, often waiting for the opportunity to interview women. As male guards wandered in, I initiated conversations with them about the prison in general and about their attitudes toward female guards. Sometimes male guards who heard that I was doing research in the prison asked to be interviewed. During the course of the research, I interviewed almost one hundred male guards in New York and Rhode Island prisons. Some of these interviews were very brief; others lasted an hour or more. These interviews were invaluable for understanding the work environment and the attitudes of male guards toward women's presence in the prison.

I also interviewed high-level personnel from the central administrative offices in the New York and Rhode Island systems. They were asked about general policies concerning women, how these policies had changed over time, and any continuing problems pertaining to women's integration into the guard force.

At each local prison, I talked with wardens, their top staff, and the middle-level supervisors (sergeants, lieutenants, and captains), who are largely responsible for assigning female guards to posts and evaluating their performance. They were asked about the integration process at their institution and any problems caused by women's presence.

Obtaining permission to interview male inmates was the most difficult problem. In Rhode Island I obtained permission to conduct interviews at the few facilities where several female guards were assigned to work full time. Twenty-seven inmates from the high-security unit and ten inmates from minimum-security were included in the study. Most of these were individual interviews, but occasionally two or more inmates were present at one time. In New York State, wardens flatly refused to allow interviews with male inmates without permission from the central office in Albany. This office never responded to my written requests.

Whenever possible, I collected relevant documents from each prison and the central administrative offices in New York and Rhode Island. These include letters, memos, internal reports, rule books, legal briefs, and administrative memorandums. Many were extremely helpful for the final analysis and provided a valuable supplement to the data collected through interviews and observations.

One of the most difficult and frustrating decisions in this research project was when to end the data collection phase. To some extent, a "natural" ending came when I had clarified three distinct job performance strategies adopted by female guards and had confirmed them through further interviews. But even after this point, many other interesting events concerning female guards occurred, and I was tempted at times to recontact my informants in the prison to update my information. Shortly after I left the field, a very important event occurred in New York. Administrators there substantially altered the policy for deploying female guards. I have briefly noted that change but was unable to return to the field to explore some important questions relating to it. What prompted the change in policy? How was it received by local prison administrators? What changes has it meant for female guards? I am still very curious about these questions but have resisted the temptation to investigate them further at this point. This dilemma exemplifies the time-bound nature of all social science research, especially that which examines social change. Social action continues after the researcher has left the field: new people enter the setting, new problems emerge, and new solutions are found. No researcher can keep up with all of it, although the desire to do so can be very compelling, particularly when the research strategy has been one that encourages emotional involvement and near total immersion in the setting. At best, the researcher can offer insights into a particular social phenomenon at a particular time that will be useful for understanding others.

Notes

Chapter 1

1. 42 U.S.C. 2000e-2 (1976).

2. Title VII was the first federal employment legislation to treat sex as a protected category, although The Equal Pay Act of 1963 did prohibit wage discrimination on the basis of sex. Before 1964, employment discrimination was explicitly prohibited only on the basis of race, religion, or national origin (Burnstein and MacLeod 1980). After 1964, all employment legislation followed the Title VII precedent and included a prohibition of sex discrimination. For example, Executive Order No. 11375 (1967) prohibits sex discrimination by employers who have federal contracts. Executive Order No. 11478 (1969) prohibits the federal government from engaging in sex discrimination in matters of employment. Title IX of the Education amendments of 1972 (20 U.S.C. 620) prohibits sex discrimination by educational institutions that use federal funds.

3. See *Business Week*, 25 November 1972, pp. 42–46.

4. William Evans (1964) points out that law is most effective in promoting social change when it provides for immediate enforcement and when those charged with enforcement are committed to the change. The 1972 amendments to Title VII provided the enforcement potential; members of the EEOC provided the initiative.

5. 42 U.S.C. 2000e-2 (1976), 703 (e).

6. EEOC Guidelines on Sex Discrimination, 29 C.F.R. 1604.2 (a) (11) (1976).

7. Rosenfeld v. Southern Pacific Company, 444 F.2d 1219 (9th Cir. 1971); Diaz v. Pan American World Airlines, 422 F.2d 385 (5th Cir. 1971); Weeks v. Southern Bell Telephone Co., 408 F.2d 228 (5th Cir. 1969).

8. Long v. California State Personnel Board, 41, Cal. App. 3d 1000, 116 Cal. Rpts. 562 (1974); City of Philadelphia v. Pennsylvania Human Relations Commissioner, 7 Pa. Commw. Ct. 500, 300 A.2d 97 (1973); Dothard v. Rawlinson, 433 U.S. 321 (1977).

9. 433 U.S. 321 (1977).

10. Among positions that Alabama had defined as inappropriate were ones that required the patrolling of dormitories, restrooms, and showers, the searching of inmates of the opposite sex, or any direct contact with inmates of the opposite sex without other persons present. This undoubtedly included a large proportion of available posts.

11. Although not using *Rawlinson* as precedent, a decision concerning the use of opposite-sex guards in New York State in 1978 was consistent with *Rawlinson*. See Carey v. New York State Human Rights Appeal Board, 61 A.D.2d 804 (1978).

12. 612 F.2d 1079 (1980).

13. 520 F. Supp. 769 (1981).

14. For example, in Avery v. Perrin [473 F. Supp. 90 (1979)], the court held that use of a female guard to deliver mail at a regularly scheduled time in a New Hampshire male prison did not violate inmate right to privacy.

15. 514 F. Supp. 201 (1981).

16. 494 F. Supp. 890 (1980).

17. 621 F.2d 1210 (1980).

18. Geoffrey Alpert (1984) suggests that social scientists design research that will provide a better foundation for judicial decision making. He points specifically to the case of female guards in men's prisons as an example in which the courts have been required to make decisions without any empirical evidence on the issues raised by sexual integration. As research on female guards accumulates, then, the legal situation may very well change.

19. The same problems have arisen with efforts by the military to divide all jobs into combat and non-combat-related categories. See Quester (1982) and Segal (1982) for discussion of these difficulties and how they affect sexual integration of military jobs.

20. In many states, including New York and Rhode Island, a current constraint on deployment is a union contract which grants employees seniority rights in matters of assignment. With few exceptions, guards can bid for the prison, shift, and post of their choice, removing these deployment decisions from the discretion of administrators.

21. Although the current study involves a single case study of a rather unique occupation, Wolf and Kendall (1955) point out that the "deviant case" is often useful for defining the edges of theory.

Chapter 2

1. Most of the major sociological studies of American prisons focus on maximum-security facilities. Some of the generalizations made from this literature may not apply to the minimum-security prisons, work-release facilities, or prison camps that house a large portion of inmates. All of the prisons in a single state, however, are administered by the same central agency and, of course, are subject to the same state and federal laws.

2. Many state legislatures have revamped their penal codes in recent

years, setting more stringent guidelines for administration of the prisons (Hawkins 1976; McGee 1981). New York State law, for example, now sets detailed standards for handling cases of inmate misbehavior (New York State Correction Law 250–253, 6 (1970)). Prison administrators must promulgate administrative rules that implement these legislative mandates.

3. Before the 1960s, the courts had taken a "hands off" stance toward state prison systems on the grounds that prisoners were "slaves of the state" (Ruffin v. Commonwealth, 62 Va. 790 (1871)). Prison administrators possessed near absolute power to set the conditions of confinement.

4. Before prison systems became more centralized and bureaucratic, wardens at each individual prison were free to run them as personal "fiefdoms," unconstrained by higher-level administrators or legal guidelines for operation. Jacobs (1977) traces the history of this change in the Illinois system, McCleery (1961) in the Hawaii system.

5. Treatment and service personnel (such as teachers, counselors, and medical staff) do not generally fall within this paramilitary chain of command, but are directly responsible to the warden or the deputy warden in charge of treatment and programs.

6. In the 1940s and 1950s, for example, researchers found inmate solidarity and adherence to an inmate code that stressed loyalty among prisoners and opposition to the staff and its values (Clemmer 1940; Sykes 1958). These subcultures emerged, according to Sykes and Messinger (1960) as a functional adaptation to the economic, social, and sexual deprivations of prison life. In 1962, Irwin and Cressey suggested that at least some inmate subcultures are imported from the outside and reflect values that inmates bring to prison with them. In the early 1970s, the most prominent inmate subculture became based on political activism, open defiance of prison rules, and violence against prison staff (Irwin 1980). For a review of the extensive literature on prisoner subcultures, see Bowker (1977).

7. In a California prison described by Rundle (1973), the racial group with the most power had access to the television, determining what programs would be watched. Carroll (1974) and Bartollas et al. (1976) described similar patterns in which blacks intimidate whites to control music, television, and recreation areas. See also Jacobs (1979a).

8. Irwin (1980) describes how the sub rosa economic system of the prison has been taken over and expanded by powerful gangs. They often gain access to desired commodities by stealing them from the least powerful inmates.

9. Park (1976) notes that the increase in prison violence can be accounted for, in part, by the increase in violent offenders in the prison population. In 1973, 71 percent of newly incarcerated inmates in California had a history of violence. Prison administrators, of course, have no control over the type of inmates they receive.

10. After widespread support for rehabilitative programs during the 1950s and 1960s, enthusiasm began to wane as prison scholars questioned

their effectiveness (Martinson 1974; Lipton et al. 1975) and their rationale (Morris 1974; Fogel 1975; Hawkins 1976). Today, although many treatment programs continue to operate, there is less optimism about their value in changing inmate behavior.

11. According to John Irwin (1980), prison administrators have had a lot of influence over the decisions made by parole boards and have been able to "threaten" inmates with a longer sentence if they misbehave. However, advocates of determinate or flat sentencing, such as Federal Bureau of Prisons Director Norman Carlson (Bureau of the Prisons 1981) and Andrew von Hirsch (von Hirsch and Hanrahan 1979), claim that parole is not an effective means of prison discipline and that indeterminacy may create more discipline problems than it solves because inmate uncertainty over release date leads to tensions, frustration, and anger.

12. In Jackson v. Bishop, 404 F.2d 571 (1968), corporal punishment was defined as cruel and unusual punishment. Many states, however, had already prohibited its use.

13. In Hutto v. Finney, 437 U.S. 678 (1978), the court prohibited the prolonged use of solitary confinement as a form of discipline. Bone v. Saxbe, 660 F.2d 609 (1980), set minimum health and hygiene standards for segregation.

14. Wolf v. McDonnell, 418 U.S. 539 (1974).

15. Only guards who work in the towers or on perimeter patrol have regular access to guns. Those who work inside the prison cannot carry guns because there is too much chance that inmates would overpower guards and take the weapons. Many inmates, however, regularly carry homemade, but lethal, weapons.

16. The average guard to prisoner ratio in this country is one to six, although there is substantial variation between states (Parisi et al. 1979). But because the staff is spread over three separate shifts (and additional allowance must be made for weekends, vacations, absenteeism, and sick leave), Bowker (1980) estimates that at any one time, the actual ratio is closer to one to thirty or thirty-five. In addition, many guards work on those posts necessary to prevent escapes—walls, outside gates, and control rooms—rather than in direct supervision of inmates. Therefore, it is a small number of guards actually supervising large numbers of inmates.

17. When inmates commit serious crimes, they can be prosecuted in the criminal court system in the jurisdiction in which the prison is located, but criminal prosecution is often hampered by a lack of reliable witnesses and a lack of admissable evidence. Therefore, many criminal violations occurring in the prisons are handled administratively and inmates receive prison discipline rather than an additional criminal sentence.

18. At the extreme, inmates may be able to "force" guards to bring in contraband for them in exchange for continued cooperation or in exchange for the guards' own personal safety. This potential for complete "corruption of authority" is what motivates prison officials to warn all new guards against any kind of "arrangements" with inmates.

19. Bowker (1980) found that inmates may protect some guards from injury during prison riots. Knowing this, a guard may be motivated to be "a nice guy" and ignore petty rule violation by inmates.

20. The guards' fear is hardly paranoia. Sylvester et al. (1977) calculate that a guard, over a twenty-year career, has a one in 200 possibility of being killed in the line of duty.

21. According to Blau and Scott (1962) this change is typical of organizations undergoing centralization. A large organization with geographically dispersed units must rely increasingly on the use of written reports by subordinates to maintain control over the units.

22. New York State Department of Correctional Services, Directive #4909 (1977).

23. A large proportion of training time at the academies in New York and Rhode Island is spent on teaching trainees these report-writing skills.

24. Thomas (1972) notes the same reaction by guards in English prisons, where the rehabilitative ideal was being implemented at about the same time as in American prisons.

25. What is most ironic about guards' longing for the "good old days" is that, by all accounts, they were not that good. Jacobs (1977), for example, points out that until recently, most guards were under the autocratic (and often unjust) control of wardens and had little job security.

26. Some guards fail to adopt the values, beliefs, and attitudes of the guard subculture. They reject the emphasis on masculinity and the notion that inmates cannot be trusted. They may also fail to socialize with co-workers after work hours. Some guards, especially those hoping to move up through the ranks, remain more committed to organizational goals than to fellow officers.

27. Most of these were illegal job actions. At the same time, many unions used legal channels (such as the federal courts) to force administrative changes. The New York union filed a lawsuit seeking relief from prison overcrowding (Wynne 1978a). In both New York and California, guard unions used the courts to challenge administrative policies for the hiring and promotion of minority guards (Wynne 1978a; Zimmer and Jacobs 1981).

28. Some contracts allow a few posts to be excluded from the general seniority system because prison administrators claim that special qualifications are necessary. The Rhode Island contract, for example, exempts posts in the hospital, the "Behavioral Conditioning Unit" in maximum-security, and "Cellblock South" in medium-security. The contract also provides for a Review Committee (made up of two administrators and a union representative) to decide whether a bid should be granted in cases where the warden of the facility involved feels the guard is not capable of performing the bid (Article X, Agreement between State of Rhode Island and the Rhode Island Brotherhood of Correctional Officers, July 1977). Thus, Rhode Island's seniority provision, which offers more protection to workers than that in any other state (Zimmer 1985), still leaves some room for administrative discretion in matters of assignment.

29. The probationary period lasts one year in New York and six months in Rhode Island.

30. Wynne (1978b) claims that union leaders often have direct access to political leaders in the state legislature and that the increased power of guards has resulted in a decrease in the resources that are allocated to treatment and educational programs for inmates. In states like Montana, where the state legislature sets the pay scales for state employees, guard strikes aim to influence politicians rather than prison administrators (Jacobs and Zimmer 1981).

31. In fact, in recent years, guards have transferred some of their anger toward the job to the union and union leaders. The 1979 strike by New York guards was, at least in part, a rank-and-file rebellion against the union for not delivering on its promise to bargain firmly with the state (Zimmer and Jacobs 1981).

32. The amount of seniority needed to obtain a noncontact post differs from prison to prison. At some stable institutions with a low turnover rate, guards may advance up the seniority list slowly. At other institutions, two years on the job may place one near the top of the list and enable a guard to choose a noncontact job.

Chapter 3

1. Although the occupational choice literature generally fails to make this disclaimer, it is important to remember that the choices people make are never entirely free. Structural and economic constraints operating on the labor market affect the kinds of jobs available (Blau et al. 1956). Employers themselves make selections both on the basis of candidates' "human capital" (Becker 1957, 1980; Mincer 1958; Staehle 1943) and their own stereotypes about particular groups of people (Phelps 1972; Thurow 1975). According to Doeringer and Piore (1971), women have been more constrained than men in making free occupational choices because many employers, believing in female inferiority, prevent women from capitalizing on their qualifications. By making it illegal for employers to discriminate against women, Title VII has been responsible for providing women with at least more occupational choice than they had previously.

2. A recent study by Glenna Spitze and Linda Waite (1980) found contrary results. Using data from the National Longitudinal Study of Young Women, they found that sex-role attitudes played virtually no role in women's decision to participate in the labor force, although they did affect women's job satisfaction.

3. Other studies have successfully linked family characteristics to women's traditional and nontraditional occupational choices. See, for example, Tangri (1972), O'Donnell and Anderson (1978), Treiman and Terrell (1975), Astin (1969), and Auster and Auster (1981).

4. This is fairly common among male guards as well. Many originally aspire to police work and then "settle" for a job in corrections.

5. One traditionally male blue-collar occupation in which money seems to have been less of a factor is trucking. Muriel Lembright and Jeffrey Riemer (1981) found that women chose these jobs primarily to be near their husbands or boyfriends who were also truckers.

6. The scant evidence available concerning women who work in female prisons indicates that money and lack of other opportunities are the major attractions there as well (Feinman 1980; Giallombardo 1966).

7. Much of the research on occupational choice focuses exclusively on either college students or working professionals. Very little is known about how blue-collar workers choose jobs. Kay Deaux and Joseph Ullman (1982) point out the extent to which this class bias pervades the entire study of work and occupations.

8. It is not only female prison guards who work at jobs for which they feel women are basically illsuited. Durning (1978) found that anywhere from 5 to 15 percent of the female cadets at Annapolis at any one time agreed that the Navy should limit opportunities for females.

9. Although there is a lot of research to connect women's sex-role attitudes to their behavior, the causal sequence may have been misinterpreted. Marvin Harris (1981) and Valerie Oppenheimer (1970, 1982) both present strong arguments that, at least in terms of labor force participation by women, liberated behavior preceded liberal sex-role attitudes. It could be that the liberal sex-role attitudes of "pioneer" women found by Nagely (1971), Crawford (1978), and Fitzgerald (1976) appeared after employment in nontraditional jobs. This still does not explain the traditional sex-role attitudes of female prison guards, but it is possible that as traditional as those attitudes are, they are less conservative than prior to employment in the prisons. This question of the causal effect of sex-role attitudes on occupational choice simply cannot be answered using data gathered after employment has begun.

10. These data came from forms which guard recruits filled out when applying for the job. Because the information on college experience is self-reported, it may be inflated. This should not necessarily invalidate the comparisons between male and female recruits, however.

11. Deaux and Ullman (1983), Walshok (1981), and Lembright and Riemer (1982) found the same kind of typically female occupational experiences in the backgrounds of the women they studied who had recently moved into male-dominated blue-collar jobs.

12. Data obtained from New York State Training academy records, Albany, New York.

13. As James Jacobs (1979b) points out, there are somewhat different issues involved in the use of male guards in women's prisons and the use of female guards in men's prisons. While the privacy issues are similar, female inmates may be in danger of sexual abuse and violence by male guards. He therefore concludes that the "courts should be less reluctant to permit a BFOQ classification for guard positions in women's prisons" (p. 416). The

courts have not been directly confronted with this issue and there has been no differentiation between the employment protections given to male and female guards. A lawsuit filed by female inmates over the danger of sexual abuse (rather than privacy per se) could change that and add another dimension to the current legal ambiguities surrounding sexual integration in corrections.

14. The Rhode Island department is able to more easily train all new guards in every facility because all of the institutions are located together in a giant institutional complex in Cranston, Rhode Island.

15. Some of the differences among women have important consequences for their adjustment to the job and their strategies for performing the job. These matters will be covered in detail in Chap. 6.

16. One way in which female guards do differ from the general population of women is that they are much more likely to be minority group members. Approximately 50 percent of the women are black and Hispanic, most of them recruited from major metropolitan areas. Deaux and Ullman (1983) found the same proportions among the female steel workers they studied, and it appears to be the case that as women move into traditionally male occupations, minority women move into blue-collar jobs and white women into professional jobs. If that trend continues, occupational integration by sex will have little impact on the racial segregation of the work force.

Chapter 4

1. The category "sex" was first included in the Civil Rights Act by opponents to the bill who hoped it would guarantee the bill's defeat by splitting the coalition supporting it (Orfield 1975). In fact, the announcement to include sex as a protected category was met with laughter throughout the House chambers, and even Esther Peterson, head of the Department of Labor's Women's Bureau, spoke against its inclusion, stating that it would "not serve the interests of women at this time" (Robinson 1979:416). The American Association of University Women also opposed the inclusion of sex for fear it would cause the bill's defeat and deny needed protection to minorities. The bill, of course, was eventually passed, with the category sex included, and according to Orfield (1975), this occurred only because President Johnson urged congressional liberals to get the bill passed quickly—and not take time to tamper with it—while President Kennedy's assassination remained fresh in people's minds and increased support for legislation he had sponsored. Sachs and Wilson (1978) report that there is "every indication that Congress did not act with full knowledge of what it was doing" (p. 210).

2. According to *New York Times* coverage of the amendments' passage, the only serious congressional debate concerned the nature of the new enforcement powers to be given to the EEOC (25 January 1972, p. 25; 9 February 1972, p. 1; 18 February 1972, p. 23; 22 February 1972, p. 43; 23 February 1972, p. 1; 9 March 1972, p. 28).

3. An outspoken opponent of the ERA, Phyllis Schlafly, devoted an entire publication, the *Phyllis Schlafly Report*, to the defeat of the ERA and the promotion of traditional roles for women. One volume even included the story of a female prison guard working at San Quentin as an example of "an excess of equality" (April 1973, p. 3). Additional antifeminist literature, such as Schlafly's *The Power of the Positive Woman*, George Gilder's *Sexual Suicide*, Marabelle Morgan's *The Total Woman*, and Helen Andelin's *Fascinating Woman*, also appeared during this period and gained avid followers among both men and women.

4. There had, in fact, been considerable opposition to women working in support positions in men's prisons. As late as 1971, eight states still did not hire women for any jobs in men's prisons (Morton 1979). In New York, the Department of Correctional Services (with support from the Human Rights Appeal Board) prohibited women from many jobs in men's prisons, including that of cook, until ordered to reverse its policy by the state court. See State Division of Human Rights on complaint of Frances E. Cox v. New York State Department of Correctional Services, 61 A.D.2d (1978).

5. One important group left out of this analysis is female prison employees who work in nonguard positions (nurse, secretary, counselor). My contact with these women was minimal, but the Task Force Report on the Status of the Female Employee, prepared by the Federal Bureau of Prisons in 1980, indicates that nonsecurity female staff often ostracize female guards and make derogatory remarks about their motives for taking the job.

6. Mady Segal (1982) found the same reason for male opposition to women in the military. "One important component of the stereotype of the ideal man, and of a male-dominated society, is the protection of women. Men feel they have failed to live up to this ideal if they allow their women into combat. In addition, if women are members of combat units, then the men in the units may act to protect the women in ways that interfere with the functioning of the units" (p. 283).

7. *Corrections Magazine*, Letters to the Editor, February 1981.

8. The seniority provisions in both contracts make no mention of sex. When these provisions were first negotiated in the early 1970s there was no reason for the unions or the correctional departments to foresee that sex would ever enter into assignment decisions.

9. The Rhode Island union was actually better able to use the seniority provision to help women than was the New York union because in New York, seniority grievances can go only to the "third step"—the State Office of Employee Relations. In Rhode Island, seniority grievances can be taken to arbitration.

10. Very seldom does a seniority system work to women's advantage. Sachs and Wilson (1978) claim that union seniority systems generally operate against women's employment interests because they block the advancement of newly hired women and often require that women be the first workers laid off during recessions. In the current situation, the seniority

system was advantageous only to those women who had been working in female prisons and acquired seniority there. Newly hired female guards reaped no benefit from the seniority system.

11. This conflict between organizational goals and personal attitudes has affected other unions as well. Barrett (1979) says: "Among blue collar workers a genuine conflict exists between union solidarity and the question of women's rights. The problem becomes acute when equal employment opportunity for women comes into conflict with seniority systems" (p. 48).

12. The other respondents gave as their reasons, in order of importance, (1) female guards fill some special need, such as to search female visitors, (2) qualified female applicants applied for the job, (3) expansion of the work force made females more acceptable, and (4) there was a shortage of suitable male applicants.

13. Several union officials made this claim. Only one high-level administrator in New York (who asked to remain anonymous) asserted that DOCS policy toward women was a strategy to subvert, albeit to a limited degree, the union seniority system. Most administrators are naturally reluctant to reveal any ulterior motives for their actions.

14. The committee that investigated the 1971 Attica riot said that this tendency of older, experienced guards to bid for low-contact jobs contributed to guards' loss of control before the riot (Attica 1972). This view has been criticized by Jacobs and Crotty (1978).

15. Forts v. Ward, 621 F.2d 1210 (1980).

16. New York State DOCS Directive #2230 (1976).

17. New York State DOCS Directive #2230 (1981) states that assignments will be made without regard to sex except for strip searches and congregate shower facilities. When inmates are transported outside the facility at least one transporting officer shall be of the same sex as the inmate. The directive explicitly states that pat-frisks of inmates will be performed by officers regardless of sex.

18. The amendments state that "no person in any state shall on the ground of race, color, religion, national origin, or sex be excluded from participation in, be denied the benefits of, or be subjected to discrimination under or denied employment in connection with any program or activity funded in whole or in part with (LEAA) funds . . ." (Section 518(c) of the Crime Control Act of 1965 as amended in 1973).

19. From Respondents' Memorandum of Law in the matter of Rhode Island Brotherhood of Correctional Officers v. Rhode Island Department of Corrections, No. 77-C-190.

20. The department, here, was relying on a famous prisoners' rights case, Palmigiano v. Garrahy, 443 F. Supp. 956 (1977).

21. Letter from LEAA Office of Civil Rights Compliance to Department of Corrections chief counsel, George Cappello, 19 January 1979.

22. Letter from Harry Dogan (LEAA) to John Moran, Director, Rhode Island Department of Corrections, 21 May 1979.

23. Palmigiano v. Garrahy, 443 F. Supp. 956 (1977).

24. The establishment and purpose of this committee is contractually agreed upon by the department and the union (Agreement between State of Rhode Island and the Rhode Island Brotherhood of Correctional Officers (1977) Article X (10.2)). The committee consists of the deputy assistant director, an associate director (warden) from one of the system's prisons, and a union representative.

25. Inter-departmental Communication to Chief of Employee Relations from Associate Director R. R. Brule, 12 January 1979.

26. Interview with Director John Moran, July 1981, Cranston, Rhode Island.

27. Interview with Assistant Director Matthew Gill, August 1981, Cranston, Rhode Island.

28. *New York Post*, 22 May 1981, p. 3.

29. If anything, it has become more liberal. Many of the restrictions on assigning female guards in the 1976 guidelines were removed a few months after Commissioner Coughlin made this statement.

30. A few others favored the presence of a few women, if assigned to limited duties. Many wardens favored having a female guard to search female visitors.

Chapter 5

1. Most states require a high school diploma or an equivalency exam, but some have no educational requirements at all. Some states give applicants a written examination, others an oral one. Most states also require that applicants be physically fit and be nonfelons (CONtact, Inc., Report for Hiring Correctional Officers, June 1980, Lincoln, Nebraska).

2. There is a great deal of variation in the turnover rate from one state system to another. Twenty-seven states report at least a 25 percent turnover of staff per year. Six of those have turnover rates over 50 percent, with Louisiana the highest at 74 percent. The annual turnover rate in New York is reported to be 4 percent. Rhode Island did not respond to this survey (See May 1976).

3. At the time of this research, the standards in New York and Rhode Island were very similar. Applicants had to be eighteen years old, have a high school diploma or equivalent, pass a written examination designed primarily to assess reading and writing skills, and meet minimum health standards. Prior conviction of a felony bars appointment; conviction of a misdemeanor may do so. Rhode Island included an oral screening at which the Director for Training and two guards assessed the character and potential performance of each applicant.

4. There is not a lot of room for discrimination in hiring, although many states include a personal interview as one of the entrance requirements and examiners must make subjective evaluations of each applicant's potential for becoming a satisfactory guard. It would not be surprising if sex biases

sometimes influenced these evaluations and hindered women's employment opportunities.

5. The major exception to this general rule is that, in both states, female trainees will not perform strip searches of male inmates. When the guidelines were in effect in New York, female trainees did not receive training on posts (such as those in shower areas) that would be forbidden to opposite-sex guards.

6. This kind of discrimination is not reported by women who did their initial training in a women's prison. The following discussion of discrimination applied almost exclusively to women who went directly from the training academy to a men's prison for their first assignment.

7. It is not necessarily different women who report receiving harsher and more lenient treatment than their male counterparts. A few women reported both experiences because they worked under more than one supervisor during the probationary period.

8. Fewer women reported harsher than more lenient treatment by supervisors, but this could be because women in the former group are more likely to terminate their employment during the probationary period *because* of the harsh treatment. Interviews with women who have left prison employment would be very useful for learning more about discriminatory treatment during on-the-job training in men's prisons.

9. No supervisors admitted to giving women harder assignments during the probationary period.

10. Deaux and Ullman (1982) also found that supervisors in the steel mills refused to assign women to jobs they considered inappropriate even though such practice was contrary to the general policy handed down to them by their supervisors.

11. Again, it is important to stress that not all women who receive differential treatment define it as "discrimination." Some women were in favor of differential treatment as long as it meant receiving more favorable assignments than the men. Naturally, no women were grateful to receive harsher assignments, and all who did readily defined such treatment as discrimination.

12. Lamber and Streib (1974) found that the exclusion of women from informal socializing is particularly prevalent in criminal justice occupations. It was one of the primary complaints made by women who had recently joined formerly all-male, criminal justice work groups (Baunach and Rafter 1982).

13. Guideline Number 4, Guidelines for Assignments of Male and Female Correctional Officers, New York State Department of Correctional Services (DOCS) Directive #2230 (1976).

14. Guideline Number 3 (see note 13).

15. These differences are due in large part to differences in the way the guidelines are interpreted, but they also result from real differences between the prisons. For example, in some of the smaller prisons, all housing units

have only one guard on duty; all are therefore automatically unavailable to females. In large prisons, housing units have two or more guards on duty at all times, so that women can bid for some housing unit posts.

16. See DOCS Directive #2230.

17. In a few cases, women have successfully challenged narrow interpretations of the guidelines by bidding for a forbidden post and challenging the denial of their request by using the union's seniority provision. The status of a few posts was changed through this technique, but it was of limited value because seniority grievances in New York cannot be taken to arbitration. A few women told me of their intention to file a Title VII lawsuit against the department, claiming that the guidelines constituted illegal sex discrimination, but the department rescinded the guidelines before any such cases were filed.

18. The same guidelines discriminate against male guards who work in women's prisons, but much less so because male guards have many more options than female guards and can avoid discriminatory treatment merely by transferring to one of the many male prisons in the state. Not all female guards could choose to work in the state's one female prison.

19. See Forts v. Ward, 621 F.2d 1210 (1980).

20. An added advantage of solving the privacy problem with such barriers is that they provide inmates with more real privacy—not just privacy from women.

21. 447 F. Supp. 1346 (D.Del. 1978).

22. In New York, administrators have also done very little to monitor the way in which these vague guidelines were interpreted at each prison. Supervisors' confusion over the "proper" way to interpret them should have been apparent to central administrators.

23. There are, of course, cases of sexual harassment perpetrated by women against men and by both men and women against members of the same sex, but the most common situation is sexual harassment of women by their male co-workers and supervisors.

24. There continues to be a lot of debate over which behaviors should be included in the concept of sexual harassment. For discussion of the most important issues, see Bayles (1974), Hughes and May (1980), and Tong (1984).

25. 29 CFR Chapter XIV, 1604.11(a).

26. 29 CFR Chapter XIV, 1604.11(d).

27. Tompkins v. Public Service Electric and Gas Co., 568 F.2d 1044 (1977); Barnes v. Costle, 561 F.2d 983 (1979); Miller v. Bank of America, 600 F.2d 211 (1979).

28. Continental Can Co., Inc. v. Minnesota, 22 F.E.D. 1808 (Minn. 1980).

29. A major exception is the case of Kyriazi v. Western Electric Co., 461 F. Supp. 894 (1978).

30. 641 F.2d 934 (1981).

31. A task force report prepared by the Federal Bureau of Prisons (1980) also found "haranguing of female officers" and "vociferous harassment from a vocal minority of male staff" that touched nearly all female guards working in men's prisons.

32. The Merit Systems Protection Board Study (1981), the most comprehensive study of sexual harassment to date, also found the large majority of harassment incidents to be of the least serious variety. This does not mean, however, that such behaviors are not serious; it merely means they are less serious than the reported cases of rape, attempted rape, and sexual assault.

33. Peterson's (1982) study of female guards also found that sexual rumors involving the women were rampant in men's prisons. She concludes that although some of the rumors may have been grounded in fact, the rumors far outnumbered the actual incidents of sexual contact between women and co-workers or women and inmates.

34. Rhode Island Executive Order #80-9 (24 March 1980); New York State Policy Statement on Sexual Harassment in the Workplace, issued by the Governor's Office on Employee Relations (12 May 1981).

35. Memorandum to all employees from the DOCS Commissioner Thomas Coughlin (12 June 1981).

36. The reasons given by female guards for failing to file normal complaints are very similar to the reasons given by women in other studies of sexual harassment. See Merit Systems Protection Board (1981), Committee on Post Office and Civil Service (1980), Crull (1980), Goodman (1981).

37. The Merit Systems Protection Board Study (1981) found that when women in the federal government made official complaints of sexual harassment, the most common management response was to do nothing. To make matters worse, many male managers responded with open hostility to women who complained.

38. Sandra Gleason (1981) found that women make this same kind of cost-benefit analysis when deciding whether to pursue cases of employment discrimination.

39. The Federal Bureau of Prisons (1980) task force also found a lack of policy to cover these matters. The report suggests that "a consistent policy regarding the proper response of female staff to exhibitionism, pinching, sexual slurs, etc., should be developed at the executive staff level" (p. 15).

40. Rutland (1978) found this same condition among female police officers who believed that their performance would determine future policy concerning women's role in law enforcement.

Chapter 6

1. The literature on male prison guards also fails to provide enough evidence of male strategies for performing the job to allow valid comparisons. Although a few researches (Hall et al. 1968; Matthiesen 1965; Lombardo 1981; Carroll 1974) focus on differences between male guards, most focus on the occupational role itself and the dilemmas and contradictions inherent in it.

2. This attitude toward danger is similar to that of the female social workers studied by Mayer and Rosenblatt (1975). They were willing to go into ghetto areas, where they were uncomfortable and often afraid, simply because they were committed to their careers. Like men in dangerous jobs, women are not able to totally overcome their fear, but they are able to continue working in spite of it if the job itself is worth keeping.

3. What is most ironic about this view is that some substantial proportion of male inmates are incarcerated for crimes of violence against women and, if we are to believe the general statistics on male battering of wives and girl friends, many others have a history of violent attacks against women. Still, the myth that men "instinctively" protect women persists and was supported by several women in the inventive role.

4. The guard rulebook in Rhode Island, for example, warns guards to "talk to inmates only in the line of duty and when an inmate appropriately asks for or appears to need assistance. . . . Don't talk with inmates just for the sake of talking." (Rhode Island Department of Corrections, High Security Center, Guide for Correctional Officers, 18A, p. 8)

5. In support of women's belief that inmates will protect them from the attack of other inmates, 65 percent of the male prisoners responding to Peterson's (1982) questionnaire said they would be more likely to protect female than male guards who were being attacked by other inmates.

6. This entire matter of strategy adoption could be clarified further by interviews with women who terminated their employment shortly after their experience of working in a men's prison. The current study deals only with women who successfully adopted one of the three strategies. Perhaps other strategies are tried by other women who then find them inadequate for adjusting to the job and solving work-related problems.

7. William Foote Whyte (1982) points out the importance of looking for situations in which the actors themselves are trying out "social inventions" or different solutions to the problems they face. Such inventions, he maintains, emerge even in "inhospitable environments." The inventive role for performing the job of prison guard is an example of such resourcefulness and creativity. Whyte suggests that an important task of the sociologist is to discover and describe these inventions, identifying how and why they work for individuals in particular settings.

Chapter 7

1. In his study of the police, Arthur Niederhoffer (1967) says that very little police behavior can be attributed to the internal dynamics of officers' personalities. Instead, "the police system transforms a man into a special type of authoritarian personality required by the police role" (p. 103).

2. A male guard interviewed by Lombardo (1980) substantiated these claims: "they [inmates] don't like to have their pride hurt and neither do I. If pride is involved, even if it's a small thing, either he apologizes or I lock him up" (p. 75).

3. When inmates were asked to compare men and women *as groups*,

they claimed that women were friendlier and pleasanter. Several inmates, however, pointed out *individual* women who did not fit this generalization. In fact, a few women consistently received very negative evaluations in this regard compared with both male guards and other female guards.

4. Even in less sex-typed jobs, the presence of women might threaten men's masculinity. Bradford et al. (1980) conclude that male executives' resitance to women is due to the connection they have always made between occupational success and their own sense of masculinity. When women can succeed on the job, the men are left with no system for proving their masculinity.

5. The military might well study the effectiveness of both integrated and all-male prison guard forces to determine whether there is any decrease in solidarity when women are present and if women's presence has any effect on male performance levels.

6. New York State Department of Correctional Service, Affirmative Action Reports, 1971–79.

7. In New York State, for example, minority guards have formed their own organization, the Minority Correctional Officer Association (MCOA), to challenge discrimination within the DOCS and the union, both of which are predominantly run by whites. (See *Buffalo Courier Express*, 4 January 1980, p. 4.)

8. New York State Correction Law, for example, now covers such matters as disciplinary procedures, punishment guidelines, and rules for the use of force. At one time such rules were totally within the discretion of prison administrators.

9. Some prison administrators might disagree with this claim, but there is no evidence at this point that the prisons in states where guards have strong seniority systems are any more volatile or unstable than prisons in states where administrators retain power over all employment decisions.

10. Bowling v. Enomoto et al., 514 F. Supp. 201 (1981); Hudson v. Goodlander et al., 494 F. Supp. 890 (1980); United States ex rel v. Levi et al., 439 F. Supp. 90 (1979); Sterling v. Cupp, 290 Oregon 611 (1981).

11. See especially Harden v. Dayton Human Rehabilitation Center et al., 520 F. Supp. 769 (1981), and Gunther v. Iowa State Men's Reformatory, 612 F.2d 1079 (1980).

12. A few women were rated as adequate (and even exceptional), but the large majority received negative evaluations. The Federal Bureau of Prisons Task Force similarly found that male supervisors tended to rate all women at the two extremes—either very good or very bad (Federal Bureau of Prisons 1980).

13. Research shows that evaluators, when asked to examine scholarly articles, works of art, job applications, and fellowship applications, rank them higher when identical materials are attributed to a man rather than a woman (Goldberg 1968; Bem and Bem 1970; Peterson et al. 1971; Rosen and Jerdee 1974, 1978; Deaux and Taynor 1973). Also, when males and

females say the same thing, listeners rate males higher in competence and can later recall more of what was said (Gruber and Gaebilin 1979). Only when women are perceived as "exceptional" are they as likely to receive as positive evaluations as men (Abramson et al., 1977; Jacobson and Effertz 1974).

14. Research comparing men's and women's performance in this job should be undertaken cautiously. Developing good indicators of job performance is always difficult, and many standard measures (such as work evaluations by supervisors—in this case male supervisors) may be biased. Even the use of more objective criteria should take into account the special constraints that operate on women and make their effective performance more difficult. As long as women must perform the job under different conditions than male guards, it will remain difficult to compare their effectiveness in a valid and meaningful way.

15. This statement is based on the opinions of persons I interviewed. Male guards, female guards, and administrators all felt that women were attacked less often by inmates. In fact, only once incident of a direct attack on a female guard was reported to me. There was, of course, also the murder of female guard Donna Payton in New York State, but the circumstances surrounding that incident are still very murky and it is not clear whether or not the fact that she was a woman was a factor in the crime.

16. It is for this reason that Gordon Hawkins (1970) has suggested that hiring the physically handicapped as guards might have some advantages.

17. Sutton and Carlson (1977) gave several personality scales to male and female police science students and found the women to be significantly less authoritarian and less punitive than the men. The authors conclude that because of these differences women will make a positive contribution to the criminal justice system.

Chapter 8

1. Dothard v. Rawlinson, 433 U.S. 321 (1977).

2. Gunther v. Iowa State Men's Reformatory, 615 F.2d 1079 (1980); Harden v. Dayton Human Rehabilitation Center, 520 F. Supp. 769 (1981).

3. See, for example, Smith v. Troyan, 520 F.2d 492 (1975), in which the 6th Circuit Court ruled that a minimum height of 5 feet 8 inches was justified for police officers because tall officers have an advantage when making arrests and giving emergency aid. The court also concluded that tall officers have a psychological advantage over their shorter counterparts.

4. 615 F.2d 1079 (1980).

5. 520 F. Supp. 769 (1981).

6. Justice Marshall's dissent to *Rawlinson* questioned the motivation of prison officials' concern with inmate privacy. He wrote, "It is strange indeed to hear state officials who have for years been violating the most basic principles of human decency in the operation of their prisons suddenly become concerned about inmate privacy. . . . I have no doubt on this record

that appellants' professed concern is nothing but a feeble excuse for discrimination."

7. 621 F.2d 1210 (1980).

8. Male inmates have made claims other than privacy violation against the use of female guards. In Madyun v. Thompson, 657 F.2d 868 (1981), inmates claimed that the presence of female guards endangered them because male inmates might fight over the women and because women would be too weak to suppress the violence. The court rejected this claim, emphasizing that it would be inmates themselves, not female guards, who would be initiating the violence.

9. Not every privacy claim has been taken seriously by the courts. In Avery v. Perrin 473 F. Supp. 90 (1979), a male inmate claimed that the use of a female guard to deliver mail violated his privacy because he might have been undressed or using the toilet. The court ruled that because the mail delivery occurred at regularly scheduled times, the inmate could protect his own privacy.

10. 494 F. Supp. 890 (1980).

11. 514 F. Supp. 201 (1981).

12. 678 F.2d 52 (1982).

13. According to the Koran, Muslim men are to avoid all physical contact with women to whom they are not married. Muslim prisoners claim that being pat-frisked by a female guard violates this proscription and thereby denies them the right to practice their religion.

14. U.S.D.C. EMich, 19 January 1983.

15. CA7, 15 April 1983.

16. The New York Court of Appeals recently reached an opposite conclusion. In Rivera v. Smith (N.Y. Ct. App. No. 534, 1984), the court held that both the New York State Constitution and State Correction Law required protection of prison inmates' religious beliefs. Because male guards were present at the time a female guard frisked a Muslim inmate, they should have been called to conduct the frisk. The decision does not, however, require that women be removed from all positions where they might be called upon to frisk a Muslim inmate.

17. In New York State, for example, there has been an increasing need to deploy women on an equal basis with men simply because the number of female guard continued to grow. From 1976 to 1981, department policies for deploying women (which restricted them from many posts) were justified on the basis of the judicial requirement that inmate privacy be protected. By 1981 these policies had become harder and harder to implement because there were more female guards than "appropriate" posts. Without any important change in the case law, the old policies were thrown out and women were to be deployed on an equal basis with men except for posts that involved direct supervision of congregate shower areas.

18. A federal district court in Oregon heard such a case. In Bagly v. Watson (11 July 1983), the court ruled that women's right to equal employment opportunity supersedes inmates' right to privacy. Female guards in

Oregon were challenging a departmental policy that prevented them from working on approximately 90 percent of prison posts. Oregon officials were relying on a 1981 Oregon Supreme Court Case (Sterling v Cupp, 625 P.2d 123), which found that prisoners had a state constitutional right to be protected from routine body searches by women. Female guards claimed that this provision violated Title VII because the denial of work on so many posts severely limited their overtime and promotion opportunities. Only if Oregon prison officials appeal this decision (in an effort to retain their current policy) will this case progress through the federal court system and set wider precedent.

19. In fact, in prison systems currently employing a large number of women, this might be the only viable option open to prison administrators because they may have more female guards than appropriate positions (i.e., those not involving an invasion of inmate privacy). Only by making more positions fit judicial standards could they protect inmate privacy and use their current staff as fully as possible. Even in those states currently without a large number of women such changes might eventually be necessary because the court might (as they have up until now) require that inmate privacy be met *without* denying job opportunities for women. That is, they have demanded that female guards be deployed in some particular fashion without providing administrators with a mechanism for limiting the number of women coming into the system.

20. Prison administrators are surely not the only employers who have failed to establish policies for successful sexual integration. Michael Rustad's (1982) study of women's integration into the military, for example, finds a near total absence of affirmative plans for guranteeing that discrimination does not take place.

21. Terburg and Ilgen (1975) explain how harmful differential treatment can be for women breaking into nontraditional jobs. "To the extent that women are denied the opportunity to experience psychological success, women may be less likely to set very difficult goals for themselves. . . . This may lead to actual differences in performance over time due to limitations in self-concept" (p. 372). The Federal Bureau of Prisons (1980) task force also found that "if females are never involved [in physical altercations], their low self-esteem in these areas will become more pronounced and will lead to self-fulfilling prophecies" (p. 5).

22. Clarice Feinman (1980) and Phyllis Baunach and Nicole Rafter (1982) demonstrate how much more difficult it is for women to be accepted in traditionally male criminal justice jobs when some women demand (and receive) preferential treatment. Male prison guards in the current study continually pointed to women in the modified role as "proof" that women were unable and unwilling to perform the whole job. This makes it much more difficult for other women to prove themselves. Similar phenomena were found by Kanter (1977) and Meyer and Lee (1978) in the nontraditional women they studied.

23. The military, for example, developed formal institutional policies for

fostering racial equality and interracial harmony as the armed forces were becoming racially integrated. It went so far as to create the Defense Race Relations Institute for this purpose. If nothing else, these kinds of policies indicate some degree of commitment to making integration work.

24. Much sexual harassment by male guards takes place in the presence of male supervisors who currently ignore (or join in) the behavior. Managers must be taught the harm of this behavior and the role they can play in halting it. And because sexual harassment by managers is even more harmful than that by peers (because of both its impact on women and its influence on male subordinates), such conduct "should be dealt with severely by the institutional supervisors" (Federal Bureau of Prisons 1980:16).

25. Kanter (1977) found the same phenomenon among the executive women she studied; they felt that asking for men's help (even during emergencies in which men might ask for help) made them appear weak and powerless.

26. The creation of a viable support system for women was one of the primary recommendations of the Task Force Report of the Federal Bureau of Prisons (1980).

27. Baunach and Rafter (1982) have suggested that as women enter male criminal justice jobs they might, in fact, become more macho. They present the following evidence from their research: "I listened to a discussion of six female police officers talking about all the people they've beaten up because that's cool, to beat people up. . . . You know, how they put handcuffs on and whacked them because it gave them a new sense of power or because it made them really accepted by their male counterparts. It was just like listening to a bunch of guys talk after roll call or after a shift. I was listening to the same garbage, only it was coming from a woman" (p. 353). Only time will tell whether women workers will be substantially altered by their criminal justice jobs.

28. Nancy Wilson (1982) suggests that if criminal justice occupations adopt a service or rehabilitative model rather than the crime control model, women will be less disadvantaged because stereotypical female attributes will coincide more closely with the job requirements. Perhaps the presence of women in these occupations will actually encourage adoption of a service orientation. (Compare this possibility with the evidence from note 26; these two perspectives—whether the job or the occupants are the more critical determinants of occupational behavior—continue to be raised by researchers with regard to all workers. See Chap. 7.)

Chapter 9

1. Several recent studies suggest that, at least in some occupations, conditions for women deteriorate as their numbers increase. Anne Harlan and Carol Weiss (1981) examine female managers in two companies and found that those in the least skewed environments suffered more negative consequences, especially in terms of performance pressure and male opposi-

tion. Kay Deaux and Joseph Ullman (1983) examined two steel companies and found that male attitudes were more negative in the one with more women employed. And finally, James Gruber and Lars Bjorn (1982) found that in the automobile industry, male sexual harassment of women became more frequent and more severe as the number of women became more proportionate to that of men.

2. Schaeffer and Lynton (1979), Deaux and Ullman (1982), and Meyer and Lee (1978) all suggest that the social class background of male workers critically affects their attitudes toward sexual integration. Further research along these lines might prove very helpful for better understanding women's occupational experiences and why they seem to differ across occupations.

3. A basic introduction into the interactionist perspective can be found in the works of Herbert Blumer (1969), I. W. Thomas (1909), and George Herbert Mead (see Morris 1934).

4. For a discussion of the usefulness of comparative analysis and the techniques available for developing integrated, grounded theory, see Barney Glaser and Anselm Straus (1967) and Charmaz (1983).

References

Abbott, Edith. 1969. *Women in Industry*. New York: Arno Press.

Abramson, P.R., et al. 1977. "The Talking Platypus Phenomenon: Competency Ratings as a Function of Sex and Professional Status." *Psychology of Women Quarterly* 2:114–24.

Acker, Joan, and Donald VanHouten. 1974. "Differential Recruitment and Control: The Sex Structuring of Organizations." *Administrative Science Quarterly* 19:152–63.

Adams, Virginia. 1980. "Women in the Army." *New Society* 54, 940:364–66.

Albrecht, Stanley, Howard Bahr, and Bruce Chadnick. 1977. "Public Stereotyping of Sex Roles, Personality Characteristics, and Occupations." *Sociology and Social Research* 61:223–40.

Alpert, Geoffrey. 1984. "The Needs of the Judiciary and Misapplications of Social Research." *Criminology* 22:441–56.

Alvarez, Rodolpho. 1979. "Institutional Discrimination in Organizations and Their Environments." *Discrimination in Organizations*, edited by R. Alvarez, 2–49. San Francisco: Jossey-Bass.

Arnold, Donald. 1970. "Introduction." *The Sociology of Subcultures*, edited by D. Arnold, 3–8. Berkeley: Glendessary Press.

Astin, H. S. 1969. *The Woman Doctorate in America: Origins, Career and Family*. New York: Russell Sage.

Attica. 1972. *Official Report of the New York State Commission on Attica*. New York: Bantam.

Auerbach, J.S. 1976. *Unequal Justice*. London: Oxford University Press.

Auster, Carol, and Donald Auster. 1981. "Factors Influencing Women's Choice of Nontraditional Careers: The Role of Family, Peers, and Counselors." *Vocational Guidance Quarterly* (March), pp. 253–63.

Auster, Donald. 1979. "Sex Differences in Attitudes toward Nursing Education." *Journal of Nursing Education* 18:19–28.

Ayoob, M. F. 1978. "Perspectives on Female Troopers." *Trooper* 3, 2:32–35, 99–101, 103, 105.

Backhouse, Constance, and Leah Cohen. 1981. *Sexual Harassment on the Job.* Engelwood Cliffs, N.J.: Prentice-Hall.

Backhouse, Constance, and Leah Cohen. 1978. *The Secret Oppression: Sexual Harassment of Working Women.* New York: Macmillan.

Baker, B.K. 1975. "How to Succeed in a Journeyman's World." *Womanpower* (Special issue of *Manpower*) 7:38–42.

Barnes, Harry, and Negley Teeters. 1943. *New Horizons in Criminology.* New York: Prentice–Hall.

Barrett, Nancy. 1979. "Women in the Job Market: Occupations, Earnings, and Career Opportunities." *The Subtle Revolution: Women at Work,* edited by R. Smith, 31–62. Washington, D.C.: Urban Institute.

Bartollas, Clemens, et al. 1976. *Juvenile Victimization.* New York: Wiley.

Baunach, Phyllis Jo, and Nicole Rafter. 1982. "Sex-Role Operations: Strategies for Women Working in the Criminal Justice System" *Judge, Lawyer, Victim, Thief,* edited by N. Rafter and E. Stanko 341–58. Boston: Northeastern University Press.

Bayles, Michael. 1974. "Coercive Offers and Public Benefits." *Personalist* 55:142–3.

Becker, Arlene. 1975. "Women in Corrections: A Process of Change." *Resolutions* 1:19–21.

Becker, Gary. 1957. *The Economics of Discrimination.* Chicago: University of Chicago Press.

Becker, Gary. 1980. *Human Capital.* Chicago: University of Chicago Press.

Becker, Howard. 1963. *Outsiders: Studies in the Sociology of Deviance.* New York: Free Press.

Bem, Sandra. 1974. "The Measurement of Psychological Androgyny." *Journal of Consulting and Clinical Psychologists* 42:155–62.

Bem, Sandra, and Daryl Bem. 1970. "Training Woman to Know Her Place: The Power of an Unconscious Ideology." *Psychology Today* 4, 6:22–26, 115–16.

Bendig, A.W., and E. Stillman. 1958. "Dimensions of Job Incentives Among College Students." *Journal of Applied Psychology* 42:367–71.

Bennett, Lawrence. 1976. "A Study of Violence in California Prisons: A Review with Policy Implications." *Prison Violence,* edited by A. Cohen et al., 149–68. Lexington, Mass.: Lexington Books.

Berk, Richard, and Peter Rossi. 1977. *Prison Reform and State Elites.* Cambridge, Mass.: Ballinger.

Beynon, H., and R. M. Blackburn. 1972. *Perceptions of Work.* London: Cambridge University Press.

Bibb, Robert, and William Form. 1977. "The Effect of Labor Market Segmentation and Sex Stratification on Wages in Blue-Collar Markets." *Social Forces* 55:974–96.

Biemer, Carol. 1977. "The Role of the Female Mental Health Professional in a Male Correctional Setting." *Journal of Sociology and Social Welfare* 4:882–87.

Binkin, Martin, and Shirley Bach. 1977. *Women and the Military*. Washington, D.C.: Brookings Institution.

Blankenship, W.C. 1971. "Head Librarians: How Many Men? How Many Women?" *The Professional Woman*, edited by A. Theodore, 93–102. Cambridge, Mass. Shenkman.

Blau, Francine, and Carol Jusenius. 1976. "Economists' Approaches to Sex Segregation in the Labor Market: An Appraisal." *Signs: Journal of Women in Culture and Society* 1:181–99.

Blau, Peter, et al. 1955. *The Dynamics of Bureaucracy*. Chicago: University of Chicago Press.

Blau, Peter, et al. 1956. "Occupational Choice, Participation, and Social Mobility." *Industrial and Labor Relations Review* 9:531–43.

Blau, Peter, and W. R. Scott. 1962. *Formal Organizations: A Comparative Approach*. San Francisco: Chandler.

Blauner, Robert. 1964. *Alienation and Freedom: The Factory Worker and His Industry*. Chicago: University of Chicago Press.

Blumer, Herbert. 1969. *Symbolic Interactionism: Perspective and Method*. Englewood Cliffs, N.J.: Prentice-Hall.

Bogart, Karen, S. Jung, and J. Flagle. 1981. *Institutional Self-Study Guide on Sex Equity*. Palo Alto, Calif.: American Institutes for Research.

Bogdon, Robert, and Steven Taylor. 1975. *Introduction to Qualitative Research Methods*. New York: Wiley.

Boles, Janet. 1979. *The Politics of the Equal Rights Amendment*. New York: Longman.

Bourne, Patricia, and Norman Winkler. 1978. "Commitment and the Cultural Mandate: Women in Medicine." *Social Problems* 25, 4:430–40.

Bowker, Joan. 1981. "An Attempt at Collectivity: Professional Confirmation and Support." *Outsiders on the Inside: Women and Organizations*, edited by B. Forisha and B. Goldman, 223–30. Englewood Cliffs, N.J.: Prentice-Hall.

Bowker, Lee. 1977. *Prisoner Subcultures*. Lexington, Mass.: Lexington Books.

Bowker, Lee. 1980. *Prisoner Victimization*. New York: Elsevier.

Bradford, David, Alice Sargent, and Melinda Sprague. 1980. "The Executive Man and Woman: the Issue of Sexuality." *Sexuality in Organizations*, edited by D. Neugarten and J. Shafritz, 17–28. Oak Park, Ill.: Moore.

Brill, A. A. 1949. *Basic Principles of Psychoanalysis*. Garden City, N.Y.: Doubleday.

Brodsky, Carroll. 1977. "Long-Term Work Stress in Teachers and Prison Guards." *Journal of Occupational Medicine* 19:133–38.

Bureau of the Prisons. 1981. *Oversight Hearings before the Subcommittee on Courts, Civil Liberties, and the Administration of Justice*. Washington, D.C. Government Printing Offices.

Candy, Sandra. 1981. "Women, Work and Friendship: Personal Confirmation and Support." *Outsiders on the Inside: Women and Organizations*, edited by B. Forisha and B. Goldman, 188–98. Englewood Cliffs, N.J.: Prentice-Hall.

Cantor, Nathaniel. 1939. *Crime and Society*. New York: Holt, Rinehart, & Winston.

Caplow, Theordore. 1954. *The Sociology of Work*. Minneapolis: University of Minnesota Press.

Carroll, Leo. 1974. *Hacks, Blacks, and Cons*. Lexington, Mass.: Lexington Books.

Center for Women Policy Studies. 1981. *Harassment and Discrimination of Women in Employment*. Washington, D.C.: Center for Women Policy Studies.

Centers, R., and D. Bugental. 1966. "Intrinsic and Extrinsic Job Motivations among Different Segments of the Working Population." *Journal of Applied Psychology* 50:193–97.

Charles, M.T. 1977. *Evaluation of Female Recruit Performance and Male/Female Perceptions of the Female Troopers Role in the 90th Michigan State Police Training Academy*. Washington, D.C.: Department of Justice.

Charmaz, Kathy. 1983. "The Grounded Theory Method: An Explication and Interpretation." *Contemporary Field Research*, edited by R. Emerson, 109–26. Boston: Little, Brown.

Christianson, Scott. 1979. "Corrections Law Developments." *Criminal Law Bulletin* 15:238–47.

Civil Rights Compliance Technical Assistance Bulletin. 1978. "Update: LEAA Enforcement of Compliance Civil Rights Compliance." *Technical Assistance Bulletin* 1, 4:6–9.

Clark, H. F. 1931. *Economic Theory and Occupational Distribution*. New York: Columbia University Press.

Clemmer, Donald. 1940. *The Prison Community*. New York: Holt, Rinehart & Winston.

Cloward, Richard, et al. 1960. *Theoretical Studies in the Social Organization of the Prison*. New York: Social Science Research Council.

Cohen, Albert. 1970. "A General Theory of Subcultures." *The Sociology of Subcultures*, edited by D. Arnold, 96–108. Berkeley: Glendessary.

Committee on Post Office and Civil Service. 1980. *Sexual Harassment in the Federal Government*. Washington, D.C. Government Printing Office.

Conrad, John and Simon Dinitz. 1977. "Position Paper for the Seminar on the Isolated Offender." Unpublished paper, Academy for Contemporary Problems, Columbus, Ohio.

Cormier, Bruno. 1975. *Watcher and the Watched*. Plattsburgh, N.Y.: Tundra Books.

Coser, Rose Lamb, and Gerald Rokoff. 1970. "Women in the Occupational World: Social Disruption and Conflict." *Social Problems* 18:535–53.

Crawford, Jim. 1978. "Career Development and Career Choice in Pioneer and Traditional Women." *Journal of Vocational Behavior* 12:129–39.

Cressey, Donald. 1973. "Adult Felons in Prison." *Prisoners in America*, edited by L. Ohlin, 117–50. Englewood Cliffs, N.J.: Prentice-Hall.

Crouch, Ben M. 1980. "The Guard in a Changing Prison World." *The Keepers: Prison Guards and Contemporary Corrections*, edited by B. M. Crouch, 5–45. Springfield, Ill.: Charles C. Thomas.

Crouch, Ben M., and James Marquart. 1980. "On Becoming a Prison Guard." *The Keepers*, edited by B. Crouch, 63–110. Springfield, Ill.: Charles C. Thomas.

Crozier, Michel. 1964. *The Bureaucratic Phenomenon*. Chicago: University of Chicago Press.

Crull, Peggy. 1980. "The Impact of Sexual Harassment on the Job: A Profile of the Experiences of 92 Women." *Sexuality in Organizations*, edited by D. Neugarten and J. Shafritz, 67–71. Oak Park, Ill.: Moore.

Davis, Kingsley, and Wilbert Moore. 1945. "Some Principles of Stratification." *American Sociological Review* 10:242–49.

Deaux, Kay, and Tim Emswiller. 1974. "Explanations of Successful Performance on Sex-Linked Tasks: What Is Skill for the Male Is Luck for the Female." *Journal of Personality & Social Psychology* 29: 80–85.

Deaux, Kay, and J. Taynor. 1973. "Evaluation of Male and Female Ability: Bias Works Two Ways." *Psychological Reports* 32:261–2.

Deaux, Kay, and Joseph Ullman. 1983. *Women of Steel*. New York: Praeger.

Deaux, Kay, and Joseph Ullman. 1982. "Hard-hatted Women: Reflections on Blue-Collar Employment." *Women in the Workforce*, edited by H. J. Bernardin, 29–47. New York: Praeger.

DeFleur, Lois, David Gillman, and William Marshak. 1978. "Sexual Integration of the U.S. Air Force Academy: Changing Roles for Women." *Armed Forces and Society* 4:607–22.

Doeringer, Peter, and Michael Piore. 1975. "Unemployment and the Dual Labor Market." *Public Interest* 38.

Doeringer, Peter, and Michael Piore. 1971. *Internal Labor Markets and Manpower Analysis*. Lexington, Mass.: Heath.

Dowdall, J. A. 1974. "Structural and Attitudinal Factors Associated with Female Labor Force Participation." *Social Science Quarterly* 55:121–30.

Drolet, Jean-Paul. 1976. *Women in Mining: The Progress and the Problems*. Ottawa: Printing and Publishing.

Duffee, David. 1974. "The Correction Officer Subculture and Organizational Change." *Journal of Research in Crime and Delinquency* 11:155–72.

Duffee, David. 1980. *Correctional Management: Change and Control in Correctional Organizations*. Englewood Cliffs, N.J.: Prentice-Hall.

Dunnette, Marvin, and Stephen Motowidlo. 1982. "Estimating Benefits and Costs of Antisexist Training Programs in Organizations." *Women in the Workforce*, edited by J. J. Bernardin, 156–82. New York: Praeger.

Durning, Kathleen. 1978. "Women at the Naval Academy: An Attitude Survey." *Armed Forces and Society* 4:569–88.

Elder, G. H., and R. C. Rockwell. 1976. "Marital Timing in Women's Life Patterns." *Journal of Family History* 1:34–53.

Epstein, Cynthia. 1971. "Women Lawyers and Their Profession: Inconsistency of Social Controls and Their Consequences for Professional Performance." *The Professional Woman*, edited by A. Theodore, 669–84. Cambridge, Mass. Schenkman.

Epstein, Cynthia. 1975. "Institutional Barriers: What Keeps Women Out of the Executive Suite?" *Bringing Women into Management*, edited by F. Gordon and M. Strober, 7–22. New York: McGraw Hill.

Epstein, Cynthia. 1980. "The New Women and The Old Establishment: Wall Street Lawyers in the 1970's." *Sociology of Work and Occupations* 7:291–316.

Epstein, Cynthia. 1981. *Women in Law*. Garden City, N.Y.: Anchor.

Ermer, V. E. 1978. "Recruitment of Female Police Officers in New York City." *Journal of Criminal Justice* 6:233–46.

Erskine, Hazel. 1971. "The Polls: Women's Roles." *Public Opinion Quarterly* 35:275–90.

Esselstyn, T. C. 1966. "The Social System of Correctional Workers." *Crime and Delinquency* 12:117–24.

Evan, William. 1964. "Law as an Instrument of Social Change." *Applied Sociology: Opportunities and Problems*, edited by A. Gouldner and S. Miller, 285–93. New York: Free Press.

Falk, Gail. 1973. "Women and Unions: A Historical View." *Women's Rights Law Reporter* 1:54–65.

Farley, Lin. 1978. *Sexual Shakedown: Sexual Harassment of Women on the Job*. New York: McGraw-Hill.

Feather, N. T., and J. G. Simon. 1975. "Reactions to Male and Female Success in Sex-linked Occupations: Impressions of Personality, Causal Attrition and Perceived Likelihood of Difference Consequences." *Journal of Personality and Social Psychology* 30:846–55.

Federal Bureau of Prisons. 1980. "Task Force Report on the Status of the Female Employee." Unpublished report.

Feinman, Clarice. 1980. *Women in the Criminal Justice System*. New York: Praeger.

Feldberg, Roslyn, and Evelyn Glenn. 1979. "Male and Female: Job versus Gender Models in the Sociology of Work." *Social Problems* 26:524–38.

Feldman, D. C. 1976. "A Contingency Theory of Socialization." *Administrative Science Quarterly* 21:433–52.

Ferree, Myra. 1974. "A Woman for President? Changing Responses: 1958–1972." *Public Opinion Quarterly* 38:390–99.

Fishbourne, Francis, and W. Walsh. 1976. "Concurrent Validity of Holland's Theory for Non-college-degreed Workers." *Journal of Vocational Behavior* 8:77–84.

Fitzgerald, L. F. 1976. "Sex, Occupational Membership, and the Measurement of Psychological Androgyny." Paper presented at American Psychological Association Meetings, Washington, D.C., September 1976.

Fitzmaurice, Patricia. 1978. "Employment and Assignment of Male and Female Correction Officers." Unpublished report. Albany, N.Y.: Department of Correctional Services.

Fitzpatrick, John. 1980. "Adapting to Danger: A Participant Observation Study of an Underground Mine." *Sociology of Work and Occupations* 7, 2:131–158.

Fleming, Alice. 1975. *New on the Beat: Woman Power in the Police Force.* New York: Coward, McCann & Geoghegan.

Flynn, Edith Elisabeth. 1982. "Women as Criminal Justice Professionals: A Challenge to Change Tradition." *Judge, Lawyer, Victim, Thief,* edited by N. Rafter and E. Stanko, 305–40. Boston: Northeastern University Press.

Fogel, David. 1975. *We Are the Living Proof: The Justice Model for Corrections.* Cincinnati: W. H. Anderson.

Forer, B. R. 1953. "Personality Factors in Occupational Choice." *Educational and Psychological Measurement* 10:361–71.

Forisha, Barbara. 1981a. Introduction. *Outsiders on the Inside: Women and Organizations,* edited by B. Forisha and B. Goldman, xiii–xxiv. Englewood Cliffs, N.J.: Prentice-Hall.

Forisha, Barbara. 1981b. "The Insider and the Outsider: Women in Organizations." *Outsiders on the Inside: Women and Organizations,* edited by B. Forisha and B. Goldman, 9–30. Englewood Cliffs, N.J.: Prentice–Hall.

Forisha, Barbara, and Barbara Goldman. 1981. "Conclusion: Integrating Love and Power." *Outsiders on the Inside: Women and Organizations,* edited by B. Forisha and B. Goldman, 303–06. Englewood Cliffs, N.J.: Prentice-Hall.

Fottler, M. P. 1976. "Attitudes of Female Nurses toward the Male Nurse; A Study of Occupational Segregation." *Journal of Health and Social Behavior* 17:98–110.

Fox, James. 1982. *Organizational and Racial Conflict in Maximum-Security Prisons.* Lexington, Mass.: Lexington Books.

Frank, Benjamin. 1966. "The Emerging Professionalism of the Correctional Officer." *Crime and Delinquency* 12:272–76.

Freedman, Estelle. 1974. "Their Sisters' Keepers: An Historical Perspective on Female Correctional Institutions in the United States: 1870–1900." *Feminist Studies* 2:77–95.

Gabriel, Richard A. 1980. "Women in Combat? Two Views." *Army Magazine* (March), p. 190.

Gaffey, R.L. , and W.B. Walsh. 1974. "Concurrent Validity and Holland's Theory." *Journal of Vocational Behavior* 5:41–51.

Gans, Herbert. 1962. *The Urban Villagers.* New York: Free Press.

Gardner, Burleigh. 1945. *Human Relations in Industry.* Chicago: Irwin.

Gardner, Ralph. 1981. "Guard Stress." *Corrections Magazine* (October), pp. 7–14.

Giallombardo, Rose. 1966. *Society of Women.* New York: Wiley.

Ginzberg, Eli, et al. 1951. *Occupational Choice.* New York: Columbia University Press.

Glaser, Barney, and Anselm Straus. 1967. *The Discovery of Grounded Theory.* New York: Aldine.

Glaser, Daniel. 1964. *The Effectiveness of a Prison and Parole System.* New York: Bobbs-Merrill.

Gleason, Sandra. 1981. "The Probability of Redress: Seeking External Support." *Outsiders on the Inside: Women and Organizations,* edited by B. Forisha and B. Goldman, 171–87. Englewood Cliffs, N.J.: Prentice-Hall.

Goffman, Erving. 1959. *The Presentation of Self in Everyday Life.* Garden City, N.Y.: Doubleday.

Goldberg, P. A. 1968. "Are Women Prejudiced against Women?" *Transaction* (April), pp. 28–30.

Goldman, Nancy Loring. 1982. Introduction. *Female Soldiers—Combatants or Noncombatants,* edited by N. Goldman, 3–17. Wesport, Conn.: Greenwood.

Goldstein, Herman. 1977. *Policing a Free Society.* Cambridge, Mass.: Ballinger.

Goodman, Jill Laurie. 1981. "Sexual Harassment: Some Observations on the Distance Traveled and the Distance Yet to Go." *Capital University Law Review* 10:445–70.

Goodman, Jill Laurie. 1978. "Women's Work: Sexual Demands on the Job." *Civil Liberties Review* (March/April).

Gordon, Milton. 1970. "The Concept of the Sub-culture and Its Application." *The Sociology of Subcultures,* edited by D. Arnold, 31–38. Berkeley: Glendessary.

Gouldner, Alvin W. 1954. *Patterns of Industrial Bureaucracy.* New York: Free Press.

Gouldner, Alvin W. 1959. "Organizational Analysis." *Sociology Today,* edited by R. Merton, 400–28. New York: Basic.

Governor's Investigative Corrections Task Force. 1980. Final Report to the Honorable Pierre S. DuPont IV, Governor of the State of Delaware, October 1980.

Graham, Camille. 1981. "Women Are Succeeding in Male Institutions." *American Correctional Association Monographs* 1:27–36.

Gray, Thomas. 1975. "Selecting for a Police Subculture." *Police in America,* edited by J. Skolnick and T. Gray, 46–56. Boston: Little, Brown.

Gripton, James. 1974. "Sexism in Social Work: Male Takeover of a Female Profession." *Social Worker* 42:40.

Gross, Neal, and Anne Trusk. 1976. *The Sex Factor and the Management of Schools.* New York: Wiley.

Grosser, George. 1968. "External Setting and Internal Relations of the Prison." *Prison Within Society,* edited by L. Hazelrigg, 9–26. Garden City, N.J.: Doubleday.

Gruber, James, and Lars Bjorn. 1982. "Blue-Collar Blues: The Sexual Harassment of Women Autoworkers." *Work and Occupations* 9:271–98.

Gruber, K.J., and J. Gaebilin. 1979. "Sex Differences in Listening Comprehension." *Sex Roles* 5:299–310.

Gutek, Barbara, and C. Y. Nakamura. 1982. "Gender Roles and Sexuality in the World of Work." *Gender Roles and Sexual Behavior: Changing Boundaries*, edited by E. Allgeier and N. McCormisk. Palo Alto, Calif.: Mayfield.

Gysbers, N. C., J. A. Johnston, and T. Gust. 1968. "Characteristics of Homemaker and Career-oriented Women." *Journal of Counseling Psychology* 15:541–46.

Haas, Jack. 1977. "Learning Real Feelings: A Study of High Steel Ironworkers' Reactions to Fear and Danger." *Sociology of Work and Occupations* 4:147–70.

Hage, Jerald, and Michael Aiken. 1970. *Social Change in Complex Organizations*. New York: Random House.

Hall, Jay, Martha Williams, and Louis Tomaino. 1968. "The Challenge of Correctional Change: The Interface of Conformity and Commitment." *Prison within Society*, edited by L. Hazelrigg, 308–28. New York: Anchor.

Hall, Marjorie, and Robert Keith. 1964. "Sex-Role Preference among Children of Upper and Lower Social Class." *Journal of Social Psychology* 62:101–10.

Hall, Richard. 1977. *Organizations: Structure and Process*. Rev. Ed. Englewood Cliffs, N.J.: Prentice-Hall.

Haller, M., and L. Rosenmayer. 1971. "The Pluridemensionality of Work Commitment." *Human Problems* 24:501–18.

Hammond, Judith, and Constance Mahoney. 1983. "Reward-Cost Balancing among Women Coalminers." *Sex Roles* 9:17–29.

Handbook on Women Workers. 1975. U.S. Department of Labor, Woman's Bureau, Bulletin 297.

Haney, Craig, et al., 1973. "Interpersonal Dynamics in a Simulated Prison." *International Journal of Criminology* 1:69–97.

Harlan, Anne, and Carol Weiss. 1982. "Sex Differences in Factors Affecting Managerial Career Advancement." *Women in the Workplace*, edited by P. Wallace, 59–100. Boston: Auburn House.

Harlan, Sharon, and Bridget O'Farrell. 1982. "After the Pioneers: Proposals for Women in Nontraditional Blue-Collar Jobs." *Work and Occupations* 9:363–86.

Harragan, Betty. 1980. *Knowing the Score*. New York: St. Martin's.

Harris, Louis, and Associates. 1972. *The 1972 Virginia Slims Opinion Poll*. New York: Louis Harris and Associates, Inc.

Harris, Marvin. 1981. *American Now*. New York: Simon & Schuster.

Hart, William. 1981. "In Michigan, Officers Rebel Then Inmates Riot." *Corrections Magazine* 7, 4:52–56.

Hartmann, Heidi. 1976. "Capitalism, Patriarchy, and Job Segregation." *Signs: Journal of Women in Culture and Society* 1:137–69.

Hawkins, Gordon. 1976. *The Prison–Policy and Practice*. Chicago: University of Chicago Press.

Hawkins, Gordon. 1970. *Perspective on Correctional Manpower and Train-*

ing: Staff Report. Washington, D. C.: Joint Commission on Manpower and Training.

Hennig, Margaret, and Anne Jardim. 1977. *The Manager Woman.* New York: Doubleday.

Hetherington, E. Mavis, and Ross Parke. 1979. *Child Psychology.* New York: McGraw–Hill.

Hoffman, Lois. 1974. "Fear of Success in Males and Females: 1965–1971." *Journal of Consulting and Clinical Psychology* 42: 157–75.

Hoffman, Lois, and F. Ivan Nye. 1974. *Working Mothers.* San Francisco: Jossey-Bass.

Holland, John. 1959. "A Theory of Vocational Choice." *Journal of Counseling Psychology* 6:35–45.

Holland, John. 1973. *Making Vocation Choices.* Englewood Cliffs, N.J.: Prentice-Hall.

Holland, T. et al. 1979. "Preference of Prison Inmates for Male vs. Female Institutional Personnel." *Journal of Applied Psychology* 64:654–68.

Homans, George. 1969. "The Western Electric Researchers." *Readings on Modern Organizations,* edited by A. Etzioni, 99–113. Englewood Cliffs, N.J.: Prentice-Hall.

Horne, Peter. 1980. *Women in Law Enforcement.* Springfield, Ill.: Charles C. Thomas.

Horner, Matina. 1970. "Femininity and Successful Achievement: A Basic Inconsistency." *Feminine Personality and Conflict,* edited by J. M. Bardwick et al., 45–74. Monterey, Calif.: Brooks/Cole.

Howell, Mary. 1973. "Employed Mothers and Their Families." *Pediatrics* 52:252–63.

Huber, Joan. 1976. "Toward a Sociotechnological Theory of the Women's Movement." *Social Problems* 23:371–88.

Hughes, H. M. 1972. "Vocational Choice, Level, and Consistency: An Investigation of Holland's Theory on an Employed Sample." *Journal of Vocational Behavior* 2:377–89.

Hunt, Janet, and Larry Hunt. 1977. "Dilemmas and Contradictions of Status: The Case of the Dual Career Family." *Social Problems* 24:407–16.

Ireson, Carol. 1978. "Girl's Socialization for Work." *Women Working: Theories and Facts in Perspective,* edited by A. Stromberg and S. Harkess, 176–200. Palo Alto, Calif.: Mayfield.

Irwin, John. 1970a. "Notes on the Present Status of the Concept SubCulture." *The Sociology of Subcultures,* edited by D. Arnold, 164–70. Berkeley: Glendessary.

Irwin, John. 1970b. *The Felon.* Englewood Cliffs, N.J.: Prentice-Hall.

Irwin, John. 1980. *Prisons in Turmoil.* Boston: Little, Brown.

Irwin, John, and Donald Cressey. 1962. "Thieves, Convicts and the Inmate Culture." *Social Problems* 10:142–55.

Jacobs, James. 1977. *Stateville: The Penitentiary in Mass Society.* Chicago: University of Chicago Press.

Jacobs, James. 1978. "What Prison Guards Think: A Profile of the Illinois Force." *Crime and Delinquency* 20:185–96.

Jacobs, James. 1979a. "Race Relations and the Prisoner Subculture." *Crime and Justice: An Annual Review*. Vol. 1. Edited by N. Morris and M. Tonry, 1–27. Chicago: University of Chicago Press.

Jacobs, James. 1979b. "The Sexual Integration of the Prison's Guard Force: A Few Comments on *Dothard* v. *Rawlinson*." *Toledo Law Review* 10:389–418.

Jacobs, James. 1980. "The Prisoners' Rights Movement and Its Impacts." *Crime and Justice: An Annual Review of Research*, edited by N. Morris and M. Tonry, 1–34. Chicago: University of Chicago Press.

Jacobs, James, and Norma Crotty. 1978. *Guard Unions and the Future of the Prisons*. Ithaca, N.Y.: New York School of Industrial and Labor Relations.

Jacobs, James, and Mary Grear. 1977. "Drop-outs and Rejects: An Analysis of the Prison Guard's Revolving Door." *Criminal Justice Review* 2:57–70.

Jacobs, James, and Lawrence Kraft. 1978. "Integrating the Keepers: A Comparison of Black and White Prison Guards in Illinois." *Social Problems* 25:304–18.

Jacobs, James, and Harold Retsky. 1975. "Prison Guard." *Urban Life* 4:5–29.

Jacobs, James, and Lynn Zimmer. 1981. "The Montana Prison Strike: A Case Study." Paper presented at SSSP Meetings, Toronto, August 1981.

Jacobson, M. B., and J. Effertz. 1974. "Sex Roles and Leadership: Perceptions of the Leaders and the Led." *Organizational Behavior and Human Performance* 12:383–96.

Johnson, Elmer. 1981. "Changing World of the Correctional Officer." *Prison Guard/Correctional Officer*, edited by R. Ross 77–85. Toronto: Butterworths.

Johnson, Robert. 1977. "Ameliorating Prison Stress: Some Helping Roles for Custodial Personnel." *International Journal of Criminology and Penology* 5:263–73.

Joint Commission on Correctional Manpower and Training. *1969. A Time to Act*. Washington, D.C.: Joint Commission on Manpower and Training.

Jurgensen, C. E. 1947. "Selected Factors Which Influence Job Preferences." *Journal of Applied Psychology* 31:553–64.

Kadushin, A. 1976. "Men in a Woman's Profession." *Social Work* 21:440–47.

Kanter, Rosabeth. 1977. *Men and Women of the Corporation*. New York: Basic.

Katz, Fred, and Harry Martin. 1962. "Career Choice Processes." *Social Forces* 41:149–54.

Kerr, Clark, and Abraham Siegal. 1954. "The Interindustry Propensity to Strike." *Industrial Conflict*, edited by A. Kornhauser et al., 189–212. New York: McGraw-Hill.

Kohn, Melvin, and Carmi Schooler. 1982. "Job Conditions and Personality: A Longitudinal Assessment of Their Reciprocal Effects." *American Journal of Sociology* 87:1257–86.

Krajick, Kevin. 1979. "Delaware Scandal Leads to 22 Arrests." *Corrections Magazine* 5, 4:67.

Lacey, D. W. 1971. "Holland's Vocational Models: A Study of Workgroups and Need Satisfaction." *Journal of Vocational Behavior* 1:105–22.

Lamber, Julia, and Victor Streib. 1974. "Women Executives, Managers, and Professionals in the Indiana Criminal Justice System." *Indiana Law Review* 8:297–372.

Lane, Raymond. 1981. "A Man's World: An Update on Sexual Harassment." *Village Voice*, December 16, 1981, p. 20.

Larwood, Laurie, et al. 1980. "Attitudes of Male and Female Cadets toward Military Integration." *Sex Roles* 6, 3:381–90.

Laws, Judith Long. 1975. "The Psychology of Tokenism: An Analysis." *Sex Roles* 1:51–67.

Lee, Patrick. 1973. "Male and Female Teachers in Elementary Schools: An Ecological Analysis." *Teachers College Record* 75:83.

Lembright, Muriel, and Jeffrey Riemer. 1982. "Women Truckers' Problems and the Impact of Sponsorship." *Work and Occupations* 9:457–74.

Lembright, Muriel, and Jeffrey Riemer. 1981. "Driving for Tradition—Women Truckers and Occupational Motives." *Free Inquiry* 8:139–42.

Liebow, Elliot. 1967. *Tally's Corner*. Boston: Little, Brown.

Lipton, D., et al. 1975. *The Effectiveness of Correctional Treatment: A Survey of Treatment Evaluation Studies*. New York: Praeger.

Lofland, John. 1971. *Analyzing Social Settings*. Belmont, Calif.: Wadsworth.

Lombardo, Lucien. 1981. *Guards Imprisoned*. New York: Elsevier.

Lucas, Rex A. 1969. *Men in Crisis: A Study of a Mine Disaster*. New York: Basic.

MacKinnon, Catharine. 1979. *Sexual Harassment of Working Women*. New Haven: Yale University Press.

Mahoney, T. 1961. "Factors Determining the Labor Force Participation of Married Women." *Industrial and Labor Relations Review* 14:563–77.

Marquart, J. W., and J. B. Roebuck. 1984. "The Use of Physical Force by Prison Guards." Paper presented at American Sociological Association Meetings, San Antonio, August.

Martin, Roger. 1980. *Pigs and Other Animals*. Arcadia, Calif.: Myco.

Martin, Susan. 1980. *Breaking and Entering: Policewomen on Patrol*. Berkeley: University of California Press.

Martinson, Robert. 1974. "What Works?—Questions and Answers about Prison Reform." *Public Interest* 35:22–54.

Mason, Karen Oppenheim. 1976. "Change in U.S. Women's Sex Role Attitudes, 1964–1974." *American Sociological Review* 41:573–96.

Matthiesen, Thomas. 1965. *The Defences of the Weak*. London: Tavistock.

Mattick, Hans W. 1976. "The Prosaic Sources of Prison Violence." *Criminal Behavior and Social Systems*, edited by A. L. Guenther, 529–40. Chicago: Rand McNally.

Maupin, Joyce. 1974. *Working Women and Their Organizations*. Berkeley: Union Wage Educational Committee.

May, Edgar. 1976. "Prison Guards in America." *Corrections Magazine* 2, 6:3–5, 12, 35–40, 44–48.

Mayer, John, and Aaron Rosenblatt. 1975. "Encounters with Danger: Social Workers in the Ghetto." *Sociology of Work and Occupations* 2:227–45.

McCleery, Richard. 1960. "Communication Patterns as Bases of Systems of Authority and Power." *Theoretical Studies in Social Organization of the Prison*, edited by R. A. Cloward et al., 49–77. New York: Social Science Research Council.

McCleery, Richard. 1961. "The Governmental Process and Informal Social Control." *The Prison: Studies in Institutional Organization and Change*, edited by D. Cressey, 149–88. New York: Holt, Rinehart & Winston.

McCorkle, Lloyd. 1970. "Social Structure in a Prison." *The Sociology of Punishment and Correction*, edited by N. Johnson et al., 73–96. New York: Wiley.

McDowell, Sophia. 1978. "Toward a Social Psychology of Women Soldiers— A Social Typology of Female Army Personnel in a Field Environment." Paper presented at Society for Study of Social Problems, August.

McGee, Richard. 1981. Prisons and Politics. Lexington, Mass.: Lexington.

McIlwee, Judith. 1982. "Work Satisfaction among Women in Nontraditional Occupations." *Work and Occupations* 9:299–36.

McNamara, John. 1967. "Uncertainties of Police Work: The Relevance of Police Recruits' Background and Training." *The Police: Six Sociological Essays*, edited by D. Bordua, 163–252. New York: Wiley.

Mead, Margaret. 1980. "A Proposal: We Need Taboos on Sex at Work." *Sexuality in Organizations*, edited by D. Neugarten and J. Shafritz, 53–56. Oak Park, Ill.: Moore.

Merit Systems Protection Board. 1981. *Sexual Harassment in the Federal Workplace: Is It a Problem?* Washington, D. C.: Government Printing Office.

Meyer, Herbert, and Mary Lee. 1978. *Women in Traditionally Male Jobs: The Experience of Ten Public Utility Companies*. R and D Monograph #65, Department of Labor, Employment and Training Administration. Washington, D. C.: Government Printing Office.

Miller, Delbert, and William Form. 1980. *Industrial Sociology*. New York: Harper & Row.

Miller, Joanne, et al. 1979. "Women and Work: The Psychological Effects of Occupational Conditions." *American Journal of Sociology* 85:66–94.

Mincer, Jacob. 1958. "Investment in Human Capital and Personal Income Distribution." *Journal of Political Economy* 66:281–302.

Mischel, Walter. 1976. *Introduction to Personality*. New York: Holt, Rinehart & Winston.

Morris, Charles. 1934. *Mind, Self, and Society*. Chicago: University of Chicago Press.

Morris, Norval. 1974. *The Future of Imprisonment*. Chicago: University of Chicago Press.

Morris, Norval, and Gordon Hawkins. 1970. *The Honest Politician's Guide to Crime Control*. Chicago: University of Chicago Press.

Morris, Terrance, and Pauline Morris. 1980. "Where Staff and Prisoners Meet." *The Keepers: Prison Guards and Contemporary Corrections*, edited by B. Crouch, 247–68. Springfield, Ill.: Thomas.

Morton, Joann B. 1979. "Women in Correctional Employment: Where Are They Now and Where Are They Headed?" Proceedings of the 109th Annual Congress of Correction of the American Correctional Association, Philadelphia, August.

Murton, Thomas. 1979. "Prison Management: The Past, the Present and the Possible Future." *Prisons: Present and Possible*, edited by M. Wolfgang, 5–54. Lexington, Mass.: Lexington.

Murton, Thomas. 1976. *The Dilemma of Prison Reform*. New York: Holt, Rinehart, Winston.

Nabors, Robert. 1982. "Women in the Military: Do They Measure Up?" *Military Review* 62:50–61.

Nagel, William. 1973. *The New Red Barn*. New York: Walker.

Nagely, Donna. 1971. "Traditional and Pioneer Working Mothers." *Journal of Vocational Behavior* 1:331–41.

Niederhoffer, Arthur. 1967. *Behind the Shield: The Police in Urban Society*. New York: Doubleday.

Nieva, Veronica, and Barbara Gutek. 1981. *Women and Work: A Psychological Perspective*. New York: Praeger.

O'Donnell, D. A., and D. G. Anderson. 1978. "Factors Influencing Choice of Major and Career of Capable Women." *Vocational Guidance Quarterly* 26:215–21.

O'Farrell, Bridget. 1975. "Affirmative Action for Women in Craft Jobs: Change in the Small Industrial Work Group." Paper presented at the American Sociological Association meetings, San Francisco, August.

O'Farrell, Bridget. 1982. "Women and Nontraditional Blue Collar Jobs in the 1980s: An Overview." *Women in the Workplace,* edited by P. Wallace, 135–66. Boston: Auburn House.

O'Farrell, Bridget. 1980. *Women in Nontraditional Blue Collar Jobs: A Case Study of Local I*. Washington, D.C.: Government Printing Office.

O'Farrell, Bridget, and Sharon Harlan. 1982. "Craftworkers and Clerks: The Effects of Male Co-worker Hostility on Women's Satisfaction with Nontraditional Jobs." *Social Problems* 29:252–65.

Oppenheimer, Valerie Kincaid. 1970. *The Female Labor Force in the United States: Demographic and Economic Factors Determining Its Growth and Changing Composition*. Population Monograph Series no. 5. Berkeley: Institute of International Studies.

Oppenheimer, Valerie Kincaid. 1982. *Work and the Family: A Study in Social Demography*. New York: Academic Press.

Orfield, Gary. 1975. *Congressional Power: Congress and Social Change*. New York: Harcourt Brace Jovanovich.

Parisi, Nicolette, et al. 1979. *Source Book of Criminal Justice Statistics—1978*. Washington, D.C.: Government Printing Office.

Park, James. 1976. "The Organization of Prison Violence." *Prison Violence,* edited by A. Cohen et al., 79–88. Lexington, Mass.: Lexington Books.

Pavalko, Ronald. 1971. *Sociology of Occupations and Professions*. Itasca, Ill.: Peacock.

Peterson, Cheryl Bowser. 1982. "Doing Time with the Boys: An Analysis of Women Correctional Officers in All-Male Facilities." *The Criminal Justice System and Women*. New York: Clark Boardman.

Phelps, Edmund. 1972. "The Statistical Theory of Racism and Sexism." *American Economic Review* 62:659–61.

Pheterson, G., S. B. Kiesler, and P. A. Goldberg. 1971. "Evaluation of the Performance of Women as a Function of Their Sex, Achievement, and Personal History." *Journal of Personality and Social Psychology* 19:114–18.

Polsky, Howard. 1962. *Cottage Six*. New York: Wiley.

Potter, Joan. 1979. "Guard Unions: The Search for Solidarity." *Corrections Magazine*. (September): pp. 25–35.

Prediger, Dale, and Gary Hanson. 1976. "Holland's Theory of Careers Applied to Women and Men: Analysis of Implicit Assumptions." *Journal of Vocational Behavior* 8:167–84.

President's Commission on Law Enforcement and Administration of Justice. 1972. "State Correctional Institutions for Adults." *Correctional Institutions*, edited by R. Carter et al., 35–51. New York: Lippincott.

Price, Barbara, and Susan Gavin. 1982. "A Century of Women in Policing." *The Criminal Justice System and Women*, edited by B. Price and N. Sokoloff, 399–412. New York: Clark Boardman.

Priest, Robert, Alan Vitters, and Howard Prince. 1978. "Coeducation at West Point." *Armed Forces and Society* 4:589–606.

Psathas, George. 1968. "Toward a Theory of Occupational Choice for Women." *Sociology and Social Research* 52:253–69.

Quester, George. 1982. "The Problem." *Female Soldiers—Combatants or Noncombatants*, edited by N. Goldman, 217–36. Westport, Conn.: Greenwood.

Quinn, Robert. 1977. "Coping with Cupid: The Formation, Impact and Management of Romantic Relationships in Organizations." *Administrative Science Quarterly* 22:30–45.

Rand, L. 1968. "Masculinity or Femininity? Differentiating Career-oriented and Homemaking-oriented College Freshmen Women." *Journal of Counseling Psychology* 15:444–50.

Reckless, Walter. 1955. *The Crime Problem*. New York: Appleton-Century-Crofts.

Regoli, Robert M., Eric Poole, and Roy Lotz. 1981. "An Empirical Assessment of the Effect of Professionalism on Cynicism among Prison Guards." *Sociological Spectrum*. 1:53–66.

Report of the National Advisory Commission of Civil Disorders. 1968. *U. S. Riot Commission Report*. New York: Bantam.

Riemer, Jeffrey. 1979. *Hard Hats: The Work World of Construction Workers*. Beverly Hills, Calif.: Sage.

Riemer, Jeffrey. 1978. " 'Deviance' as Fun—a Case of Building Construction Workers at Work." *Social Problems: Institutional and Interpersonal Perspectives*, edited by K. Henry, 322–32. Glenview, Ill.: Scott-Foresman.

Ritzer, George. 1977. *Working: Conflict and Change.* Englewood Cliffs, N.J.: Prentice-Hall.

Robinson, Alice. 1973. "Men in Nursing: Their Careers, Goals and Images Are Changing." *RN* 36:37.

Robinson, Donald. 1979. "Two Movements in Pursuit of Equal Employment Opportunity." *Signs: Journal of Women in Culture and Society* 4:413–33.

Roe, Anne. 1956. *The Psychology of Occupations.* New York: Wiley.

Rosen, B., and T. Jerdee. 1978. "Perceived Sex Differences in Managerially Relevant Characteristics." *Sex Roles* 4:837–44.

Rosen, B., and T. Jerdee. 1974. "Effects of Applicants' Sex and Difficulty of Job on Evaluations of Candidates for Managerial Positions." *Journal of Applied Psychology* 59:511–12.

Rosenbaum, David. 1972. *New York Times,* Editorial, 27 February.

Rosenblatt, Aaron, et al. 1971. "Predominance of Male Authors in Social Work Publications." *The Professional Woman,* edited by A. Theodore, 103–18. Cambridge, Mass.: Schenkman.

Roscow, I., and K. Rose. 1972. "Divorce among Doctors." *Journal of Marriage and the Family* 34:587–89.

Ross, Beth. 1978. *Changing of the Guard.* Madison: League of Women Voters.

Rossi, Alice. 1965. "Barriers to the Career Choice of Engineering, Medicine, or Science among American Women." *Women and the Scientific Professions,* edited by J. A. Mattfeld and C. G. VanAken, 51–127. Cambridge, Mass.: MIT Press.

Rouceck, Joseph. 1935. "Sociology of the Prison Guard." *Sociology and Social Research* 20:145–51.

Rowe, Mary. 1981. "The Minutiae of Discrimination: The Need for Support." *Outsiders on the Inside: Women and Organizations,* edited by B. Forisha and B. Goldman, 155–70. Englewood Cliffs, N.J.: Prentice-Hall.

Rundle, Frank. 1973. "The Roots of Violence at Soledad." *The Politics of Punishment,* edited by E. O. Wright, 163–72. New York: Harper & Row.

Rustad, Michael. 1982. *Women in Khaki.* New York: Praeger.

Rutland, C. M. 1978. Comparative Analysis of the Relationship between Social Background Factors and Training Performance of Male and Female Security Specialists. Master's thesis, California State University at Sacramento.

Sachs, Albie, and Joan Wilson. 1978. *Sexism and the Law.* New York: Free Press.

Safilios-Rothschild, Constance. 1970. The Study of Family Power Structure: A Review, 1960–1969." *Journal of Marriage and the Family* 32:539–52.

Schaeffer, Ruth, and Edith Lynton. 1979. "Corporate Experiences in Improving Women's Job Opportunities." Conference Board Report no. 755. New York: Conference Board.

Schmitz, John. 1972. "Look Out! They're Planning to Draft Your Daughter." *American Opinion* (November): p. 1.

Schoonmaker, Meyressa. 1975. "Women in Probation and Parole." *Crime and Delinquency* 21:109–15.

Schrag, Clarence. 1961. "Some Foundations for a Theory of Correction." *The Prison: Studies in Institutional Organization and Change,* edited by D. Cressey, 309–57. New York: Holt, Rinehart, & Winston.

Schreiber, Carol. 1979. *Men and Women in Transitional Occupations.* Cambridge, Mass.: MIT Press.

Schwartz, Herman. 1972. "Prisoners' Rights: Some Hopes and Realities." *Annual Chief Justice Earl Warren Conference on Advocacy in the United States.* Cambridge, Mass.: Roscoe Pound–American Trial Lawyers Foundation.

Schwartz, Howard, and Jerry Jacobs. 1979. *Qualitative Sociology.* New York: MacMillan.

Segal, Bernard. 1962. "Male Nurses: A Study in Status Contradiction and Prestige Loss." *Social Forces* 41:31–38.

Segal, Mady Wechsler. 1982. "The Argument for Female Combatants." *Female Soldiers—Combatants or Noncombatants,* edited by N. Goldman, 267–90. Westport, Conn.: Greenwood.

Seidman, Joel, et al. 1958. *The Worker Views His Union.* Chicago: University of Chicago Press.

Seifert, Kevin. 1973. "Some Problems of Men in Child Care Center Work." *Child Welfare* 52:72–73.

Sherman, Lewis. 1973. "A Psychological View of Women in Policing." *Journal of Police Science and Administration* 1:383–94.

Sichel, Joyce, et al. 1978. *Women on Patrol: A Pilot Study of Police Performance in New York City.* Washington, D.C.: Government Printing Office.

Silberman, Charles. 1978. *Criminal Violence, Criminal Justice.* New York: Vintage.

Silver, H., and P. McAtee. 1972. "Health Care Practice: An Expanded Profession of Nursing for Men and Women." *American Journal of Nursing* 72:78–80.

Singer, S. L., and B. Stefflre. 1954. "Sex Differences in Job Values and Desires." *Personnel and Guidance Journal* 32:483–84.

Skolnick, Jerome. 1969. "Why Cops Behave the Way They Do." *Deviance: Studies on the Process of Stigmatization and Societal Reaction,* edited by S. Dinitz et al., 40–47. New York: Oxford University Press.

Smith, C. P., and C. H. Smith. 1970. "Why Don't Women Succeed?" *New Society* 16:557–79.

Smith, Ralph. 1979. "The Movement of Women into the Labor Force." *The Subtle Revolution: Women at Work,* edited by R. Smith, 1–30. Washington, D.C.: Urban Institute.

Sobol, M. G. 1963. "Commitment to Work." *The Employed Mother in America,* edited by F. Nye and L. Hoffman, 70–82. Chicago: Rand-McNally.

Spitze, Glenna, and Linda Waite. 1980. "Young Women's Early Experiences." *Sociology of Work and Occupations* 7:3–32.

Staehle, H. 1943. "Ability, Wages and Income." *Review of Economics and Statistics* 25:77–87.

Stark, Rodney. 1972. *Police Riots.* Belmont, Calif.: Wadsworth.

Staudohar, Paul. 1976. "Prison Guard Labor Relations in Ohio." *Industrial Relations* 15:177–89.

Stiehm, Judith. 1982. "Elected Women: Skewers of the Political System." *Women and the World of Work*, edited by A. Hoilberg, 55–64. New York: Plenum.

Stotland, Ezra. 1976. "Self-Esteem and Violence by Guards and State Troopers at Attica." *Criminal Justice and Behavior* 3:85–96.

Stout, Ellis. 1973. "Women in Probation and Parole." *Crime and Delinquency.* 19:61.

Sumner, George. 1976. "Dealing with Prison Violence." *Prison Violence,* edited by A. Cohen et al., 169–76. Lexington, Mass.: Lexington Books.

Super, Donald. 1953. "A Theory of Vocational Development." *American Psychologist* 8:185–90.

Suttles, Gerald. 1968. *The Social Order of the Slum*. Chicago: University of Chicago Press.

Sutton, Markley, and Helena Carlson. 1977. "Attitude and Personality Differences among Men and Women Studying Police Science." *Journal of Social Psychology* 102:61–62

Sweet, James. 1973. *Women in the Labor Force*. New York: Seminar.

Sykes, Gresham. 1956. "The Corruption of Authority and Rehabilitation." *Social Forces* 34:157–62.

Sykes, Gresham. 1958. *The Society of Captives*. Princeton, N.J.: Princeton University Press.

Sykes, Gresham, and Sheldon Messinger. 1960. "The Inmate Social System." *Theoretical Studies in the Social Organization of the Prison,* edited by R. Cloward, 5–19. New York: Social Science Research Council.

Sylvester, Sawyer, et al. 1977. *Prison Homicide*. New York: Wiley.

Tangri, S. S. 1972. "Determinants of Occupational Role Innovation among College Women." *Journal of Social Issues* 28:177–99.

Taylor, Shelley, and Susan Fiske. 1976. "The Token in a Small Group: Research Findings and Theoretical Explanations." *Psychology and Politics,* edited by J. Sweeney, 110–17. Collected Papers.

Tenny, Evabel. 1953. "Women's Work in Law Enforcement." *Journal of Criminal Law, Criminology and Police Science* 44:239–46.

Terborg, James, and Daniel Ilgen. 1975. "A Theoretical Approach to Sex Discrimination in Traditionally Male Occupations." *Organizational Behavior and Human Performance* 13:352–76.

Terborg, James, Mary Zalesny, and Mark Tubbs. 1982. "Socialization Experiences of Women and Men Graduate Students in Male Sex-typed Career Fields." *Women in the Workforce,* edited by H. J. Bernardin, 124–55. New York: Praeger.

Theodore, Athena. 1971. "The Professional Woman: Trends and Prospects." *The Professional Woman*, edited by A. Theodore, 1–38. Cambridge, Mass.: Schenkman.

Thomas, J. E. 1972. *The English Prison Officer since 1850: A Study in Conflict*. London: Routledge & Kegan Paul.

Thomas, W. I. 1909. *Source Book for Social Origins*. Chicago: University of Chicago Press.

Thurow, Lester. 1975. *Generating Inequality*. New York: Basic.

Tiedeman, D. V. 1965. "Career Pattern Studies: Current Findings with Possibilities." Harvard Studies in Career Development, no. 40, Graduate School of Education, Harvard University, Cambridge, Mass.

Tiger, Lionel. 1969. *Men in Groups*. New York: Random House.

Toch, Hans. 1977. *Police, Prisons, and the Problem of Violence*. Washington, D.C.: Government Printing Office.

Tong, Rosemarie. 1984. *Women, Sex, and the Law*. Totowa, N.J.: Rowman & Allanheld.

Treiman, D. J., and K. Terrell. 1975. "Sex and the Process of Status Attainment: Comparison of Working Women and Men." *American Sociological Review* 40:174–200.

Turner, Ralph. 1964. "Some Aspects of Women's Ambitions." *American Journal of Sociology* 70:271–86.

Tuten, Jeff. 1982. "The Argument against Female Combatants." *Female Soldiers—Combatants or Noncombatants*, edited by N. Goldman, 237–66. Westport, Conn.: Greenwood.

Vandever, Jan. 1978. "Nursing Students: Stereotypically Feminine." *Psychological Reports* 43:10.

Van Maanen, John. 1975. "Police Socialization." *Administrative Science Quarterly* 32:207–28.

Van Maanen, John, and E. H. Schein. 1979. "Toward a Theory of Organizational Socialization." *Research in Organizational Behavior* 1:209–64.

Vaught, Charles, and David Smith. 1980. "Incorporation and Mechanical Solidarity in an Underground Coal Mine." *Sociology of Work and Occupations* 7:159–87.

von Hirsch, Andrew, and Kathleen Hanrahan. 1979. *The Question of Parole: Retention, Reform, or Abolition?* Cambridge, Mass.: Ballinger.

Wagman, M. 1965. "Sex and Age Differences in Occupational Values." *Personnel and Guidance Journal* 44:258–62.

Wagman, M. 1966. "Interests and Values of Career and Homemaking Oriented Women." *Personnel and Guidance Journal* 44:794–801.

Waite, L. J., and R. M. Stolzenberg. 1976. "Intended Childbearing and Labor Force Participation of Young Women: Insights from Nonrecursive Models." *American Sociological Review* 41:235–52.

Walshok, Mary Lundenstein. 1981. *Blue-Collar Women: Pioneers on the Male Frontier*. Garden City, N.Y.: Anchor.

Walum, Laurel Richardson. 1977. *The Dynamics of Sex and Gender: A Sociological Perspective*. Chicago: Rand-McNally.

Ward, Richard, and David Vandergoot. 1981. "Correction Officers with Case Loads." *Prison Guard/Correctional Officer*, edited by R. Ross, 127–34. Toronto: Butterworths.

Weber, George. 1961. "Emotional and Defensive Reactions of Cottage Parents." *The Prison: Studies in Institutional Organization and Change,* edited by D. Cressey, 189–228. New York: Holt, Rinehart & Winston.

Weldy, William O. 1976. "Women in Policing: A Positive Step toward Increased Police Enthusiasm." *Police Chief* (January): pp. 46–47.

Wertheimer, Barbara. 1984. "Union Is Power: Sketches from Women's Labor History." *Women: A Feminist Perspective,* edited by J. Freeman, 337–52. Palo Alto, Calif.: Mayfield.

West, Constance. 1982. "Why Can't a Woman Be More Like a Man?" *Work and Occupations* 9:5–30.

Westley, Laurie. 1982. *A Territorial Issue: The Study of Women in the Construction Trades.* Washington, D.C.: Center for National Policy Review.

Wetherby, Terry. 1977. *Conversations: Working Women Talk about Doing a Man's Job.* Millbrae, Calif.: Les Femmes.

White, Martha. 1975. "Women in the Professions: Psychological and Social Barriers to Women in Science." *Women: A Feminist Perspective,* edited by J. Freeman, 227–37. Palo Alto, Calif.: Mayfield.

Whyte, William Foote. 1943. *Street Corner Society.* Chicago: University of Chicago Press.

Whyte, William Foote. 1948. *Human Relations in the Restaurant Industry.* New York: McGraw-Hill.

Whyte, William Foote. 1982. "Social Inventions for Solving Human Problems." *American Sociological Review* 47:1–13.

Williams, Robin M. Jr. 1977. *Mutual Accommodation: Ethnic Conflict and Cooperation.* Minneapolis: University of Minnesota Press.

Wilson, Nancy Koser. 1982. "Women in the Criminal Justice System: An Analysis of Status Conflict." *Judge, Lawyer, Victim, Thief,* edited by N. Rafter and E. Stanko, 359–74. Boston: Northeastern University Press.

Woelfel, John. 1981. "Women in the United States Army." *Sex Roles* 7:785–800.

Wolf, K., and P. Kendall. 1955. "The Two Purposes of Deviant Case Analysis." *Language of Social Research,* edited by P. Lazarsfeld and M. Rosenberg, 167–74. Glencoe, Ill.: Free Press.

Wolkin, Kenneth. 1972. "Pioneer vs. Traditional: Two Distinct Vocational Patterns of College Alumnae." *Journal of Vocational Behavior.* 2:275–82.

Women's Labor Project. 1980. *Bargaining for Equality.* San Francisco: National Labor Center.

Wynne, John. 1978a. *Prison Employee Unionism: The Impact on Correctional Administration and Programs.* Washington, D.C.: Government Printing Office.

Wynne, John. 1978b. "Unions and Bargaining among Employees of State Prisons." *Monthly Labor Review* 101:10–16.

Yanico, Barbara, et al. 1978. "Androgyny and Tradition versus Nontraditional Major Choice among College Freshmen." *Journal of Vocational Behavior* 12:261–69.

Yarkin, K. L., J. Harvey, and B. Bloxom. 1981. "Cognitive Sets, Attribution, and Overt Behavior." *Journal of Personality and Social Psychology* 41:243–52.

Yinger, J. Milton. 1960. "Contraculture and Subculture." *American Sociological Review* 25:625–35.

Zald, Mayer. 1962. "Power Balance and Staff Conflict in Correctional Institutions." *Administrative Science Quarterly* 7:22–49.

Zimmer, Lynn. 1985. Job Bidding on the Basis of Seniority in the Prison Context. Paper presented at Society for Study of Social Problems, Washington, D.C.

Zimmer, Lynn, and James Jacobs. 1981. "Challenging the Taylor Law: Prison Guards on Strike." *Industrial and Labor Relations Review* 34:531–44.

Index